W9-ABF-700

WITHDRAWN

Salem Academy and College
Gramley Library
Winston-Salem, N.C. 27108

The Modern Language Association of America

Approaches to Teaching
World Literature

Joseph Gibaldi, Series Editor

PT
1930
.A6
1987

Approaches to Teaching Goethe's *Faust*

Edited by

Douglas J. McMillan

Consultant Editor
Cyrus Hamlin

The Modern Language Association of America
New York   1987

Salem Academy and College
Gramley Library
Winston-Salem, N.C. 27108

Copyright © 1987 by The Modern Language Association of America

Library of Congress Cataloging-in-Publication Data

Approaches to teaching Goethe's Faust.

(Approaches to teaching world literature)
Bibliography: p.
Includes index.
1. Goethe, Johann Wolfgang von, 1749–1832. Faust.
2. Goethe, Johann Wolfgang von, 1749–1832—Study and
teaching. I. McMillan, Douglas J., 1931–
II. Hamlin, Cyrus. III. Series.
PT1930.A6 1987 832'.6 86-33191
ISBN 0-87352-501-9
ISBN 0-87352-502-7 (pbk.)

A version of Jane K. Brown's chapter, "The Genre of *Faust*," appeared in her *Goethe's* Faust: *The German Tragedy*. Copyright © 1986 by Cornell University. Used by permission of the publisher, Cornell University Press.

Cover illustration of the paperback edition: *Night: Faust in His Study* (1828), lithograph, by Eugène Delacroix. Courtesy of Lilly Library, Indiana University, Bloomington, Indiana.

Published by The Modern Language Association of America
10 Astor Place, New York, New York 10003

CONTENTS

PREFACE TO THE SERIES

In *The Art of Teaching* Gilbert Highet wrote, "Bad teaching wastes a great deal of effort, and spoils many lives which might have been full of energy and happiness." All too many teachers have failed in their work, Highet argued, simply "because they have not thought about it." We hope that the Approaches to Teaching World Literature series, sponsored by the Modern Language Association's Committee on Teaching and Related Professional Activities, will not only improve the craft—as well as the art—of teaching but also encourage serious and continuing discussion of the aims and methods of teaching literature.

The principal objective of the series is to collect within each volume different points of view on teaching a specific literary work, a literary tradition, or a writer widely taught at the undergraduate level. The preparation of each volume begins with a wide-ranging survey of instructors, thus enabling us to include in the volume the philosophies and approaches, thoughts and methods of scores of experienced teachers. The result is a sourcebook of material, information, and ideas on teaching the subject of the volume to undergraduates.

The series is intended to serve nonspecialists as well as specialists, inexperienced as well as experienced teachers, graduate students who wish to learn effective ways of teaching as well as senior professors who wish to compare their own approaches with the approaches of colleagues in other schools. Of course, no volume in the series can ever substitute for erudition, intelligence, creativity, and sensitivity in teaching. We hope merely that each book will point readers in useful directions; at most each will offer only a first step in the long journey to successful teaching.

Joseph Gibaldi
Series Editor

PREFACE TO THE VOLUME

To know Goethe's *Faust* is to know the humanities. No other poet and no other work of literature present the modern human being better than Goethe and his *Faust* do. At the same time, no other poet and no other work of world literature are more difficult to present to American and Canadian undergraduates. Translation (when used) is only one of many difficulties. Others include Goethe's special uses of language, mythology, history, and science, to mention just four. Whether one is presenting *Faust* in German or in English, one needs help, and it is the intent of this volume, as it is of the series of which it is a part, to offer such help.

The Faust theme has been a part of German culture at least since the days of the tenth-century Benedictine nun, poet, and dramatist Hrotsvit von Gandersheim, two of whose eight sacred poetic legends deal with Faustian material. Hrotsvit's poem *The Fall and Conversion of Theophilus* deals with a contract between Theophilus and the devil and with the power of Mary, Christ's mother, to have the devil return the contract. Her *Basilius* also presents the theme of the conflict between good and evil, with good triumphing over the devil (Haight 16–17). Hrotsvit was the first German poet to present the Faust theme and the first to emphasize the significance of the role of woman as mediator in the salvation of a man. Goethe's *Faust* perfects and immortalizes the presentation of this theme and this role.

My own closest connection with Goethe, one that I feel deeply and use to good effect in introducing students to the poet and to his *Faust*, is a lyric that in my opinion is the quintessence of poetry and the essence of *Faust*:

> Wandrers Nachtlied
>
> Über allen Gipfeln
> Ist Ruh,
> In allen Wipfeln
> Spürest du
> Kaum einen Hauch;
> Die Vögelein schweigen im Walde.
> Warte nur, bald
> Ruhest du auch.

Wanderer's Nightsong

O'er all the hill-tops
    Is quiet now,
In all the tree tops
    Hearest thou
Hardly a breath;
    The birds are asleep in the trees:
    Wait, soon like these
Thou, too, shalt rest.   (Middleton 59;
    trans. Henry Wadsworth Longfellow)

The rest the Wanderer will soon enjoy could also be the spiritual goal of Faust. Throughout the drama, this is possibly what Faust is seeking, without knowing it. Throughout the drama, too, of course, he is struggling, striving so that he can be fully human, but possibly, too, so that he can be saved (at rest). Students respond fully to this little lyric by Goethe and become eager to take on the poet's *Faust*.

They need other help and encouragement, naturally, and this volume contains suggestions, first, by the teachers of German literature, Romance literatures, English and American literature, comparative literature, world literature, history, and psychology who responded to the MLA survey and, second, by the teachers who contributed the essays that constitute part 2 of this volume.

Part 1 offers a discussion of selected materials available to the teacher of *Faust*: editions and translations, aids to teaching, background works, and background and critical studies. The second part of the volume contains twenty-four essays, including an introduction by consultant editor Cyrus Hamlin on the current problems of teaching *Faust* in North America. These essays, which make up the major portion of the volume, are divided into three sections: teaching backgrounds, teaching Goethe's *Faust*, and teaching the Faust legend. The reader will note in the essays a certain tension between authors who advocate a more strictly literary approach (e.g., Flax, Atkins, Lange) and those who take interdisciplinary and interart approaches (e.g., Brown, Walker, Potter). I take this tension to be positive and to reflect the many and varied uses and purposes of *Faust*. The topics of the essays are very wide-ranging—indeed, moving all the way from the genre of *Faust* through a valuable variety of approaches to a discussion of a course on the devil in literature. An appendix of participants in the survey, a list of works consulted, and an index complete the volume.

A book like this is the product of many minds and many hands. Without the participation of the teachers and scholars in the survey, there could have been no volume; each respondent to the survey has my sincere thanks.

Among the essay contributors, all of whom were unusually generous in giving their time and assistance, I wish particularly to thank Edith Potter for helping compile the list of audiovisual materials and Christoph E. Schweitzer and Kathleen Harris for their suggestions of recommended and required texts. I especially also wish to thank Cyrus Hamlin, who, as consultant editor, gave valuable guidance and support over a relatively long period of time.

Thanks are due as well to the members of the MLA Committee on Teaching and Related Professional Activities for their sponsorship. The suggestions of the consultant readers made this a better book than it otherwise would have been. The general editor of the series, Joseph Gibaldi, has been an inspired and inspiring colleague at every step of the preparation of this volume; it is a pleasure to have had his guidance, wisdom, and support, and I thank him for all this and more. The copyeditor, Roslyn Schloss, also is most deserving of my special thanks.

It would be unconscionable of me not to remember the introduction to German literature and culture that was given to me early in my career and that has been a continuous inspiration in all that I do. Special thanks are due to Karola Geiger, who taught me German at De Paul University, and to Kurt Franz May and Joseph Kunz, who taught me German, and Max Horkheimer, who taught me philosophy, while I was a Fulbright student at Johann Wolfgang von Goethe University in Frankfurt.

This project received funds from the Committee for Teaching Effectiveness, administered by the East Carolina University Faculty Senate. That support and the research assistance of Connie Taylor were of great help. I extend thanks also to Jane Adams for her considerable help in preparing the typescript.

For longtime support and encouragement I thank Virginia Luckhardt, and Inge and Tim McMillan. This book is dedicated to Franklin Cooley, my *Doktorvater*.

DMcM

Part One

MATERIALS

Douglas J. McMillan

Editions and Translations

German Editions

About half the survey respondents who teach *Faust* in German use the Hamburger Ausgabe (Hamburger edition), edited by Erich Trunz. This reasonably priced and reliable edition has the complete text in one volume, plus excellent notes, commentary, and bibliography. One instructor cautions, however, that the edition "does require above-average knowledge of German for best use."

About a quarter of the respondents teaching *Faust* in German use the University of Wisconsin Press (formerly the Heath) edition, prepared by Heffner, Rehder, and Twaddell. The new version preserves all the features of the D. C. Heath original edition. Volume 1 contains a lengthy introduction with very useful background information and the complete text of *Faust*. Volume 2 contains extensive notes that help elucidate allusions and passages and a glossary tailored to the text. Many prefer this edition because all commentary is in English; as one instructor commented, "Most undergraduates can't cope with a purely German edition." At least one respondent, however, believes that the volume of notes and vocabulary leaves something to be desired.

Those who choose the Reclam edition, relatively few in number, cite the low cost as their main reason. One instructor likes to use this edition along with Friedrich and Scheithauer's *Kommentar zu Goethes* Faust, also published by Reclam, which includes a *Wörterbuch* (glossary) and a bibliography. But another respondent notes that the print may be uncomfortable for some readers. Those selecting the DTV (Deutscher Taschenbuch Verlag) edition, edited by Peter Boerner, mention the modest price and praise the quality of the printing, editing, and notes. Finally, although very few respondents to the survey select the Insel edition, edited by Anton Kippenberg et al., those who do consider it excellent, complete, and reasonable in price.

Readers should also know that there are two major Goethe editions in preparation: one by Hanser Verlag (the Münchener Ausgabe) and one by Deutscher Klassiker Verlag, a subsidiary of Suhrkamp (the Frankfurter Ausgabe).

Translations: Dual-Language Editions, English Translations, Anthology

Respondents' answers concerning translations ran the expected gamut, from "one cannot teach *Faust* in any language but German" to "American students have to be taught *Faust* in English." A sampling of other responses is instructive. "In English one reads Goethe through a veil." "Clearly *Faust* should be taught in German to students who can handle the language." "I prefer to teach the work in German but appreciate the need to provide competent instruction in English translation." "I try to make the students aware of the effect of the German by explaining connotations that get lost in English or by reading some passages in German to give them the experience of hearing it in the original." "When teaching in English, I have to dispense with some allusions, subtleties, and more detailed connections and echoes restricted to German literature. Thus my teaching in English has become broader, also gaining in universality and general application." "*Faust* is too important a text to be read only by the few students who learn German well enough to read it in the original. I have always found my courses in translation more rewarding to teach because students have fewer purely linguistic problems, have a better overview of the text, have more interest for and training in literary issues, bring a much wider range of reading and experience to bear on the text." "Should be taught in English on the undergraduate level; the difficulty of the German is just too great for an undergraduate." "I believe that *Faust* is so exciting to contemporary students that the language should place no barriers in their way!"

The only dual-language edition of *Faust* recommended in the survey responses was Walter Kaufmann's, which about a quarter of the respondents use or have used. Respondents noted particularly the commentary and the inclusion of all of part 1, with selections from part 2. A typical comment is, "It comes closest to the spirit of Goethe's original, especially because one can follow the original on the opposite side. One great drawback—Kaufmann omitted many parts of the second part of *Faust*." Peter Salm's dual-language version of part 1, available in a revised edition, was not mentioned by the respondents.

The translation most often used, according to the survey, is that by Walter Arndt (ed. Hamlin). In a second category are the translations by Philip Wayne, Charles Passage, and Louis MacNeice, which a significant number of instructors use. In a third category are the translations by C. F. MacIntyre, Bayard Taylor, George Madison Priest, Barker Fairley, and Bayard Quincy Morgan, each favored by a few enthusiastic respondents.

It should also be noted that the Suhrkamp/Insel Goethe in English, a proposed twelve-volume edition of the collected works, has begun to appear. *Faust I and II* is edited and translated by Stuart Atkins. Although this *Faust* was not in print when the survey was taken, several respondents noted it as a text that they would use as soon as it became available. Atkins's translation is lively and truly modern, and the edition includes a helpful introduction and useful notes.

Walter Arndt's translation in the Norton Critical Edition series is used by

about one-third of the respondents who teach *Faust* in English. Most cite
the fine translation, excellent commentary, critical apparatus, notes, and
selection of essays as reasons for using this edition. A few instructors recommend this edition more for the editorial matter than for the translation.
At least one instructor noted the reasonable price for a book containing so
much, including the complete text of *Faust*. One user sums up what many
others said or implied: "Excellent background, critical essays, and explan-
atory and interpretive notes, plus a translation that tries to respect the
intricate, varied playfulness of Goethe's verse."

About half the respondents, in roughly equal numbers, use the Wayne,
Passage, or MacNeice translations. The Wayne translation is recommended
for several reasons: parts 1 and 2 are available in separate volumes; the
translation is clear, "close to the original, and in good English"; the commentary is helpful; and the work is accessible and reasonably priced. One
instructor uses the Passage translation because it is "complete and . . . the
poetry in general good. I at least can hear Goethe's German under most of
the English verses." Another says, "The translation is quite good; the notes
are . . . very helpful." One respondent approaches his praise in a somewhat
negative way: "the least objectionable of those in print." Most users praise
the translation and the apparatus equally. One respondent considers the
MacNeice translation "the best" (though incomplete because MacNeice leaves
out much of part 2). Another calls it "accurate and relatively poetic."

Finally, we turn to the large group of translations used by few but enthusiastic respondents. One instructor writes, "I consider the George Madison Priest translation one of the best. I wish it were available in an inexpensive
paper edition." Another finds the Fairley translation complete and "relatively
the most satisfying translation." Some think MacIntyre lively and very readable. Taylor is cited for its "flavor" and "genius." And the Morgan prose
translation is, for one, a useful supplement to teaching a verse version.

The only anthology still in print recommended by respondents is the
Norton Anthology of World Masterpieces, volume 2, with the MacNeice
translation of *Faust*. Use of the Norton anthology is often a departmental
choice. Many regret its omission of part 2. The anthology has an excellent
introduction on Romanticism and a good account of Goethe's life, with a list
of critical works in English. Volume 1 contains Marlowe's *Doctor Faustus*;
such Romantics as Rousseau, Blake, Wordsworth, and Coleridge appear side
by side with Goethe. This arrangement is particularly advantageous for comparative literature courses.

Required and Recommended Student Readings

Introduction

Although most respondents to the survey say that they focus almost exclusively on the text of *Faust* in class and that reading *Faust* is usually a rather heavy assignment for the students in itself, they usually require a few additional readings and recommend many others.

In assigning and suggesting readings, the respondents clearly favor one book: the Norton Critical Edition of *Faust*, translated by Walter Arndt and edited by Cyrus Hamlin. This impressive paperback contains a translation of the complete text of *Faust* plus detailed notes, background materials, sources, Goethe's comments on the drama, contemporary reactions, modern criticism, and a selected bibliography.

All the other suggestions for required and recommended readings fall generally (but with some unavoidable overlap) into four groups: general introductions to Goethe, background studies, critical works, and influence studies.

General Introductions to Goethe

The most commonly required or recommended reading for a general introduction to Goethe is his autobiography, *Poetry and Truth (Dichtung und Wahrheit)*, available in a number of good editions and translations. Also worthy of note is the little paperback volume *Who Is Goethe?*, edited by Katharina Mommsen and translated by Leslie Willson and Jeanne Willson, which is based mainly on autobiographical selections from Goethe's writings.

The second most frequently required or recommended general introduction is the Norton Critical Edition, edited by Cyrus Hamlin. Various sections of this volume (especially the autobiographical writings and the contemporary criticism) and Hermann Weigand's essay "Goethe's *Faust*: An Introduction for Students and Teachers of General Literature" are often assigned as required reading. Also popular is Richard Friedenthal's *Goethe: His Life and Times (Goethe: Sein Leben und seine Zeit)*, which one teacher calls a "fresh, controversial approach."

Other required or strongly recommended introductions include *The Life of Goethe* by Albert Bielschowsky (although dated), *Goethe as Revealed in His Poetry* by Barker Fairley (particularly recommended for those who read little German), *Goethe: A Critical Introduction* by Henry Hatfield (a brief biography with competent analyses of the principal literary works, including salient lyrics), *Goethe's Life in Pictures*, edited by W. Hoyer (good text explanations go with the illustrations), *The Life and Works of Goethe* by George Henry Lewes (also dated yet highly recommended), and *Goethe, Poet and Thinker* by Elizabeth M. Wilkinson and L. A. Willoughby (again, particularly recommended for those who read little German).

Background Studies

The background reading most often required or recommended is *The Tragical History of Doctor Faustus* by Christopher Marlowe. The chief literary treatment of the theme before Goethe, this play can be read with great profit by those about to begin the study of Goethe's *Faust*. Also often recommended are biblical selections (especially Genesis, Job, and John 1.1–3 in Luther's translation) and compilations of classical myths, such as Bulfinch, Graves, and Murray.

A highly recommended and readily available short survey of the *Faust* theme in Western literature is "Motif in Literature: The Faust Theme" by Stuart Atkins.

The ten books most often required or recommended are, in the order of importance, Philip Mason Palmer and Robert Pattison More, *The Sources of the Faust Tradition from Simon Magus to Lessing* (for one respondent, "this book—unfortunately out of print but available in some libraries—is an invaluable aid to the study—and teaching—of *Faust*. It contains, among many other documents of the Faust legend, the text of the *English* Faust *Book*"); Harold Jantz, *The Form of* Faust, and *Goethe's Faust as a Renaissance Man* (according to one respondent, the latter is "important for its perspectives on Renaissance Europe—philosophical, scientific, literary, etc.—as preconditions for the development of Goethe's work as the culmination of the Faust tradition"); W. H. Bruford, *Culture and Society in Classical Weimar*; Otto Heller, Faust *and Faustus: A Study of Goethe's Relation to Marlowe*; Harry Gerald Haile, ed., *The History of Doctor Johann Faustus*; Eudo Mason, *Goethe's* Faust: *Its Genesis and Purport*; Leonard Ashley Willoughby, *The Classical Age of German Literature, 1748–1805*; John William Smeed, *Faust in Literature*; and Eliza Marian Butler, *The Fortunes of Faust*.

Other required or recommended background books include *Goethe's* Faust: *A Literary Analysis* by Stuart Atkins ("in part heavy-going but well-organized, often . . . useful"), Faust: *Sources, Works, Criticism*, edited by Paul A. Bates (highly recommended for those with little German), and *Germany: 2000 Years* by Kurt F. Reinhardt ("an authoritative, well-written history, convenient for ready reference concerning the various periods, especially the sixteenth century").

Critical Works

If asked to assign just one critical work, most respondents would choose Stuart Atkins, *Goethe's* Faust: *A Literary Analysis*, which one instructor describes as "a sequential close reading that covers the entire play almost speech by speech" and another calls "probably the most outstanding commentary in English on the work as a whole." In the order of their importance the following were also recommended: two books by Harold Jantz, *The Form of* Faust and *The Mothers in* Faust; Karl Viëtor, *Goethe the Poet*; Rolf Christian Zimmermann, *Das Weltbild des jungen Goethe*; Harold Jantz, *Goethe's Faust as a Renaissance Man*; Albert Schweitzer, *Goethe*; George Santayana, *Three Philosophical Poets: Lucretius, Dante, and Goethe* (although dated, this book brilliantly shows Goethe's high place in Western civilization); Barker Fairley, *Goethe's* Faust: *Six Essays* ("a lucid presentation of Goethe's 'creative' process"); Ronald Gray, "Faust's Divided Nature"; Erich Heller, "On Goethe's *Faust*"; and Alexander Gillies, *Goethe's* Faust: *An Interpretation*.

Also mentioned were Alan P. Cottrell, *Goethe's* Faust: *Seven Essays*; Barker Fairley, *A Study of Goethe*; A. R. Hohlfeld, *Fifty Years with Goethe*; and Liselotte Dieckmann, *Goethe's* Faust: *A Critical Reading*. For students who know German, these critical works are highly recommended: Faust II. Teil: *In der Sprachform gedeutet* by Kurt May and *Goethes* Faust I: *Leitmotivik und Architektur* by Paul Requadt.

Several respondents recommended a book not yet available at the time of the survey, Jane K. Brown's *Goethe's* Faust: *The German Tragedy*, a sequential reading that focuses on the play's relation to the European tradition. Aimed primarily at those who teach *Faust* in general literature courses, it does not require a knowledge of German literature.

Influence Studies

The most commonly assigned modern works devoted to the Faust theme are Thomas Mann's *Doktor Faustus* and Mikhail Bulgakov's *The Master and Margarita*. Others include *Thomas Mann's* Doctor Faustus by Gunilla Bergsten; *Visages de Faust au XXe siècle* by André Dabezies; *Der nordische Faust: Adam Homo, Peer Gynt, Hans Alienus* by Rafael Koskimies; *Faust and the City* by Anatolii V. Lunatscharski; *Mon Faust* by Paul Valéry; and *Faust im Kino* by Ernest Prodolliet.

Aids to Teaching

Although some participants in the survey suggest that the numerous audio-visual aids available are not helpful (a few even think them harmful), most respondents use them frequently. The most popular visual aid is the 133-minute 16mm color version of the play produced by Gustav Gründgens at the Deutsches Schauspielhaus in Hamburg. This German-dialogue film of part 1 is directed by Peter Groski and stars Will Quadflieg as Faust, Gustav Gründgens as Mephistopheles, Eduard Marks as Wagner, Ella Büchi as Margaret (Gretchen), Elizabeth Flickenschildt as Marthe, Max Eckard as Valentine, and Heidi Leupolt as Lieschen. A shorter, black-and-white version, in German but with brief introductory English titles, more effectively conveys the meanings of the drama in some dramatic and atmospheric ways. This six-unit version is meant to be used primarily in normal-length class sessions, whereas the 133-minute version should be viewed in its entirety in one showing. The acting is so fine that even those who understand no German should benefit from viewing it.

Other occasionally shown films include the 1926 silent film *Faust*, directed by F. W. Murnau and starring Gösta Ekman, Emil Jannings, and Camilla Horn, and the 1968 *Doctor Faustus*, based on Christopher Marlowe's drama, starring Elizabeth Taylor and Richard Burton.

In addition to or instead of the Gründgens film, many respondents use the Deutsche Grammophon recording of the Gründgens performance of part 1. (Part 2 is also available.) Some users of the record comment as follows: "The recording is better than the film, but it is time-consuming," "good for oral reading, declaration," "useful to indicate the theatricality of the play," "especially useful for 'Nacht,' for the exchanges between Faust and Mephistopheles, and for bringing Gretchen to life for students."

One instructor uses a segment of Kenneth Clark's television series *Civilization*: "The program called 'The Worship of Nature' has some material on Goethe. If not pressed for time, the instructor will find this item to be both useful and entertaining for the students."

Some survey respondents suggest music: "I like to have a session in which I play music related to *Faust*. The opening of Haydn's *Creation* (for 'Prologue in Heaven'), Schubert's 'Gretchen am Spinnrade,' Berlioz's *Damnation of Faust*, and Mahler's Eighth Symphony (for 'Mountain Gorges')"; "I generally bring in at least one musical version, usually the Carl Orff *Schulwerk* (four songs from *Faust*), which are attention-getting and appealing"; "I use musical interpretations of *Faust*, i.e., Gounod's *Faust*, Liszt's *Faust Symphony*, Mahler's Eighth Symphony, Boito's *Mefistofele*, etc."; "I use the Elly Ameling recording of 'Gretchen am Spinnrade.' I also like Marian Anderson's old recording of the same song, but it is no longer available." A selected list of recordings with musical settings for *Faust* is included in the list of works cited. For a complete list of compositions consult Schuh 75 and Sternfeld.

Edith Potter's chapter in this volume provides excellent guidance for those who might wish to incorporate audiovisual aids into their teaching of *Faust*. Further comments are found in the chapters by Richard Erich Schade, Roslyn Abt Schindler, and Carsten E. Seecamp.

Some instructors use slides to present works of art and other illustrations. Most often mentioned are the Delacroix illustrations: "In my honors course on art and literature I analyze the Delacroix illustrations vis à vis their iconographic traditionality and their relationship to the text: for example, the Delacroix illustration of Faust in his study partakes of the tradition of 'scholar-in-study' icon, etc."; "The Delacroix prints demonstrate the contemporary reception of *Faust* as profoundly as any other documents. And they give the students a closer relationship to the dramatic interplay of the figures: each of the Delacroix prints is a small stage set for itself filled with the tension, action, and cross-purposes of the given characters. The students really enjoy this approach"; and "I use Delacroix prints from slides, and I provide the students with small Xerox copies of them." (For further suggestions see Schade's chapter.)

Finally, some instructors suggest combinations of audiovisual aids: "works of art relevant to *Faust* and pictures of various types of stage sets in producing it"; "music from Gounod's *Faust* and pictures of scenes from the play"; "I use Delacroix's illustrations of *Faust* scenes, music by Gounod and Berlioz to convey conventional interpretations, selected translated scenes from Flaubert's *The Temptation of Saint Anthony* to prepare for discussion of the psychology of temptation. When I have a film budget I show Bergman's *The Devil's Eye*, *The Exorcist*, and similar films." Student dramatization is yet another kind of audiovisual aid. One instructor writes, "If the students wish to act out a puppet play or scenes from *Faust I*, I try to help."

The Instructor's Library

Introduction

The problem of making suggestions here is formidable. Volume 1 (1965) of the *Goethe-Bibliographie*, edited by Hans Pyritz et al., for instance, contains 10,701 entries, 1,101 on *Faust*; the second volume, covering 1955–64, contains 2,489 entries, 303 on *Faust*; and (to pick just one relatively recent year) the 1983 *MLA International Bibliography* contains 277 entries under Goethe, 51 under *Faust* alone. The total number of valuable items available on Goethe and on *Faust* is astronomical. Or, as one respondent said: "To be familiar with *Faust I and II* is of essential importance. After that the deluge."

Nevertheless, the respondents to the survey did make some suggestions concerning the instructor's library. One instructor valiantly submitted the following guide, and I present it here complete, for instructors who teach the drama in English: "If I were allowed to highlight a small number of books that would be useful to the English speaker having to teach *Faust* in a survey or humanities course they would be: *Criticism*: Cyrus Hamlin's commentary in his edition of *Faust: A Tragedy*; Stuart Atkins, *Goethe's Faust*; Jane K. Brown, *Goethe's Faust*; and maybe Alexander Gillies, *Goethe's Faust*. *Background (Romanticism)*: Meyer Howard Abrams, *Natural Supernaturalism*; Marshall Brown, *The Shape of German Romanticism*; and Ernst Cassirer, *Rousseau, Kant, and Goethe*. *Background (historical)*: Walter Horace Bruford, *Germany in the Eighteenth Century*. *Background (Renaissance)*: Harold Jantz, *Goethe's Faust as a Renaissance Man*, and Edgar Wind, *Pagan Mysteries in the Renaissance*. *Specialized study*: Alan P. Cottrell, *Goethe's Faust*; Harold Jantz, *The Form of Faust*; and Eudo Mason, *Goethe's Faust*." Any new instructor will find all the books suggested above very helpful.

Reference Works

Three reference items were widely recommended by survey participants. The two-volume *Goethe-Bibliographie*, edited by Pyritz et al., is thought "convenient and recent" as well as "the most comprehensive bibliography of Goethe studies in general and therefore particularly of those relating to *Faust*." Similarly, some instructors consider "Anmerkungen zu Goethes *Faust*" by Erich Trunz in volume 3 of his Hamburger Ausgabe of Goethe's works "the most generally satisfactory," "absolutely essential," and "the most widely used." Finally, respondents referred to *Goethe: Faust*, edited by Georg Witkowski, as "the edition with the fullest commentary" and as "next to Trunz in value."

Salem Academy and College
Gramley Library
Winston-Salem, N.C. 27108

Other suggested reference works include Eckermann's *Gespräche mit Goethe*, edited by Ernst Merian-Genast ("a priceless mine of direct information regarding Goethe's views of his works"), and *A History of German Literature* by J. G. Robertson.

Other bibliographies include *Faust-Bibliographie*, edited by Hans Henning; *Goethe-Jahrbuch*; and the *MLA International Bibliography*.

Background Studies

Four books stand out among those recommended as background studies for the instructor's library. The Hamlin edition of *Faust* was recommended for its "helpful overview of *Faust* criticism," "useful background material and selected criticism as well as a useful selected bibliography." Philip Mason Palmer and Robert Pattison More's *The Sources of the Faust Tradition from Simon Magus to Lessing*, according to respondents, "gives a good all-around background" and "highlights Goethe's originality and superiority." Emil Staiger's *Goethe* was called an "essential," "critical, basic, mainline study." Elizabeth M. Wilkinson and L. A. Willoughby's *Goethe: Poet and Thinker* contains, for one instructor, "excellent general essays on Goethe that give him contemporary relevance."

Other highly recommended background studies include *The Classical Centre* by T. J. Reed ("beautifully written by a person who is extremely well informed"), *The Age of Goethe* by Stuart Atkins, *Culture and Society in Classical Weimar* by Walter Horace Bruford, and *The Life and Work of Goethe* by John George Robertson. For those who read German, the following are also very highly recommended: *Goethe: Sein Leben und seine Werke* by Albert Bielschowsky and *Das Weltbild des jungen Goethe* by Rolf Christian Zimmermann.

Critical Studies

The respondents to the survey were particularly enthusiastic in recommending the following twelve critical studies (presented here in order of importance): Stuart Atkins, *Goethe's* Faust ("the best reading of *Faust* in English"); Eudo Mason, *Goethe's* Faust ("significant and stimulating"); George Santayana, *Three Philosophical Poets* ("clearly demonstrates Goethe's role in world literature and in philosophy"); Liselotte Dieckmann, *Goethe's* Faust ("beautifully identifies puzzling aspects of the work"); Barker Fairley, *Goethe's* Faust ("a critical, basic, mainline study," "the most 'teachable' insights into *Faust*"); Harold Jantz, *The Form of* Faust; Henry Hatfield, *Goethe*; Harold Jantz, *Goethe's Faust as a Renaissance Man*; Wilhelm Emrich, *Die Symbolik von* Faust II ("most stimulating" and "no doubt the definitive treatment of the vast symbolism of the second part of *Faust*"); Harold Jantz, *The Mothers in* Faust ("I recommend it but issue a caveat about the exclusive significance the author claims"); Heinrich Rickert, *Goethes* Faust ("essential," "a recommended book with a comparative perspective"); and Reinhard Buchwald, *Führer durch Goethes Faustdichtung* ("an interesting analysis with excellent notes").

Other critical studies suggested are, in order of importance, Arnold Bergstraesser, *Goethe's Image of Man and Society*; Alan Cottrell, *Goethe's* Faust; Victor Lange, *Goethe*; and Karl Viëtor, *Goethe the Poet*. For those who read German, the two following books are also very highly recommended: Kurt May, Faust II. Teil: *In der Sprachform gedeutet*, and Dorothea Lohmeyer, *Faust und die Welt*. Of course, the studies listed here contain additional items in their bibliographies for those who require additional books and articles.

Part Two

APPROACHES

Teaching Goethe's *Faust*: Introductory Remarks

Cyrus Hamlin

There is a paradox to the teaching of Goethe's *Faust*, which will be familiar to anyone who has tried. Few texts of world literature captivate the imagination and challenge the intellect of students so powerfully as this sprawling cosmo-drama. Even at the introductory level, in translation, where no more than a passing glance is possible for a week or two in the midst of a whirlwind syllabus, something overwhelming gets across. At the same time, however, a kind of bewilderment sets in, indeed a primal confusion on the basic questions of critical and pedagogic procedure, that leaves both teacher and students wondering what to say and do in the face of Goethe's enigmatic and seemingly inexplicable poetic and dramatic sleights of hand. No single work that I know in the canon of Western literature can lay claim to such an intensity of opposing and seemingly incompatible responses. What can we as teachers do with *Faust*? And is there any way around this dilemma for students?

My own view would be that the dilemma of response is or should be a central part of the challenge, and even one legitimate source of pleasure, in the study of *Faust*. We should recognize this and look for ways to make such a paradox productive for critical discourse. At the same time we may be able to help our students gain access to the drama more effectively if we can define the basis of this dilemma from the outset in terms that will facilitate the exercise of reading through the text. My purpose in these brief introductory remarks is to suggest a few possibilities for such definition.

17

I

The difficulty of *Faust* is inherent in the work itself, a reflection of the circumstances in which it was first composed and the historical context— poetic, cultural, intellectual, social—that fostered the work and that the work itself may have helped create. Goethe's *Faust*, however comprehensive and even universal its vision concerning the human condition, remains a product of its own age, the age of Goethe, the age of Romanticism, of idealist philosophy, and of the bourgeois and industrial revolutions at the close of the eighteenth century and the outset of the nineteenth. As such, it must be referred to its own time for clarification of its singular complexity and challenge to readers. Although this claim might seem self-evident, the history of interpretations shows that the opposite has often been the case. On the one hand, reference is made to the origin of the Faust legend in the sixteenth century and to the proximity of the earliest chapbook—not to mention the hypothetical career of the historical Dr. Faustus—to certain values and motives appropriate to the Renaissance and the Reformation, whereby the challenge of science and black magic both for a pact with the devil and for subsequent damnation assumes a specific philosophical, theological, and ethical significance. All this might well hold true for the sixteenth-century origin of the Faust legend and especially for its literary and artistic representations—notably in Christopher Marlowe's famous play, though not only there. Yet Goethe's drama from earliest inception utterly transforms that tradition into a radical variant appropriate to its own world and time.

On the other hand, from the earliest stages of interpretation among the Hegelians and other nineteenth-century critics, Goethe's *Faust* has been used to document the most disparate prevailing ideologies and doctrines. This has been true, above all, within the established orthodoxy of German literature for its own cultural and educational institutions. Nowhere has *Faust* been more abused than in school. The most blatant instances would be arguments based on the drama that seek to justify doctrines of German nationalism, especially during the late 1930s under Hitler, or socialism, as more recently in East Germany, where Walter Ulbricht commented that Goethe's hero should be regarded as a precursor for the current socialist regime. Nor is the reading of *Faust* free from such ideological bias beyond the borders of Germany, even in current criticism in North America. We may now be asked to bear witness as radical semioticians and poststructuralists rediscover this text for the particular felicities of their theories. Such configurations for criticism may lend a legitimate excitement, along with an inevitable attendant confusion, to the best and most controversial debates of our time, both in and out of the classroom. Yet the proper approach to *Faust* must still be found in the claims that it imposes on its own, and these are for the most part historically conditioned, no matter how valid they still may be for our concerns.

The complexities of Goethe's *Faust* may be divided into those that are thematic to the drama as such and those that reflect the form and technique of the text as composition and verbal structure. This distinction, though artificial, may be helpful for isolating specific difficulties that students face in approaching the work. I shall attempt briefly to outline both with regard to the historical context of Goethe's concern.

The crux for any reading of *Faust* must be the force of the Faustian will and the kinds of goals it seeks to achieve. This problematic of the will is established at the very outset of the drama, in the scene "Night," where Faust confronts the Earth Spirit. Readers have recognized since the initial fragment of the drama was published by Goethe in 1790 that this scene constitutes a fundamental and programmatic transformation of the traditional legend, where hitherto the learned doctor had always conjured the devil with some kind of black magic in order to secure the use of infernal powers by contract for his soul. Here the issue for Faust is the desire for experience, the will to know all of life in its immediate, indeed unmediated, force, as signified by the Earth Spirit that he conjures. The outcome is a categorical rejection and denial of everything he desires, the very opposite of a contract for his soul. Goethe's central insight into the tragic implications of Faustian striving, however ironically portrayed, is established in this scene. To suggest to students that this rejection of the will reflects the spirit of Romantic idealism in the era of the Kantian revolution in philosophy may not help them understand Goethe's drama, especially if they are unfamiliar with the problematic of "reason and science" ("Vernunft und Wissenschaft," *Faust* 1851). Yet here above all Goethe conveys the spirit of his own age in a manner that has nothing whatsoever to do with the original legend of a pact with the devil and the issue of damnation to everlasting torment in hell.

Also essential for the study of *Faust* is to clarify precisely how Mephistopheles complicates both the form and the substance of the drama in dynamic, ironic, and varied theatrical manner. Here the dialogue scenes between Faust and Mephistopheles, from the devil's first appearance through the pact and wager, provide a crucial contrast with the fundamentally monological and absolutist stance of the protagonist in the opening scene. The playful and witty verbal exchange serves as vehicle for the mediated forms of experience that the devil offers for Faustian desire: a detour from the absolute spirit through the real world of human activity and involvement, a compromise of everything that Faust seeks to possess as totality. To argue that Mephistopheles, too, can be interpreted within the broader context of Romanticism, much in the post-Goethean manner of ironic writers such as Byron, Pushkin, Heine, or Stendhal, may seem farfetched and even forced;

yet the use of dialogue as an ironic form of exchange invites precisely such comparison. Above all, the extent to which Goethe's devil appears as master of theater, costume, spectacle, and disguise, a master role player and deceiver in the great theatrical tradition of rogue or jester (one thinks both of the comic actor in "Prelude in the Theater" and the actual court jester whose role Mephistopheles usurps in act 1 of part 2), should not be ignored.

II

Three separate though related issues for teaching *Faust* deserve mention, each of which also reflects central concerns of Goethe's time. For convenience I call them the problem of individuality, the problem of knowledge, and the problem of transcendence. Each was inherited by Goethe from the full complexity of the European tradition. Each also undergoes in the course of the drama fundamental, if not revolutionary, transformations that reflect central features of European Romanticism. A few comments on each may suggest how a reader of *Faust* might further explore the implications of these problems for the drama.

The Faustian spirit is absolutist in its claims for itself, radically subjectivist in its bias, and ultimately doomed to compromise, breakdown, or complete resignation. Faust's demand for knowledge of the world and experience of life, ranging from the project of sexual seduction in part 1 to a direct involvement in political and economic affairs of the empire in part 2, bears comparison, on the one hand, with the hero of *Don Giovanni*, Goethe's favorite opera, first performed just two years before the *Faust* fragment was published, and, on the other, with Napoleon Bonaparte, whose public career from his first military victories to his first triumphant campaigns as emperor coincided with the completion and publication of part 1. The Romantic hero, both as man of action and as sensitive soul, whether conquering nature and striving for absolute power or cultivating the inner life of feeling and searching for the ideal of beauty in myth and art, finds its single highest prototype in Faust. The representative qualities of Goethe's character have always been recognized, even by the earliest readers of the drama. Less apparent as a feature of Romantic destiny has been the counterspirit of subversion and compromise that Mephistopheles imposes on the Faustian will. Much of the variety, complexity, and dramatic fascination of Faust's career throughout Goethe's play depends on a dynamics of negativity and denial that Faust's absolutist and subjective will is made to suffer at the hands of the devil. The principle of error attributed to human striving by the Lord in "Prologue in Heaven" works itself out at every stage in the drama. Such a career of consistent failure in both its ironic and its tragic perspectives is central to

Goethe's entire drama, almost as if the author were here passing judgment on his age.

The problem of knowledge in *Faust* proceeds from a modest origin in the early stages of composition, when academic satire must have come easily to the young poet Goethe, at best a reluctant university student (somewhat in the manner perhaps of the student who appears in the scene "Study"). The tone and manner of such satire includes the archaic, rough-hewn quality of the doggerel (*Knittelvers*) in Faust's opening monologue and the bestial debauchery of the drunken students in "Auerbach's Tavern in Leipzig" (the only scene in the drama with a specific geographical location, common to both the historical Faustus—whose supposed visit to the tavern is commemorated in primitive murals still on display there—and Goethe himself, who often visited this famous watering place during his student days in that city). Out of such modest beginnings proceed the elaborate social satires contained in later stages of the drama: from the scene on Easter Sunday, where the populace of the town emerges from the city gate, to the various groups assembled in "Walpurgis Night" and the "Dream" as intermezzo; similarly from the elaborate carnival (*Mummenschanz*) in act 1 of part 2 to the mythological-cosmological bag of tricks in the "Classical Walpurgis Night" in act 2.

Far more significant as signal for the temper of Goethe's own time is the thematic failure of academic learning to achieve absolute knowledge. This failure, even if inherited from the traditional legend of Faust, provides a powerful, if equally ironic, commentary on the emergence of German academic philosophy from the days of Kant at Königsberg (the *Critique of Pure Reason* appeared in 1781) to those of Hegel in Berlin (through the 1820s). Especially important for the Faustian quest, whether or not a direct connection was ever intended by Goethe, were the emergence at the University of Jena in the 1790s of a systematic theory of knowledge (*Wissenschaftslehre*) introduced by Fichte and the philosophy of nature drafted by the young Schelling. Goethe, who witnessed this development at close hand nearby in Weimar, must have had the uncanny feeling that life was imitating art, as the rise and fall of Romantic thought followed an eminently Faustian path. (This sense of a parallel might even be extended to the biographical level, since both Fichte and Schelling left the University of Jena under the cloud of scandal: Fichte was fired on the charge of atheism, and Schelling departed with Caroline Schlegel, wife of the leading scholar of the Romantic school.) The satirical scenes in *Faust* involving the famulus Wagner and the young student—figures of fun in part 1—assume central significance as predominantly academic phenomena in the retrospective light of Romantic idealism. Scenes involving Wagner and the student as Baccalaureus in act 2 of the second part offer a devastating satire of Romantic scholarship and science, perhaps with specific, though veiled, allusions to the later schools of Fichte and Schelling. Even more challenging for the reader of *Faust* is to interpret the projects of the protagonist in the light of Hegelian philosophy, especially as regards theories of history and art. The Hegelians themselves were among the first to celebrate Goethe's drama as sympathetic to their philosophical endeavor (though perhaps the drama includes more of an ironic perspective on that endeavor than they were aware). Hegel himself in his lecture course on aesthetics at the University of Berlin celebrated *Faust* as "the absolute philosophical tragedy."

The problem of transcendence in *Faust* may be the most alien and seemingly irrelevant to the concerns of our secular age. Goethe himself prepared the way for such a view by systematically transforming every facet of an other-worldly dimension in the traditional Faust legend into (at best) mere theatrical device. The court of the Lord in the "Prologue in Heaven" resembles nothing so much as a self-conscious show, and the exotic sequence of mystics and anchorites, angelic choirs and attendant female spirits surrounding the Madonna in the final scene of part 2 almost suggests a parody of Baroque allegory, for which the extravagance of Mahler's musical setting in his Eighth Symphony seems eminently suitable. Even the demonic element in the drama, represented above all by Mephistopheles with all his infernal devices, seems characterized by earthly and temporal qualities. Damnation and the last judgment play little role here. The theological implications of Faust's use of magic, his translation of the biblical Logos into "deed," and even his statement of faith to Gretchen that "feeling is all" provide at best a consistent impression of radical revisionism, if not a categorical inversion of traditional Christian doctrine. Goethe's drama thus achieves a thoroughgoing secularization of the traditional legend, which originated in a self-consciously Christian polemic against excessive learning and ambition beyond appropriate human limits.

Faust nonetheless sustains and affirms a profound sense of spiritual values and powers, which do not depend at all—so it seems—on the agency of the devil but which do reflect a modified use of traditional theological symbolism. The Earth Spirit in its revealed presence may signal the earliest, perhaps the original instance of epiphany in the composition of the drama. To this may be added the scenes of hymnic celebration in the chorus of the archangels in the "Prologue in Heaven" and the Easter choruses overheard by Faust at the end of the scene "Night." The consistent vehicle for such spiritual power within the drama is "great creating nature" (to borrow Shakespeare's phrase), which is also celebrated by Faust in his monologues, notably in "Forest and Cave" and in the opening scene of part 2, "Charming Landscape." Through a supreme fiction Goethe also lends to nature its own appropriate voices and guises within various symbolic scenes, most particularly in the figure of Ariel (taken over from *The Tempest*) and his chorus of elfin spirits who sing the watches of the night in that same opening scene of part 2. The highpoint of this epiphanic dimension occurs in the festival at the Aegean Sea that concludes "Classical Walpurgis Night," where the sirens of ancient myth join various other choral voices to celebrate the triumph of the nymph Galatea and the climactic fusion of Homunculus with the element of the sea as primal event of creation, proclaimed in a universal hymn to Eros by the totality of the spirit realm.

Accompanying this thematic use of nature as vehicle and voice of spiritual powers are various manifestations of love, beginning with the image that captures Faust's eye in the magic mirror in "Witch's Kitchen." The most immediate dramatic focus for this theme is found in Gretchen's response to the protagonist's strategies of seduction, despite the suffering and eventual destruction it causes. More comprehensive and complex is the mythical-poetic marriage of Faust with Helena in act 3 of the second part. United by the pleasures of rhyme, they produce as offspring within the setting of traditional pastoral the figure of Euphorion, whom Goethe himself referred to as the "Spirit of Poesy." This power of love originates in nature and affects within the human realm a familiar pattern of renewal and rebirth, as in the scene of Easter "Outside the City Gates." Love also serves finally as the source of Faust's redemption, where the striving of his will receives the intercession of the feminine spirit ("otherwise called Gretchen") as an ultimate gift of grace. Goethe's final revision of the Faust legend thus constitutes a radical reformulation of the Christian concept of salvation.

III

Paths of interpretive inquiry into the central issues of *Faust* invariably lead beyond the role of character and the configurations of the Faustian project. The traditional pact with the devil, however transformed by Goethe, may serve as a point of origin for the dramatic action. Expanding perspectives in part 2, however, quickly leave behind all preoccupation with the hero as individual and with the perversities of his errant career. Readers must accommodate their response to a widening horizon of thematic variations on the Faustian mode: from the court of the emperor (who is himself a variant on Faust) to the boundless stage of cosmic myth and archetypal poiesis (in the "Classical Walpurgis Night" and the Helena act), concluding with the global politics of a demonic military campaign in act 4 and the tidal reclamation project and city planning in act 5. Faust himself in all this serves at best as instigator, participant, or representative instance and even seems to perform at times, no less than we ourselves do, the role of spectator to the event.

In conclusion, let me touch on two particular areas of significance that emerge ever more pervasively in part 2 as central to the form and technique of Goethe's drama. Both aspects also speak directly and powerfully to the manners and habits of our own time, as if the poet had programmed into his drama a kind of prophecy for future discourse.

First, there is established in *Faust* a technique of allegorical mimesis, through which the drama achieves an implied judgment on the culture and society that it constructs, including even economic and political systems. At first, as mentioned, this occurs in forms of satire, as in the scene of the populace "Outside the City Gate" or in the more ambitious sequence of "Walpurgis Night" and its intermezzo. In part 2 such satire extends to a form of pageantry and mythical phantasmagoria (in the carnival scene and the "Classical Walpurgis Night"), all of which could seem quite alien and arbitrary to the career of Faust, like willful digressions. Faustian dimensions may always be found, however, at various levels of allegorical figuration. The same holds true for the larger arena of events in the political realm, notably the project for fiscal reform in act 1 and the general warfare in act 4, involving the rival emperor, the scene of looting by Mephistopheles's henchmen, and the judgment passed by the church on the secular realm. Is not all of that somehow an allegory for Europe in the nineteenth century? Act 5, finally, where Faust appears as urban developer whose absolutist projects arbitrarily destroy the Ovidian figures of Baucis and Philemon and the anonymous Traveller, completes a pattern of implicit social and technological critique, directed against the emerging industrialist and capitalist systems of Goethe's later years. Some early readers, including Karl Marx, clearly recognized this dimension of *Faust*. Only in our own century, however, has the validity of this all-inclusive allegorical satire come to be recognized as drama, possibly even as Goethe's most singular poetic achievement.

Second, and most important for a modern reading of *Faust*, we begin to discover a programmatic aesthetics, an implicit theory of art, which is developed within the drama as a measure for its self-reflective performance, as well as a directive for its systematic appropriation of the entire Western tradition. The Helena act especially may be understood as the critical review of a tragic history achieved through poetic appropriation, which extends over three millennia (as Goethe himself remarked): from the heroic age of Homeric Greece through the era of the Gothic, or "Germanic," Middle Ages to the final collapse of Romantic modernism, signaled by Euphorion's death as memorial to Lord Byron's involvement in the struggle for Greek independence. Even apart from the Helena act, however, a number of programmatic moments establish a developing aesthetics for the drama. Within part

1 such moments tend to assume ritualistic or even liturgical forms, as in the celebration of the Easter Mass at the end of "Night," or even in the folk festival in the village visited by Faust and Wagner on their Easter walk, and again in the slapstick amateur theatrics of the "Walpurgis Night's Dream." The climactic moment of vision for the theme of art, as critics have generally recognized, occurs at the outset of part 2, in the scene "Charming Landscape," where the image of the rainbow Faust sees emerging from the mist thrown up by the waterfall catches the light of the morning sun, signifying that the highest model of art is permanence in change (*Wechseldauer*), refracted color in which we truly *have* our life. Such a poetics receives even further elaboration at the end of act 2 in the fusion of Homunculus with the sea, a secular symbol of immaculate conception, and at the end of act 3 in the naturalistic metamorphosis of the spirit chorus. Distant echoes of this thematic concern for art also occur at the outset of act 4, when the veil of Helena, after carrying Faust back to Germany from Greece, retreats to the eastern horizon as a gigantic cumulus cloud in the shape of the "eternal feminine," and hovers there as a remote and inaccessible vision. The last scene of the drama, finally, borrowing the epiphany of the Madonna across a vast cultural gap from the end of Dante's *Paradiso*, offers yet one further instance of apotheosis for the theme of art in both its theatrical and spiritual guise, in ways that may prefigure the forms of sublime parody for a post-Christian aesthetics in the work of such modernists as James Joyce and Thomas Mann.

What should be the outcome of reading *Faust*? More to the point for the purposes of teaching, what should be the impact of such a complex and varied work in the curriculum of university literature courses? I have made a strong plea for the representative role of this work as product of its own time; yet equally I acknowledge that the play continues to exert its own pluralist and even indeterminate influence up to and including our own time. Given the challenge of reading such a wide-ranging and all-encompassing drama, it would be an error to impose even the expectation of a consensus on the outcome. Perhaps we should be content to recognize the challenge and affirm the pleasure that *Faust* can impose on even the most unsuspecting reader. To those who make the commitment to study it, the fascination and surprise of continuing discovery should carry the endeavor forward toward whatever conclusion may seem appropriate and valid for the occasion. *Faust* will continue to conjure us, however ironically in its indirections, much in the manner of Mephistopheles, to the point where the Faustian quest may relate to our own, at least as readers of the text. Who is to say where that may lead and whether the ultimate redemption of such an erring path may also be available even to the experience of reading today?

APPROACHES TO GOETHE AND *FAUST*: GENERAL DISCUSSIONS AND BACKGROUND

The Genre of *Faust*

Jane K. Brown

I am always grateful for the students—and there are several in every course—who are troubled by what they perceive as fundamental moral flaws in *Faust*. They perceive, correctly, that an alliance with the devil is a much more radical evil than a "tragic flaw," and they cannot understand how a Faust can be the hero of a genuine tragedy, much less how such a hero can finally be saved with any credibility. Then, they are troubled by the apparent psychological and emotional inconsistencies of Faust's involvement with Gretchen, by his apparent lack of concern for her emotional and moral welfare. This, as much as the openly fantastic aspects of the play and abrupt shifts of focus, strains their willingness to suspend disbelief. They are correct to be troubled, for they have been taught that tragedy deals with individuals confronting profound moral, emotional, and psychological issues, and in this view psychological consistency is the cardinal virtue. Such are the terms in which our culture has understood Aristotle's *Poetics* for the last three hundred years. The problem, however, is that *Faust* was never conceived in the neo-

Aristotelian terms into which most contemporary readers automatically cast it; it was conceived rather as a kind of giant morality play, in a tradition that I discuss here as "world theater." In order to help students contextualize and understand their reservations about the play and so free themselves to ask the play more appropriate questions, I have increasingly focused my courses both in the original and in translation on the question "What kind of play is *Faust*, what is its genre?"

At the end of the "Prelude in the Theater," Goethe's preliminary reflection on the dramatic mode of *Faust*, the director calls on his people to pace out on the narrow stage the whole circle of creation and to move from heaven through the world to hell. This is a call for "world theater," for the cosmic drama that prevailed in Europe from the late Middle Ages through the seventeenth century. Played on the streets or in theaters with names like The Globe, such drama placed the individual in the largest possible context of his or her relations to the totality of society and of the divine order. These plays, in which supernatural figures, including God, appeared freely on stage (as in the "Prologue in Heaven," which follows immediately on the director's speech) took many forms: morality, Corpus Christi play, masque, the Spanish Golden Age dramas of a Lope de Vega or a Calderón, opera and operetta, even, in many respects, Shakespearean comedy, tragedy, and romance. It was superseded—indeed vigorously suppressed—in the later seventeenth and early eighteenth centuries by the character-oriented neoclassical drama and theory of the Enlightenment. Since then tragedy, the genre to which Goethe assigned *Faust*, has been normally discussed in neoclassical terms, in the vocabulary of hero, innocent suffering, fate, tragic flaw, hubris, guilt, peripety, catastrophe. Well into the seventeenth century, however, the term "tragedy" was much more neutral in meaning, even referring often only to a stage play of serious import. Thus if *Faust* is conceived in the tradition of world theater, which developed essentially independently of the revival of Aristotle's *Poetics*, it should be read in terms of a different poetics and of different questions. This essay briefly outlines the poetics of world theater, or what is often called nonillusionist drama, then suggests, again briefly, what questions and insights about *Faust* such a poetics generates.

Before I outline a poetics of world theater, however, it might be helpful to establish some historical basis for Goethe's relation to this mode. In a ferocious segment of his autobiography (later deleted and published posthumously as the essay "Deutsches Theater") Goethe identifies police, religion, and "morally purified" taste as the main persecutors of the theater through history. "In France," he says, for example, "the pedantry of Cardinal Richelieu subdued [the theater] and squeezed it into its present form"— the "present form" being, in this context, the theater of Corneille and Racine! In Germany, Goethe continues, the theater was taken over by "shallow incompetents"; these turn out to be the leading exponents of French neo-classicism in Germany. Goethe by contrast explicitly wants to turn the devil loose on stage again and to restore the harlequin, both of whom, as standard figures in the world-theater tradition, had been driven from the stage by those same "shallow incompetents." The devil and the clown reappear combined in Goethe's own Mephistopheles. Despite the prominence generally accorded to *Iphigenie* and *Tasso*, the most neoclassical of Goethe's plays, the largest proportion of his dramatic output actually consisted of masques, libretti for operettas, allegorical festival plays, and, of course, *Faust*. Goethe's activity as director of the Weimar theater from 1791 to 1817 reflects similar concerns: he produced, for example, Terence in masks, so that the interest would focus on types rather than individuals; he was the first to produce a play by Calderón in original form on the German stage. His major contribution to the history of theater was to train his company to work as an ensemble: the stage was to provide the spectator with total pictures, like masques. He staged Shakespeare's *Julius Caesar* because he was intrigued with the mob scenes; he adapted *Romeo and Juliet* as a kind of operetta. Even this cursory overview shows clearly that Goethe's conception of drama was not the tightly unified, psychologizing neo-Aristotelian tragedy but rather the episodic thematic drama of the world-theater tradition.

There are no texts that may be called a "poetics" of this form such as abound for neoclassical tragedy. Rather, such a "poetics" must be deduced from the plays themselves. There is an excellent account of this sort for the Corpus Christi cycles in thirteenth-century England in the first two chapters of V. A. Kolve's *The Play Called Corpus Christi*; Stephen Orgel has provided equally important accounts for Stuart masque in the first chapter of *Inigo Jones: The Theater of the Stuart Court* and in *The Illusion of Power: Political Theater in the English Renaissance*. Although these accounts focus on particular, limited manifestations of the mode, nevertheless both contain important and perceptive generalizations about the form that also apply to Goethe's work. Perhaps the paradigmatic text for this tradition is Calderón's *El gran teatro del mundo (The Great Theater of the World)*, a play in which human life is portrayed as a play played before God. Much of Goethe's dramatic practice in *Faust* can be seen in schematic adumbration in this seventeenth-century text, even though there is no evidence of specific influence. Thus it is a good text for focusing a discussion of the poetics of the play at the beginning of a *Faust* course.

The essential difference between world theater and Aristotelian drama is that the first is not mimetic. The action is not an imitation of anything but rather a "game" or "play" that consistently observes certain given conventions, as the very name, "play," suggests. The frequency of the play-within-the-play motif in Shakespeare, Calderón, and *Faust* reflects the extreme self-consciousness of such texts with regard to this trait. Costumes and sets tended to be extremely stylized—either toward schematic simplicity in religious drama or toward ornate elaboration in masque and opera. English Corpus Christi drama was so little concerned with realistic portrayal that the same character was played by different actors at different parts of the cycle. This stylization kept the spectator always aware of the illusion as something to be interpreted and understood: the religious dramas presented sometimes abstruse points of doctrine that would be explained either by *raisonneurs* in the play or by expositor figures. Shakespeare still used choruses, allegorical figures, and narrators sporadically over the whole span of his career. Even in Renaissance court masque, for which the techniques and equipment of the modern illusionist stage were developed, the focus was on the almost magical capacity to evoke illusions rather than on the realism of the illusion, as Orgel demonstrates (*Illusion of Power* 55–56). Similarly the conditions of performance, whether in the street, in a converted banqueting hall, court theater, or Elizabethan outdoor theater, always reminded the spectator in some way of his or her place in the society and thus, metaphorically, of his or her place in the larger cosmic structure in which the play defined itself. The illusion on the stage was not understood to be illusion or imitation of reality, a room with the fourth wall removed, but rather a "game" that revealed the illusoriness of reality in the face of a larger context and higher truth.

The nonmimetic nature of this dramatic mode has important effects on character and plot, the two categories that dominate both Aristotelian poetics and our current language for discussing drama. E. R. Curtius defined the shift from older drama to neoclassical drama as one from theocentric to anthropocentric (142), that is, from one focused on the individual's relations to the cosmos to one focused on the individual's relations to him- or herself and other people. This distinction makes it easier to see why nonillusionist drama often has no hero at all; when there is one, the hero is typical rather than individual, readily universalizable—think, for example, of the readiness with which Goethe's Faust is seen to represent Western man or modern man. And, in general, characters tend to be allegorical, to embody qualities, powers, principles, or social roles, rather than to be rounded individuals. The concepts of tragic flaw and innocent suffering are thus irrelevant to them. Typically such characters do not engage in individualized personal relationships with one another, nor is there necessarily much concern with psychological analysis or even consistency. Even where dramatists show great psychological insight, the movement of the drama will depend more on what characters are than on either their motivations or the interaction of personality and circumstance. Goethe's Faust, for example, is placed by the "Prologue in Heaven" into a larger cosmic structure in which erring is made the necessary condition for salvation. To ask, then, how Faust develops, what he learns, how his relationship to the devil evolves is hardly meaningful; for if he ever learns not to err, he will not be human. Faust is instead a static character who repeatedly destroys other lives in his haste to realize ideals. It is the spectator or reader, who does not identify with Faust, who learns and develops in response to the play. Similarly, the issue in the so-called Gretchen tragedy is not the morality or immorality of the seduction: it is what Gretchen represents for Faust and for us, her relation to earlier and later manifestations of the ideal in the play.

In the same way, plot structure does not involve the standard Aristotelian categories of peripety or reversal, catastrophe, or unity. Not only the unities of time and space but the more fundamental unity of action are frequently ignored. Such drama is, in other words, episodic, and the connection between episodes is often as much or more at the level of theme as at the superficial level of story line. Opera, seventeenth-century Spanish drama, and, indeed, Shakespearean comedy and romance all tend to plots based on Renaissance romance narratives, which are by nature episodic and meandering. Masque has no mimetic plot at all—the interest lies rather in interpreting a series of images rather than imitating reality. The episodic nature of part 2 of *Faust* is immediately apparent; that of part 1 becomes apparent as soon as students realize they can relax and not worry about how or why the action moves from one place to the next. As an example of the implications of this view, let us consider the function of magic in the play. Mephistopheles's magic cloak or the potion in "Witch's Kitchen" seem to be rather arbitrary ways to move the plot from one point to the next. Indeed they are arbitrary, and ought to be recognized as such. The mode of the play actually rejects such connection (and in fact these links disappear between the acts of part 2), but for Goethe's audience in 1808 this mode was already the exception: the arbitrariness of Mephistopheles's magic ironically emphasizes the lack of neoclassical verisimilitude in the apparent unity of the plot and thus calls attention to the fact that the play operates according to different generic principles. Magic is entirely symbolic in the play: it represents the attempted shortcut to transcendent knowledge that Mephistopheles seems to offer to Faust in the same way that it offers shortcuts from one part of the play to the next. Thus the focus is, again, on interpreting the significance of what is visible, not on the Aristotelian category of invisible causality.

Leaving these few examples to suggest how profoundly these different conceptions of character and plot affect our reading of the play, I would like to proceed to some further formal considerations. Once sensitized to the non-Aristotelian aspects of *Faust* the reader can readily see that the text is full of miniature non-Aristotelian forms. It is obvious that act 1 of part 2 contains a Renaissance masque; it is equally obvious that act 3 contains an opera. Acts 2 and 4 depend heavily on Calderón (Atkins, "Goethe" 96–97; J. Brown 191–93, 226–27). The same elements also run all through part 1: the first part of "Outside the City Gate" is a small processional masque, the Gretchen tragedy and "Walpurgis Night" are both structured as operettas, "Walpurgis Night's Dream" is again a masque. Not only is the Gretchen sequence structured exactly like Goethe's own early operetta libretti, but the concluding redemption by the Voice from Above quotes the pardon of Macheath from John Gay's enormously popular *The Beggar's Opera*. This generic identification raises questions about the moral loftiness of the end of part 1, and because the redeemer in Gay is the poet, not God, it suggests that we might take the Gretchen tragedy to address aesthetic issues rather than moral issues.

Indeed Goethe revives in *Faust* not only the various examples of nonillusionist drama but its central self-consciousness as well: *Faust* is a veritable Chinese box of plays within plays. The process begins with the double framing of the action by the two prologues; the Easter chorus in "Night" comes from the Easter sequence, the earliest form of medieval religious drama, being performed in the neighboring church; "Auerbach's Tavern" consists of a series of vaudeville acts; the apes in "Witch's Kitchen" set up a mock court around Mephistopheles, then bring him a mock world; the climactic "Walpurgis Night" issues in the performance of the "Dream," to give only a few examples. I have argued elsewhere (J. Brown 94, 114) that the Gretchen sequence in fact functions as a play within the play, for which we see Faust donning his costume of youthfulness in "Witch's Kitchen." Because the play-within-the-play motif, as indeed the whole world-theater tradition, is revived in *Faust* it does not, of course, have the same significance as it did in Shakespeare or Calderón. If, in the seventeenth century, drama can still serve as a relatively unproblematic metaphor for life, in the secularized eighteenth century, with its modern awareness of the arbitrary nature of all signs, the motif becomes rather a metaphor for art. And so it functions in Goethe, so that his use of the world-theater tradition is not only self-conscious revival of an already self-conscious mode but meditation on the mode itself and on the proper nature of drama.

No matter how effectively Goethe revived this non-Aristotelian mode, he could not have expected simply to erase neoclassicism. When he allows his hero to be blinded just before death, this allusion to *Oedipus the King* returns us to the realm of Aristotle's *Poetics*, for which *Oedipus* was the model text. To juxtapose the paradigmatic tragic moment in the Western—and particularly here, the Aristotelian—tradition with the Baroque opera of salvation that immediately follows is to invite reflection on tragedy in a context much broader than neo-Aristotelianism, that of world theater.

How does this translate into classroom practice? First of all, as I have tried to suggest, recognizing the genre of *Faust* affects our interpretation. It leads me to focus mine on the play's analysis of the nature and function of drama in the context of the epistemological concerns of European Romanticism. Through the large number of imitations and parodies of specific texts in *Faust* this concern takes on a historical dimension, so that the play becomes an extended meditation on the Western literary tradition. In my one-semester course on *Faust*, then, I read the play (both parts) scene by scene, or groups of scenes, in conjunction with Goethe's major sources and analogues. Thus, for example, we read the prologues together with Calderón's *Great Theater of the World* to analyze the context of world theater; then we read the "Prologue in Heaven" with reference to Job, to understand both what Job implies about Goethe's use of the Faust theme and what Faust implies about Goethe's reading of Job. Similarly we read the Gretchen sequence together with the Ophelia sequence from *Hamlet*, with Nicholas Rowe's *The Fair Penitent* (as the most famous example of eighteenth-century seduction tragedy) and *The Beggar's Opera*. It is not possible to read all of *Faust* with all of its analogues in one semester, but even a portion of them introduces students to the range of the tradition as seen from the vantage point of European Romanticism. The rest offer a wealth of interesting paper topics. *Faust* can similarly function in a Great Books course to help students achieve an overview of previous texts and become self-conscious about the differences between Goethe's reading and their own readings of those texts. Indeed my students without urging use *Faust* to organize their own previously scattered perceptions about literature into a larger context: as much as a quarter of the class time is devoted to helping students relate material from other courses—from the Greeks to Emerson to the modern world theater of Claudel, Hofmannsthal, Pirandello, and Brecht—into the larger tradition *Faust* enables them to define.

Goethe and Classicism

Kathleen Harris

What is classicism? From the earliest days of the study of literature, scholars have been tempted to follow August Wilhelm Schlegel's example and set it up in opposition to Romanticism, its chronological contemporary and successor. In his first Vienna lecture on dramatic art and literature Schlegel observes: ". . . the poetry of the ancients was one of possession, ours is one of longing" (25). And critics never tire of citing the aged Goethe's maxim that "Classical is what is healthy, romantic what is sick." (*Maximen*, no. 863. References to the works of Goethe throughout this essay are by title and section, so that the reader may use any edition; the translations are mine.)

It is clear from each of these quotations that both Schlegel and Goethe are referring to the literature of antiquity when they use the term *classical*. In the wake of the nineteenth-century nationalist movement, however, Goethe himself became Germany's principal classical poet. And while this concept is still widely held in *German*-speaking countries today, scholars who come to his work from the tradition of *English* literature commonly see him as a Romantic.

There are grains of truth to be found in all these opinions, but it can be argued that the pursuit of the rhetorical opposition of classical and Romantic can mislead as much as it casts light on the student's way. The following discussion will, therefore, concentrate on defining the concept of classicism from its initial relevance for Goethe's view of the world to its impact on *Faust* and will trace in passing his thinking on "classical" literature in the German language.

Recalling the period of convalescence that he spent at home in Frankfurt after a severe bout of illness had put an end to his studies in Leipzig, Goethe noted: "I turned once more . . . to my beloved ancients, who still, like far-off blue mountains, bounded the horizons of my intellectual wishes" (*Dichtung und Wahrheit* 2.8).

This is but one of numerous statements that Goethe made on aspects of antiquity at various times during his long life. In the search to understand the poet's relation to what we call in English "classicism," it will, therefore, be necessary not only to try to define *his* concept but also to explore the meaning of the terms that have been employed both in German and in English.

First of all, a simple warning is in order: the reader should beware of literal translations. To be sure, the standard dictionary reference will tell us that "classicism" is the English equivalent of "der Klassizismus." Germans, however, also use the term "die Klassik," sometimes in the form "die deutsche Klassik," by which they usually—and primarily—mean the work of Goethe and Schiller above all. "Der Klassizismus"—a term coined by literary historians—may accordingly, but not necessarily (or entirely), be synonymous with "die Klassik," and both—or neither—represent *Goethe's* position at any given time.

In order to clear the approaches to an understanding of the issues, let us examine the force exerted by the terms as descriptors and as norms. While I refer to the interplay of politics and the search for a national identity and to the categorizations of historians of literature, my main concern is to make Goethe's position clear for readers of today, who in this particular instance are preparing for a study of *Faust*.

The Latin words *classis* 'class' (of citizen) and *classicus* 'belonging to a class' (of citizens, ships, etc.) form the linguistic starting point for our modern terms "classic," "classical," and "classicism." As Curtius points out, these criteria were initially applied to the *grammatically* correct use of language by a select number of "model" authors. Only in the course of the rediscovery of Greek and Roman literature by Western Europeans in the early sixteenth century did a broadening of the definition occur, to include the *aesthetic* notions that our dictionaries list today, such as "objectivity," "formality," "balance," "simplicity," "dignity," and "restraint." At that time, moreover, *all* the literature of antiquity, as then known (and, by extension, the world that it represented) was elevated to the status of a canon of perfection, valid for all ages to come.

Walter Muschg reminds us in "Die deutsche Klassik, tragisch gesehen" (157) that the poets of imperial Rome, filters through which the Renaissance saw ancient Greece, were the singers of power, servants of the state through their literary creations. Thus the very existence of a powerful state came to be regarded as another prerequisite for the emergence of a "classical" literature—as was true in seventeenth-century France.

That these conditions did not prevail in either seventeenth- or eighteenth-century Germany is only too evident to the student of history. Well into this century, scholars have continued to discuss whether the *wish* for a national classical literature was father to the *thought* (as Muschg argues in the last chapter of his *Tragische Literaturgeschichte*, esp. on pp. 602–03) or whether, as August Wilhelm Schlegel has it, the true successors of the ancients were simply those who rejected the doctrine of *imitation* (as propagated by Gottsched and others) and claimed for themselves the status of *competitors*. The debate can be followed in such German compilations as those of Burger (bearing in mind the caveat of his socialist reviewer Hecht—in the words of Robert Minder—that bourgeois writers of literary history have intellectually uprooted the so-called Age of Goethe from its sociohistorical setting in eighteenth-century Europe), Johannes Irmscher, and Chiarini and Dietze. Hatfield takes another approach; initially following Santayana, he postulates a number of "classicisms" through which Goethe passed between Winckelmann's Greece and *Faust* (*Goethe*, esp. pp. 57, 75, and 98). Then, setting Goethe firmly in the context of German thought between Winckelmann and Wilhelm von Humboldt, he takes his notion one step further. Pointing up both differences and similarities between what he now calls "literary classicism" and "paganism," he traces these two new concepts in Goethe's work between the *Prometheus* fragment and *Faust II* (*Aesthetic Paganism*, esp. pp. 72, 116, and 230).

The eighteenth century was, however, a stone with many facets, resisting simple definition. The "movements" so beloved of literary historians, instead of following each other in an orderly fashion, overlap, intersect, and even collide with their neighbors. Thus we find representatives of the Enlightenment almost throughout the century, making Rococo, Sentimentality, and Storm and Stress look, relatively speaking, like nine-day wonders, while the Age of Goethe spans not only parts, even the whole, of some of these epochs but also all of the Romantic period, extending considerably beyond 1800.

Among Goethe's earliest memories, predating considerably the passage cited earlier, were those of "a series of views of Rome, . . . with which my father had decorated an anteroom . . ." (*Dichtung und Wahrheit* 1.1). His impressions were accordingly drawn from a selection of the monuments of imperial and Renaissance Rome and thus conformed in all respects to the received tradition. They had no discernible impact on the small quantity of his early poetry that has survived, which follows a variety of conventional models and can, therefore, be classed as "acceptable imitation." One should nonetheless be wary of assuming that the impact was nil; the creative time lag between Goethe's reception of a new experience and the emergence of a new phase of poetic development is a characteristic that can be observed throughout his life.

A major widening of the horizons appears to have taken place in Leipzig, the initial agent probably being his drawing master Oeser, who first made him aware of the work of Winckelmann; a later visit to Mannheim, where he first saw plaster copies of a number of Greek and Roman figures and architectural fragments, provided some practical illustration of Winckelmann's text. It is accordingly more than a mere coincidence that his choice and conception of the protagonists of the Great Hymns (Prometheus, Ganymed, the nameless wanderer-poets) and of the Artists' Poems (the painter-genius in reflection and in the situations of daily living) both reflect his perception of the classical world and form part of his contribution to the discussion of genius by the poets of Storm and Stress. Occasionally he adapts a classical form, such as the dialogue pattern of the idyll ("Der Wanderer"). Traditional German verses are also present; most often the verses are entirely free.

Evidence for the persistent attraction of Italy is to be found in a drawing, done at the St. Gotthard Pass in 1775, in the course of the first journey to

Switzerland, and entitled "Parting Look at Italy." But it was only via Weimar that Goethe eventually reached Italy and that the classical world came to play a major role in his work. Ten years as court official and administrator, ten years of intense emotional involvement with Charlotte von Stein, were, however, also years of relatively little in the way of *literary* creation, though there were, to be sure, the poems of natural philosophy and a number of first drafts of narrative and dramatic works (*Wilhelm Meister, Faust, Egmont, Iphigenie auf Tauris, Tasso*). So we are hardly surprised either to learn of his "escape" to Italy in the fall of 1786 or to read his later confession to Herder: "my feet only hurt in tight shoes" (*Italienische Reise,* "Second Stay in Rome," Dec. 1787).

"The great advantage that Goethe derived from his work as a Weimar official was one that he did not foresee," notes Barker Fairley. "For the first time in his life he found himself associated with practical men, . . . [a]nd . . . he was compelled to see the world with their eyes" (*Study* 78). And it was just when he was struggling to acquire "a notion of antiquity" by studying monuments that were mostly in ruins that he recognized the capacity of his eye for geology and landscape to give him "a free, clear perception of the locality," one that was also free of imagination and emotional impression (*Italienische Reise,* "Ferrara to Rome," 27 Oct. 1786). What he calls "classical ground" is equated with the "sensuously intellectual conviction" of the presence of greatness, greatness that is at one and the same time transitory and eternal. Returning to this train of thought a little over one year later, he sums up by encouraging his readers to produce "something of significance that may from now on inspire our successors . . . to noble activity . . ." (*Italienische Reise,* "Report," Dec. 1787).

He had himself already put his stay to good use. In January he had sent Herder the new *Iphigenie auf Tauris,* reworked in verse; by early September *Egmont* was complete; and he had at least taken with him the *Tasso* fragment on the trip to Sicily. During this time, however, Goethe's experience of the Roman and Greek past had combined with the Italian present to produce a fundamental shift in his stance. From asking, in Mignon's longing verses, "Do you know the land where the lemon trees bloom?" he moves, in the *Roman Elegies* (or *Erotica Romana,* as the subtitle describes them), to a joyful expression of the experience of fulfillment in life and love, competing with his Roman forebears Tibullus, Propertius, and Ovid in the language and form of the elegy as erotic idyll. Because Goethe himself was the first (but not the only one) to censor these poems, generations of scholars have ignored their central significance, preferring instead to see in *Iphigenie* his primary statement on the "classical" values imparted by antiquity and in *Tasso* the "classical" working out of the problems of the artist in society.

With the return to Weimar in the spring of 1788 came the confrontation of the new ethos with the old. As Barker Fairley puts it in *A Study of Goethe,*

"the pull of Charlotte . . . was away from the ancients, not towards them" (142). Difficulties, both personal and social, were inevitable, especially after he took Christiane into his household, and a second visit made it plain that (as he wrote to Duke Carl August from Venice on 3 Apr. 1790) "the first bloom of inclination and curiosity" had fallen, a fact to which the *Venetian Epigrams* bear witness. And while the campaign in France of 1792 brought some small consolation to his "objective eye" by way of renewed evidence of the presence of antiquity on German soil (*Campagne in Frankreich*, "On the Way to Trier"), it was not until the first, fruitful meeting with Schiller in 1794 that Goethe found inspiration for the next stage of his intellectual and spiritual journey.

Now, for the first time, we find him applying the term "klassisch" to authors, German authors, when he asks what conditions are necessary for the development of a "classical national author" ("Literarischer Sanskulottismus," 1795). Coming to the conclusion that only a political cataclysm on the order of a French Revolution would provide the right conditions, he decides that the nation should not be reproached either for its unifying geography or its political fragmentation. And since German writers lack a cultural center and have even suffered from the dominance of a foreign (French) literature and culture, young writers might do much worse than take a careful author like Wieland for a model.

Many literary historians have called the decade between 1795 and 1805 the period of Goethe's and Schiller's "Hochklassik" (or "Hochklassizismus," depending on which terminology is favored). Analysts such as Pyritz and Staiger have also pointed to factors that were bound to circumscribe both the character and the duration of their creative relationship—factors of temperament, manner of thinking, and poetic style. Thus we find Goethe, when he reflects later on the time spent working with Schiller (in the essay of 1820 entitled "Influence of Recent Philosophy"), observing that because he himself had argued for the absolute supremacy of the Greek style of poetry and its underlying aesthetic, Schiller had been obliged to think the matter over "more sharply." As a result, "we owe the essays on naive and sentimental poetry precisely to this conflict." At the time, however, he failed to recognize that by consciously striving to be *only* a "classical" poet he was willfully restricting his poetic genius, even putting himself in an intellectual straitjacket. Certainly these years were productive: they brought forth public polemics as well as experiments with the verse forms of antiquity (*Xenien, Alexis und Dora*), a modern epic poem (*Hermann und Dorothea*), and the first sketches for those parts of *Faust* that are set in the ancient world—or one of Goethe's re-creation ("Classical Walpurgis Night," the Helena act). But he completed only one canto of *Achilleis*, and after Schiller's death in 1805, Goethe's work took another direction, one that did not bring him back to *Faust* for two decades.

This is not to say that he stopped thinking about the ancient and the modern worlds. He furnishes us with a very useful summary in the essay of 1805 on Winckelmann. Again, in the essay of 1818 entitled "Ancient and Modern" he reflects on the qualities that a truly great artist must have. Taking Raphael once more as his example, he characterizes him as one who, while he "nowhere takes on Greek airs, . . . feels, thinks, acts thoroughly like a Greek." And so we are not at all surprised to find him exhorting the reader, in closing: "Let each one be a Greek in his own way! But let him *be* one."

So what does "being a Greek in his own way" mean for our understanding of *Faust?* Emrich and, following him, Trunz have argued convincingly that the essential step for Goethe was to recognize that notions of the ancient world could only bear fruit in modern times as historical phenomena, not as ethical or aesthetic norms. This was the stumbling block that had prevented both the completion of *Achilleis* and the first attempt to integrate the Helena motif into *Faust*. (A student's report on Goethe's literary "failures" during this period would serve to illustrate this point very well, while a study of the treatment of Helena in the various *Volksbuch* versions of *Faust* would set the stage for Goethe's transformation of the figure.)

Now Goethe could explore through the drama the contribution of the ancient world to modern civilization; Faust could be permitted to bring the shade of Helena from the underworld; and Goethe's creation, the perceptive spirit Homunculus, could enter the chain of evolution. Even Mephistopheles, medieval spirit of negation, is pressed into service as "Phorkyas in profile," simulacrum of one of the ancient daughters of Phorkys, old man of the sea. Now "she" is employed by the poet as foil to Helena, both as essence of ugliness and as arouser of unwelcome memories of the legendary-historical past. (The Helena legends might well be the subject of another brief report, to point up the significance of this verbal exchange for the action that follows, both in the *Faustburg* and in Arcadia.)

By confronting the modern world with the ancient one and—at least temporarily—achieving a synthesis between them, Goethe has, of course, created a new myth. Subjects for investigation and class discussion abound, particularly in these two acts of *Faust II*. Instructors and students may care to explore some of the following topics and, I hope, be inspired to formulate more of their own, taking Phorkyas's words to Faust as their motto: "Hold on to what you have retained" (3.9945):

1. The function of Homunculus
2. The role of landscape and geology in Goethe's conception of history
3. Goethe's use of precise historical events as starting points for his poetic creation

4. The role of history and biology in the "Classical Walpurgis Night"
5. The function of Phorkyas in the verbal duel with Helena—and in Arcadia
6. Goethe's use of verse forms to create special effects and atmosphere in acts 2 and 3
7. Why was Faust not saved by *Helena*?

Goethe and Romanticism

Neil M. Flax

Whether Goethe is a Romantic ranks among the most vexed issues in German literary studies. For the teacher of *Faust* in an undergraduate literature course, it makes sense to sidestep the complex debates and work from Cyrus Hamlin's premise that "we must never forget that *Faust* is the masterpiece of a poet writing during the Romantic era" (370). Hamlin's position is also supported by René Wellek's classic essay "The Concept of Romanticism," which affirms that "Goethe perfectly fits into the European romantic movement which he, as much as any single writer, helped to create" (163).

What are the typical traits of a work of the Romantic movement? Wellek identifies them as "a view of poetry as knowledge of the deepest reality, of nature as a living whole, and of poetry as primarily myth and symbolism" (161). All these elements are crucial in *Faust*, and the standard commentaries have discussed them in great detail. In my own teaching of *Faust I* in a Great Books course, I have found it helpful to focus on two additional aspects of Romantic literature. Critics have begun to pay closer attention to these topics in recent years and have modified our thinking about Romanticism in decisive ways. The revised reading of the Romantics does not deny the importance of Wellek's themes but views them in a somewhat different light. The two topics are Romantic irony and the Romantic inquiry into the nature of language.

Romantic Irony

To introduce the basic concepts of Romantic irony, I rely on Anne K. Mellor's excellent study *English Romantic Irony*. The opening chapter gives an unusually clear summary of the German writings, chiefly by Friedrich Schlegel, which first presented the idea of Romantic irony. Mellor's book is especially helpful to the teacher of a general or comparative literature course, since it goes on to establish the affinities between German Romantic thought and the major English writers of the period. Mellor identifies the essential trait of Romantic irony as permanent, irreconcilable self-contradiction. In the Romantic-ironic work, mythic patterns are at once affirmed and rejected. Programmatic skepticism is countered by enthusiastic invention. A fictional world is both sincerely presented and sincerely undermined. The artist projects his or her ego as a divine creator and also mocks, criticizes, or rejects the created fictions as limited and false. The work presents two contradictory ideas or themes, which the author carefully balances but refuses to synthesize or harmonize.

These formulations of Mellor's seem to me to provide an ideal preparation for the reading of Goethe's *Faust*. The aptness of the phrases is no accident. They summarize ideas of Friedrich Schlegel's that were shaped in large part by his own reading of *Faust* and *Wilhelm Meister*. If we reapply Schlegel's ideas to their original source, we can trace the workings of Romantic irony in *Faust* in the following major areas. The topics are by no means exhaustive, but they suggest an approach to *Faust* that is in tune with the spirit of the German Romantic movement.

Self-reflection. One of the chief Romantic devices for bringing internal division into a literary work is to have the work overtly reflect on its own status as a work of literature. Schlegel speaks of Goethe as the great modern exemplar of this "artistic reflection and beautiful self-mirroring." The Romantic literary work, Schlegel continues, "should describe itself, and always be simultaneously poetry and the poetry of poetry" (qtd. in Mellor 15). From the outset, *Faust* presents itself, in this sense, as both theater and the theater of theater. The play begins with a sequence of three "nested" prologues: a dedication spoken by the playwright about his own reactions to the play, a conversation on the empty stage among the play's director, the author, and an actor, and a prologue in the form of a parody of divine revelation scenes in the Baroque theater. The sequence clearly illustrates the explicit self-reflection on the artistic medium that Schlegel celebrated in Romantic art. From these opening moments, as Jane K. Brown convincingly shows earlier in this volume, "*Faust* is a veritable Chinese box of plays within plays" and a sustained "meditation on . . . the proper nature of drama." (For a thorough account of artistic self-reflection in *Faust*, see Brown's chapter in the present volume and her study *Goethe's* Faust: *The German Tragedy.*)

Symmetrical Contradiction. Schlegel describes the ideal Romantic-ironic work as "[a] charming symmetry of contradictions, [a] wonderfully perennial alternation of enthusiasm and irony which lives even in the smallest part of the whole" (qtd. in Mellor 18). In *Faust*, the dual principles of enthusiasm and irony are of course embodied in the figures of Faust and Mephistopheles. Much of the dramatic energy of the play comes from the clash of these two opposing impulses. Once students have been keyed to the importance of the polarity, they easily discover many examples on their own. To the extent that there is any character development in the figure of Faust in part 1, it is seen in his growing awareness of the basic antagonism between his own ardor and the devil's cynicism. The recognition culminates in his scathing line to Mephistopheles: "Her [Gretchen's] misery cuts clean to the marrow of my life; yet you grin coolly at the doom of thousands!" (MacIntyre trans., 62. Subsequent quotations are taken from this translation, which I have found to be the most readable of the available versions of part 1.)

The implacable conflict of character types provides a good starting point for class discussions of the moral (or immoral, or amoral) implications of the

Gretchen tragedy. Also apropos here is the unresolved conclusion of the play, which simultaneously declares of Gretchen that "She is saved" and "She is damned." The Romantic principle of perpetual contradiction is sustained to the last moment of the play and beyond. (Looking ahead to the fiercely ironic conclusion of part 2, we can ask whether a Gretchen fated to be eternally drawn to Faust isn't indeed eternally damned.)

The Fertility of Chaos. Romantic literature, according to Mellor, is preoccupied with an essential human longing for system and order and an equally basic recognition that the world is ultimately chaotic. (Other works of literature may deal with the same conflict; Romantic works try to keep the conflict unresolved.) For Schlegel, the Romantic work can only embody this inescapable contradiction by perpetually oscillating between the two poles. As Schlegel puts it, once philosophy has reached its goal of understanding, it "should begin again and again from the beginning—alternating between chaos and system, chaos preparing for system and then new chaos" (qtd. in Mellor 8). Here again, Faust and Mephistopheles can easily be seen as the representatives of the two opposing principles. The action begins with Faust enthralled by mystical signs of universal order and harmony. Then he is awed by the Earth Spirit, whose activity of "weaving" remains an indelible image of ordered energy in the cosmos. The remainder of Faust's adventure is a prolonged quest to recover these momentary glimpses of a transcendent unity.

Meanwhile Mephistopheles, whom Faust calls a "wayward son of Chaos" (42) and who identifies himself as "the beloved son of Chaos" (pt. 2, line 8027), is everywhere the subverter of order and structure. Whatever realms of experience Faust runs through in the two parts of the drama—romance, family, court society, finance, myth, art, warfare, government—Mephistopheles works there as the great disrupter of familiar, established patterns of life. What is essential in teaching *Faust* as an exemplar of Romantic irony is to recognize the perfect neutrality of the work toward the dual principles of chaos and system. The moralism of earlier versions of the Faust legend has been completely eliminated. The devil is no longer the evil spirit who fits into a higher providential scheme of ultimate good. He is now the agent of some primal principle of ungoverned energy (Goethe would later call it "Daimon"), which knows nothing of good, evil, purpose, or plan in the universe and which ceaselessly destroys static and finite structures in order to throw up new forms of creation.

To be sure, Mephistopheles introduces himself to Faust as the one who "always wills evil and always works good." But he is quick to dissociate himself from this conventional morality, pointedly remarking to Faust that he is "everything that *you* call sin and destruction, in short, evil" (40; emphasis mine). Mephistopheles freely admits then that he is a spirit of sheer

negativity. His personal motto is an unforgettable expression of pure ni-
hilism: "For all that exists deserves to be destroyed." But by virtue of its
power to shatter fixed orders of experience, this negative principle called
"Chaos" is *also* a source of productive, creative energy. The paradox of
Goethe's nihilistic devil is that his actual dramatic function in the play is to
perform the work of an artist or impresario. His bet with Faust obliges him
to become a showman who leads his companion through a series of enter-
tainments fabricated out of a mysterious mixture of magic and reality. Mephistopheles's "shows" come to life in turn, occupy Faust for a brief time as
patterns filled with meaning, and then fade away like dreams. The ironic
interplay of the two characters is that Mephistopheles, the cynical creator
of these marvelous fictions, can never take any pleasure in his handiwork
—it all "deserves to be destroyed"; while Faust, no matter how often he is
duped and disappointed, never loses his longing for the powerful illusions.

Of course we should be careful of evincing too much sympathy for the
devil. Mephistopheles is in fact the object of an irony and ridicule in the
play that is at least as potent as that aimed at Faust. The mockery reaches
a delightful climax in the closing scenes, where Mephistopheles momentarily
succumbs to a bit of heavenly theater himself and thereby loses the payoff
on the wager that he has pursued for so long. As Schlegel puts it, the ultimate
goal of the Romantic artist is "transcendental buffoonery," a "mood that
surveys everything and rises infinitely above all limitations, even above its
own art, virtue, or genius" (qtd. in Mellor 17). In this spirit, Goethe the
Romantic poet mocks his own self-representation in the figure of the artist-
devil who is finally duped by a higher art, just as he mocks his ardent quest
hero Faust for his incurable credulity. But he also presents his two protagonists in full seriousness. They appear as exponents of the two primordial
principles that make up the Romantic's universe: abysmal but fertile chaos
and beautiful but ephemeral order.

Romantic Parody. In English usage, the term "parody" usually suggests
a mocking or burlesque imitation of a familiar literary work. Schlegel uses
the term in a way that is somewhat more subtle and a good deal more
applicable to one of the major traditions in modern literature. He defines
parody in *Literary Notebooks* as "a witty translation" (118; trans. mine). This
ambiguous type of parody stands both inside and outside the original model,
repeating it and criticizing it, honoring and mocking it at the same time. "A
true parody," Schlegel observes, "itself possesses what is being parodied."
A work "can only be parodied by one of its own kind" (110).

Because the figure of Faust has so often been inflated into an archetype
of modern Western civilization, or of the German soul, or of some other
large historical abstraction, it is difficult now to recover the quality of Romantic parody that pervades the play. But it is worth the effort to focus on

how Goethe's *Faust* is a "witty translation" of the older Faust materials and especially of the idea at the heart of the legend, the story of Faust's pact with the devil. In a number of ways, Goethe seeks to eliminate the traditional cautionary meanings that the Faust legend had for an earlier audience. He turns the original pact with the devil into a bet that Faust loses but then somehow doesn't have to pay up on. The hero's salvation is justified by an ethic of restless "striving" that would be very difficult to apply as a universal moral principle. When Faust's guilt for the destruction of Gretchen and her family has faded into the distant past, Faust becomes responsible for the deaths of two more innocent victims, Baucis and Philemon. Yet moments later—as if this final reminder of his true character were all that was needed—he is swept up into heaven. In effect, a story whose popular appeal rested to a great extent on its clear moral message has been transformed into a tale that defies any conventional moral reading.

Is this a viciously immoral work? Only if we think it is trying to say something about ethical behavior in traditional terms. A more plausible view is that its concern is not with questions of conventional ethics but with questions of art conceived as a new category of morality. Goethe aims to establish—in the spirit of Kant's aesthetics—the absolutely disinterested, nonutilitarian, nonpragmatic nature of the work of art. He does this in *Faust* by turning all the familiar rules and expectations about morality in literature upside down. The reversal could not be more dramatic, since the models that are parodied, the Faust chapbooks and puppet plays, represent an epitome of naively moralistic literature.

But holding true to the requisites of Romantic irony, even as *Faust* affirms the new gospel of aesthetic autonomy, the play also tests the Kantian ideal and questions its implications for the moral realm. The issue here is not simply the idea of aesthetic autonomy but the whole related German tradition of "the aesthetic education of the human race," the curious and fateful notion expounded by Lessing, Kant, Schiller, Schlegel, and Hegel and later on by Wagner, Nietzsche, and countless others. According to this notion, in aesthetic experience alone would human beings learn how to be set free. In one sense, this is precisely what happens in *Faust*. If Faust does finally earn his salvation, it is by passing through Mephistopheles's school of aesthetic illusion. But the moral costs of this education are so exorbitant that the play seems finally to negate the ideal of aesthetic autonomy even as it is enacting it. Here again, we encounter the form of Romantic irony, which provides for unresolved contradiction on all levels of the work. As a true Romantic parody, *Faust* mocks the simple moralism of its original literary model and openly declares its own aesthetic autonomy; but at the same time it works as a profoundly moral critique of German aesthetic idealism. "A true parody," to repeat Schlegel's words, "itself possesses what is being parodied."

Romantic Inquiry into the Nature of Language

The idea of the poetic symbol as the revealer of ultimate truths is, as noted earlier, one of the basic tenets of Romantic theory. Discussions of the topic often cite such well-known maxims as Goethe's "This is true symbolism, where the particular represents the more general, not as a dream or shadow, but as a living, visible, and instantaneous revelation of the unfathomable" (*Maximen und Reflexionen* 471; trans. mine) or Coleridge's description: "a translucence of the special in the individual, or of the general in the special, or of the universal in the general, above all . . . the translucence of the eternal through and in the temporal" (qtd. in Mellor 23). The Romantic symbol, then, is a sign that incarnates an idea and makes the idea visible and present. It stands in opposition to ordinary language and to allegory, which, in the Romantic view, employ arbitrary and conventional tokens to represent ideas.

But the presence of such theories of the symbol in a poet's critical writings does not guarantee that the poetical writings will work in precisely the same way. The actual operations of Romantic poetic language are much more ambivalent. In Romantic literature, as Mellor observes, "symbols are generated only to be qualified and rejected; . . . the capacities of figural discourse are celebrated even as they are finally found inadequate" (6, 11). This equivocal treatment of the symbol is a crucial feature of Goethe's *Faust*. The question of the revelatory power of symbolic signs comes up in the earliest moments of the play. Faust denounces his library of academic books for failing to reveal the inner truths of nature. He turns instead to two magical emblems in the book of Nostradamus, and they promptly provide him with something like the instantaneous revelation he was seeking. Neither the macrocosm sign nor the sign of the Earth Spirit offers Faust a lasting contact with the higher realms; the epiphanies are fleeting. But they confirm Faust in the belief that where ordinary language obstructs our vision of ultimate realities, symbolic signs can reveal these realities in their unqualified essence. Henceforth, Faust's quest will be to recover permanently that sense of divine revelation which he experienced for an instant with the two magical symbols.

What Faust discovers, however, in the course of his quest for transcendence, is that the more he relies on revelatory symbols to deliver him from routine reality, the more infallibly these symbols turn out to be just like the ordinary language he hoped to escape. The signs are obstacles rather than vehicles to transcendence. He takes the image of the beautiful woman in Mephistopheles's magic mirror, for example, as just such a revelatory symbol: "What a heavenly picture . . . the very essence of heaven" (84). But when he finally possesses the real woman, Gretchen, for whom the magical image served as a premonitory sign, the affair ends with Faust in Gretchen's prison cell, suffering an even greater measure of confinement, impotence, and despair than he knew in the narrow limits of his library.

In a similar fashion, Faust uses a series of magical symbols—secret spells from the *Clavicula salomonis*, the holy letters inscribed on the crucifix, the mystical emblem of a triangle with the eye of God in the center—to conjure forth the spirit who will help him escape from his sterile academic life. But here again the outcome of this "successful" use of revelatory signs is another defeat. Faust finds in his long association with Mephistopheles that even with supernatural help transcendence still eludes him. (For a more detailed account of this ironic pattern in *Faust*, see Flax.)

The play then is a sort of semiotic *Lost Illusions* or *Sentimental Education*. The naive hero passes through a series of episodes in which his high hopes of gaining salvation through a revelatory sign repeatedly meet with bitter disappointment. But the experiences never completely destroy his faith in the magical powers of language. The end of the play finds him still celebrating the authority of "the Word" in scriptural terms: "The Word of the Lord, it alone lends force" (line 11502). However, a crucial transformation has occurred, and this is the key to Faust's mysterious salvation: it is now his own words that he refers to as "des Herren Wort." Instead of invoking the *Erdgeist* with a magical symbol from an esoteric book, he has himself become the "Geist," or Spirit, who can command the energies of nature: "One Spirit suffices for a thousand hands" (11510). The culmination of Faust's long education in Mephistopheles's school of art is that he finally transforms himself into an artist, a creator, a conjurer of new worlds out of a compound of his own commanding words, Mephistopheles's demonic magic, and the material reality of nature. To be sure, his creation of a new paradise on earth is a self-delusion, but all art, as the play has repeatedly shown, is delusion. The important point is that Faust, as a creator, has finally tapped into the divine sources of being and is thus ready to ascend to a higher realm. But he does not achieve his transcendence by finding the right revelatory symbol in a magic book or magic mirror; rather, he turns his own ordinary words into the speech of a demonic power. The quest for a transcendental sign ends when the quester begins to speak like a god.

The *Faust* play stands then in a highly equivocal relation to the theory of poetic language that Goethe formulated and shared with the other Romantics. Through most of its length the play ironically dissolves the supposed opposition between ordinary language and revelatory symbol. But then at the last minute, coinciding with Faust's salvation, it pulls a stunning reversal and shows that there really *is* a special language that can present "an instantaneous revelation of the unfathomable." But this divine language is not set apart, as Faust mistakenly believed, by something special in the nature of the signs themselves; the revelatory power of the words resides rather in the nature of the being who speaks them. The key distinction is not between ordinary language and transcendental symbol but between ordinary speakers and divine creators.

At this point Romantic language theory merges with Romantic aesthetics, ethics, and politics. All the fierce individualism, the intense subjectivity, the extreme glorification of the creative genius that typify Romanticism are crystallized in Faust's self-transformation and elevation to higher spheres. How seriously Goethe intends this climax to be taken is hard to say. Certainly the counterpoint of Mephistopheles's burlesque defeat and the operatic profusion of orthodox Christian imagery in the final scenes suggest that Faust's apotheosis may also be an example of "transcendental buffoonery." But it is no less possible that Goethe is dead serious; much in his other writings and his most personal beliefs would support this view. Here critical concepts like Romanticism, however useful, begin to show their limits and the individual work stands alone with its own enigmatic identity.

The Problem of Gretchen

Lilian R. Furst

To students of today who ask in all good faith (as mine do) why Flaubert's Emma Bovary doesn't get a divorce from the husband she loathes and why Richardson's Clarissa Harlowe doesn't leave home, the behavior of Gretchen poses problems. By the commonsensical norms of the late twentieth century with its aspirations to egalitarianism between the genders and the classes, her relationship to Faust strains credibility. Her docility, her submissiveness, her childlike innocence, and her punctilious concept of virtue seem quaint, not to say farfetched. In fact, the very qualities that so endeared Gretchen to eighteenth-century readers and that made her the "emblem of the pure German maiden" (P. Heller 175) now represent a source of puzzlement, perhaps even irritation. How can any girl be so naive? Why doesn't it dawn on her that Faust's attentions to her are geared to seduction (especially since she does harbor doubts as to his religious beliefs and feels an instinctive revulsion to his companion, Mephistopheles)? Why don't her own Christian upbringing and tenets make her more steadfast in resistance? Why doesn't she at any point assert herself and make at least some minimal demands on Faust? Her only initiative comes in her uneasy probing of his beliefs. Otherwise she puts Faust under no obligation whatsoever and clearly assumes that he carries no responsibility toward her or even toward his child. Why does she so readily accede to suffering as the woman's lot?

Such questions can be addressed through a variety of approaches that may overlap and certainly don't exclude one another. The most obvious and immediate one is by reference to the eighteenth-century ideal of womanhood. Long before Sarah Stickney Ellis formulated the advice that has come to be associated with the Victorian woman, namely that her "highest duty is so often to suffer and be still," the ethos implicit in that dictum, an attitude of passivity, resignation, and silent acceptance of one's lot exerted a shaping influence on women's bearing and conduct. The figure of Gretchen is strongly indebted to these conventions. She embodies many of the traits that the eighteenth century prized in a young girl, above all goodness and innocence. It is worth noting that Faust twice actually calls her an "angel" (Heinemann ed., lines 3490 and 3510), thereby endowing her with the attributes most highly cherished in a woman at that time. Her modesty and purity are denoted too by her "small clean room" (stage directions preceding 2678), which acts as an objective correlative to her character. The same qualities of innocence and purity are emphasized by the other terms used of her. Not only is she frequently described as a child ("Kind"), but she envisages herself as such when she speaks of herself as "ein arm unwissend Kind" 'a poor unknowing child' (3215). Her language has the simplicity and directness of a child's, while her lyrics suggest folk songs, with their regular four-line stanzas, uncomplicated rhymes, and symmetrical repetition. This reiterated insistence on her ingenuousness results in a certain infantilization of Gretchen that coincides with the eighteenth century's condescension toward women. The reductiveness contained in "child" is confirmed by such phrases as "Liebe Puppe" 'dear doll' (3476), "Dirne" 'wench' (2619), and "Ding" 'thing' (2624), which may in some contexts be intended as terms of endearment towards a female but which nevertheless betray a distinctly patronizing attitude.[1] So Gretchen's docility can be seen as reflecting the behavior expected of a young woman of that period and the role in which she is cast by a male-directed society.

Yet such a reading of her character runs into problems of its own, first and foremost because Gretchen infringes the conventions into which I have been trying to set her. The force of her attraction to Faust leads her to break the most sacrosanct code of womanly behavior by yielding to his advances. She defends her actions, even while conceding their sinfulness, by absolute criteria of morality that transcend time-bound conventions: "Yet—everything that drove me to it / Was so good! oh God! was so dear!" (3585–86). Her appeal to the goodness of her motives is a variant of the argument that the ends justify the means. In resorting to such a plea, Gretchen is breaking out of the ethical and social frame posited for women in the eighteenth century. By advancing a personal code of conduct and by hazarding an apologia for erotic feelings, she can be taken as an early example of a Romantic heroine. The situation is considerably complicated by the role reversal in effect here. The more usual eighteenth-century scenario, of course, shows a male swept along by the violence of his passions. However, Gretchen is by no means exceptional in Goethe's works in stepping out of the woman's customary role. Beginning with Lotte in *The Sorrows of Young Werther* (1774) there is a long line of Goethean women who are as much the incarnations of masculine sense as of feminine sensibility (see Furst). But Lotte and her successors are more consistent than Gretchen. The difficulty with Gretchen stems from her conformity by and large to the submissiveness expected of women and its alliance to a mode of thought and conduct prohibited to eighteenth-century women. She becomes a self-contradictory figure as she endeavors to fashion her own program of conduct—a privilege that was in itself denied to her female contemporaries.

This inner contradiction in Gretchen makes it all the more imperative to take a broader approach to her so as to become aware of the diverse strands that have been interwoven into this persona. Such a broader approach involves a process of contextualization that helps the reader perceive Gretchen not as an isolated and perplexing figure but as the outcome of a literary tradition and of a sociohistorical predicament.

The literary tradition from which Gretchen devolves is that of innocence led astray. The theme has been traced back to classical literature, to Lucretia and Virginia (see Petriconi), who form the prototypes of the young woman whose purity is so great that she is virtually defenseless against the advances of her seducer because she has no experience or understanding of evil. However implausible such a foolish virgin may seem in our day, she was a common reality in times when women were brought up so shielded from the world as to be ignorant of its ways. Their sheltered existence within the family circle prevented the development of their powers of judgment and so made them easy prey to the predatory male provided he maintained the mask of polite courtesy. Even the highly intelligent young women of Jane Austen's novels run the danger of deception (and seduction) by specious scoundrels.

The motif of the innocent female led astray by the unscrupulous male has a lengthy literary lineage. It occurs in many major writers, including Chaucer, Lope de Vega, Calderón, Shakespeare, Molière, and Racine. The Don Juan legend too in its multiple variants is another manifestation of the same theme. About the mid–eighteenth century it comes very strongly into the forefront of the reader's consciousness through the immense popularity in Europe of Richardson's *Pamela* (1740) and *Clarissa* (1747). These novels were well known to Goethe as early as 1765, as his letters to his sister testify (6 Sept. 1765 and 14 May 1766). Although Richardson's heroines differ from Gretchen in fighting with greater or lesser success to preserve their virtue, they afford potent models of the dilemmas facing the young woman of the time. In France too the same problem is explored, albeit in a decidedly less moralistic manner, in Laclos's *Les liaisons dangereuses* (1782) and the Marquis de Sade's *Justine ou les malheurs de la vertu* (1791). There is no doubt that eighteenth-century readers would have recognized in Gretchen an almost stock figure to which they could bring a ready familiarity we no longer possess. Yet the intertextual presence of a traditional literary theme is sufficiently strong in *Faust* to warrant a historizing effort on the part of today's readers in order to grasp its vitality for an interpretation of Gretchen.

The disparity between readers of Goethe's time and those of today is even more pronounced when it comes to the sociohistorical context. But this aspect is so absolutely central to a comprehension of Gretchen that it must be taken into consideration. Goethe's contemporaries would have been quick to realize that the Gretchen episode was a treatment of a burning social issue of the day. The more advanced thinkers in later eighteenth-century Germany were much preoccupied with the plight of the *Kindermörderin*, the young woman who has borne an illegitimate child whom she kills in a frenzy of insane despair. Such a figure is the focus of a spate of plays that enjoyed popular success and notoriety in the mid-1770s in Germany, though they are now largely forgotten except by specialists in the field. *Die Kindermör-*

derin by Heinrich Leopold Wagner (1775) and *Die Soldaten* by Jakob Michael Reinhold Lenz (1776) are the most effective of these dramas. They may well have been provoked by the public execution in Frankfurt on 14 January 1772 of Susanna Margarete Brandt for the crime of infanticide. Note the coincidence of her middle name with that of Goethe's heroine. The execution was witnessed by members of his circle and became a topic for heated discussion. The youthful Goethe and his peers, who included Heinrich Wagner and Lenz, formed a loosely allied group that came to be known as the Sturm und Drang (usually rendered as Storm and Stress, although the German word *Drang* has a more positive and certainly more thrusting connotation than the English *stress*). During a period of extreme political conservatism in the small states and principalities into which Germany was fragmented before its unification in 1870, these Young Turks of their time engaged in revolutionary social criticism against the ills and abuses of the day. One of the principal objects of their attacks was the class system, which permitted extraordinary privileges to the "haves" at the expense of the "have-nots." The exploitation of innocent young girls of the lower class by irresponsible officers and playboy gentlemen out for a little amusement and sexual gratification became a primary target for their criticism. It is this indignation at prevailing conditions and rebellion against the dominant mores that gave the impetus for the child murderess plays.

That then is the background and the source of the Gretchen episode in *Faust*. It has a direct precipitate in the many references throughout the dialogues between Faust and Gretchen to the social disparity between them. The very first words they exchange carry a pointed allusion to the question of class: when Faust accosts her with the allocution "Mein schönes Fräulein" (2005), Gretchen's instant response is: "Bin weder Fräulein, weder schön" (2007). Both terms chosen by Faust are intended as compliments: "schön" can be translated simply as "fair," "beautiful," or "pretty"; "Fräulein," however, is not so easily rendered because it has here a definite class connotation. "Maiden" is too class-neutral because it can denote any young unmarried woman; but the customary translation, "lady," while still overtly class-related in British English, is much less so in American parlance since the title "Lady" does not exist. Moreover, it can refer to either a married or an unmarried woman, and in conjunction with the adjective "fair" it becomes an unfortunate cliché. Gretchen's denial of her beauty may be regarded as an indication of her modesty, and Faust does in fact persist in calling her "schön." But he never again uses "Fräulein," obviously acknowledging the justice of her refutation of this upper- and middle-class style of address as inappropriate to her social standing. Gretchen, by contrast, constantly speaks to and of Faust as "Herr" 'gentleman' and surmises that he comes "aus einem edlen Haus" 'from a noble family' (2681). Marthe too deems Faust a "gentleman"

(2900) and, clearly impressed by his status, tells Gretchen that he takes her for a "Fräulein" (2906). So from the outset this element of class is a crucial factor in the relationship between Faust and Gretchen. To the normal pleasure that any young girl would feel at the attention of a suitor must be added the flattery and pride stirred in Gretchen at being attractive to a gentleman. Her interest in Faust is heightened by his social superiority; the possible prospect, however remote in realistic terms, of rising in the world through connection with him may well make her more receptive to his gallantries.

The social chasm separating them remains a motif throughout the play. The class distinctions sharpen as they draw closer to each other. Faust's extravagant gifts of jewelry are judged by Gretchen fit to be worn by "eine Edelfrau" 'a woman of the nobility' (2972) at the most glittering gala. Although, in her poverty, she is drawn to the gold for its monetary value, she is even more excited by the glimpse of the aristocratic world that the gems afford her. At the same time she has growing fears of condescension and, presumably, of a decline of interest on Faust's part as she becomes increasingly conscious of the full extent of the social, financial, and intellectual gulf between them. She contrasts his "edle Gestalt" 'noble figure' (3395) and "hoher Gang" 'lofty gait' (3394) with her own rough hands worn by lowly domestic chores (3111–12). Her acute awareness of his social position engenders anxieties of loss and so indirectly animates her desire to please. Instead of dividing them, the class difference therefore becomes a force to drive Gretchen into Faust's arms despite her knowledge of the fate that awaits a girl who yields to a "spiffy youth" (3571). In the gossip at the well, Lieschen tells Gretchen of Bärbel's pregnancy and of her desertion by her lover. The pattern follows that between Faust and Gretchen: flattery, courtship, and gifts, succeeded inevitably, according to Lieschen, by pregnancy, abandonment, disgrace, and despair for the girl. Gretchen does not, for obvious reasons, share Lieschen's righteous moral condemnation. The brief scene is significant from several angles: it foreshadows Gretchen's own fate (though Faust is not a faithless lover and tries to rescue her from prison); even more important, it underscores the commonness of this situation, and it places Gretchen firmly within the parameters of a tradition well established in the social as in the literary sphere. Mephistopheles's cynical dismissal of Faust's agonized outcry with the curt rejoinder "She is not the first" ("Gloomy Day," line 18) completes the contextualization and invites us to read the Gretchen episode in the light of both a problem of the day and a long-standing convention.

The links to that problem and convention become quite apparent from the compositional history of *Faust*. The story of Gretchen was originally conceived as a separate drama contemporaneous with Wagner's and Lenz's treatment of the same theme. Subsequently it was subsumed into the tragedy of Faust as one of Faust's first adventures after his pact with Mephistopheles, a testing of his new capacity for life on his release from his stifling study. The amalgamation of the two distinct sets of material could not be accomplished without certain problems, some of which remain unresolved. The titanic cosmic striving of Faust's early debates with Mephistopheles suddenly gives way in the Gretchen scenes to a much cozier type of drama reminiscent of the *bürgerliches Trauerspiel* 'bourgeois tragedy' popularized by Lessing's *Miss Sara Sampson* (1755) and *Minna von Barnhelm* (1767). With the change of pace, tone, and tension in the Gretchen episode, *Faust* undergoes a break in style. This statement is not meant as a negative critique since multiplicity of styles is the generic hallmark of *Faust*. However, the modulations between the Gretchen episode and the other scenes demand a rapid adjustment on the reader's part. The difficulty of adequately dealing with the episode is further compounded by the fragmentary nature of the Gretchen material, which forces the audience, as later in the dramas of Büchner, to piece together the happenings from hints and inferences.

Reading between the lines allows a psychoanalytic approach to Gretchen. Its starting point is Gretchen's account to Faust of her life story on their first protracted meeting in the garden scene. After telling him of her father's death, her brother's absence in the army, and her mother's strictness over the housekeeping, she reminisces at some length (3121–49) about her little sister for whom she had cared until the baby's death because of their mother's precarious health. As she speaks of the joys and pains of looking after an infant, she voices a very striking mothering impulse. In this respect Gretchen resembles Lotte in *Werther*, who has assumed the role of little mother to her younger siblings on her mother's death. But whereas Lotte is surrounded by a clamorous brood of living children, Gretchen mourns the loss of her baby sister. She laments her loneliness, and she appears to lack a sense of self-worth, having repudiated beauty and social standing. Perhaps she even experiences an unacknowledged sense of guilt, viewing the baby's death as evidence of her wanting skills as a care giver. The psychological stress of what she perceives as her failure may contribute to her desire to please Faust, that is, to be successful at something. Under these circumstances it is arguable that Gretchen may have a subconscious longing for a child to replace her lost sister and to give meaning to her own existence through sustenance of another being dependent on her. Such a reading may help to explain how a girl as overtly virtuous as Gretchen comes to fall for Faust's advances. The lure is not mere profit or gratification of her vanity and her sexual desires but the hope of satisfying a deeper psychological need in a bleak life.

But the moral and social climate of the later eighteenth century did not permit an unmarried mother to find happiness in the rearing of her child.

Ultimately Gretchen becomes a victim of society through its harsh censure of her public transgression of its rigid codes. Her child is the concrete manifestation and therefore the symbol of her delinquency. In a fit of insanity she not only kills the infant but also wills her own destruction by refusing to go along with Faust's attempts to free her from jail. Her guilt at her seduction, pregnancy, and infanticide is intensified by her sense of complicity in her mother's death from the sleeping draft she has given her at Faust's instigation. The burden of culpability and sinfulness becomes too heavy for Gretchen, and it breaks her.

Gretchen's story epitomizes the fate of innocence ill-equipped to cope with the grim realities of the world. To the eighteenth century it would have appeared, at least to some extent, as a cautionary tale. Yet despite her downfall in this world, Gretchen is in some mysterious yonder realm saved and redeemed. With this ending Goethe disassociated himself from the confining morality of his age to uphold Gretchen's own conviction of her essential goodness. She is to the very end an equivocal figure, neither wholly a saint nor wholly a whore. In the last resort, what makes her problematic also makes her very human as a portrayal of womanhood and, in some measure, a commensurate female counterpart to Faust, "a good man" who "in his dark and secret longings / Is well aware of the right path" ("Prologue in Heaven," 328–29).

NOTE

[1] Bub (11) cites Spalding and Brooks: ". . . *das Ding*, for person only pejorative; *das Ding*, for girl, young woman no longer pejorative, but character determined by adjectives" (1: 478). It would be more accurate to admit that some remnant of the pejorative meaning persists nonetheless, though it may be mitigated by the conditioning adjective.

Goethe and Science

A. G. Steer

One often neglected approach to Goethe's *Faust* takes the route of science. Teachers who have the time may wish to present a detailed introduction such as I present here. Others with less time may wish to adapt portions of this important material to short units in their teaching. Goethe's scientific studies are important not for the extent to which they foreshadowed modern developments but for their influence on his literary works. The fact that a few of his scientific convictions were erroneous does not change that fact. The poet's writings on these subjects were not only voluminous but diverse. Striking here is his almost religious dedication to science, even though he was not, in the traditional sense of the word, devout. His father had seen to it that he learned the languages of the Bible, Greek and Hebrew. He was *Bibelfest* (well versed in the Bible), as we can see from *Faust*. In addition, he was well versed in church history. The consistency with which he pursued his various scientific endeavors rivaled that with which he pursued literary goals. The broad and continuous consultation he sought with contemporary scientists was unusual, and the scientific collections that he amassed were famous in his day. His mineralogical collections were found after his death to contain some 17,800 specimens. The devotion employed here was no accident—it was spurred first by alchemy and then later by the pantheistic philosophy of Spinoza.

During Goethe's lifetime (1749–1832) the basic modern sciences—chemistry, physics, botany, geology—were in their infancy. Most of the other sciences did not yet exist. Chemistry, as the offspring of alchemy, is generally considered to have started its separation from its parent with Robert Boyle's *The Sceptical Chymist* of 1661, yet it continued the struggle to disentangle itself for another century. As late as 1782 the British Royal Society appointed a committee to investigate the claims of a certain James Price to have transmuted base metals into gold (Gray, *Goethe* 3). So it is not surprising if the youthful Goethe, in 1770, took alchemy seriously.

The appeal of this arcane material to the young university student was enormously increased by a fact that has been largely forgotten, namely, that two of the then prevalent strains of religiosity, pietism and mysticism, used the language of alchemy. The mystic Jacob Boehme (1575–1624) used this terminology in the attempt to illuminate and describe his religious experiences. For instance, he sometimes used the philosopher's stone to refer to Christ, sometimes to the mystical union between devotee and God. Later the Swedish mystic Emmanuel Swedenborg (1688–1772) used similar language for similar reasons. Goethe came into contact with the thinking of these groups through a friend of his mother's, Susanna von Klettenberg, during his illness and convalescence following his return from the University of Leipzig in 1769.

His precise ailment is still unclear, but when he came forty years later to write his autobiography, *Dichtung und Wahrheit*, he apparently understood that it had, in modern terms, psychosomatic overtones. He there refers to himself as one "who seemed to suffer more in soul than in body" (Hamburger Ausgabe 9: 339; trans. mine throughout). In the same autobiography he describes how, as a convalescent, with the help of his tutor, he set up an alchemist's furnace, acquired the necessary equipment and materials, and attempted to repeat some of the experiments of the great alchemists.

These interests culminated in a unique experience: Goethe perceived the "miracle" of alchemy of his own person. His physician at this time was a Johann Friedrich Metz, a member, with Frl. von Klettenberg, of the local group of mystical pietists. He had hinted that he possessed a miraculous "universal cure" that he had made himself in his own alchemical laboratory. When Goethe's illness took a turn for the worse and his life was despaired of, the doctor was prevailed on to use his magic cure (9: 343–44). Goethe dates his recovery from that point. It is easy to see how a mystical potion, administered to a believer, might have functioned by suggestion. When the youth finally felt himself well enough to continue his university studies in 1771, this time at the University of Strassburg, he was apparently convinced that he owed his recovery to the alchemical potion.

In Strassburg he met Johann Gottfried Herder, the great philosopher and critic. The younger man at once realized the importance that this incisive mentality could have for him and a close friendship developed that was to last, with vicissitudes, until Herder's death in 1803. Herder's sharp and creative mentality could show itself in abrasive language, as Goethe soon found out when he mentioned alchemy, for Herder was one of those who understood how chemistry had already replaced this outmoded set of superstitions. The younger man had spread much of his poetry and literary plans before Herder, who criticized and inspired. But Goethe notes that he carefully refrained from mentioning *Faust*, sketches and first drafts of which already existed, because of its alchemical material.

The fact that Goethe eventually became the finest lyric poet to have used the German language was due in part to Herder's spurring him on at this time to collect and adopt as models the German *Volkslied* (9: 408–09). In circulating through the back country of Alsace listening to the people sing, Goethe could not have described himself as an anthropologist or a folklorist; the words did not yet exist. As will be seen, this close connection with the folk song and with folklore was to have great importance for *Faust*.

When Goethe returned to Frankfurt he was less interested in practicing law than in literary pursuits. *Götz von Berlichingen* dates from this period, as does coeditorship of a literary journal, *Frankfurter Gelehrte Anzeigen*, and of course the novel that established his world fame, *Die Leiden des jungen Werthers*. In this period also falls his first study of Spinoza. The poet's instinctive and passionate love of nature had been encouraged by Herder and was now reinforced by Spinoza, whose central idea, *deus sive natura* 'God or nature' assumed such importance for Goethe that he later characterized his relationship to it as a *Wahlverwandtschaft* 'elective affinity.' So there again was the connection between religion and science. For if God is nature, then the study of nature is the real theology.

In 1821 Goethe planned an essay on the history of his own scientific studies, which unfortunately he never wrote, although an outline did survive (Artemis Ausgabe 16: 904–05). Here he noted for 1769–71, "At home: alchemical groping." Following that, for the years 1772–75: "Long pause, filled out with youthful passions." It was at the end of this period that he accepted the invitation of Karl August, Duke of Sachsen-Weimar, to join his court. Then follows the note: "Real beginning [of his scientific studies]. In Weimar; through Buchholz." The latter was the ducal apothecary, who not only maintained his own garden to raise curative herbs but also had broader scientific interests. The sketch continues: "Character of the latter. Really patron. Well-to-do, active, ambitious. Seeks honor in demonstrating everything that's new. Has skilled chemical assistants."

Goethe always kept himself abreast of developments in chemistry, although he made no original contributions. The 1770s and 1780s were characterized by expanding knowledge of gases. For instance, oxygen was discovered by Priestley in 1774. The hot-air-balloon ascensions of the Montgolfier brothers in Paris in 1783 were related to this new interest in gases, and Goethe repeated their experiment in 1784 in Weimar. In 1809 he based his novel *The Elective Affinities* on a chemical analogy: if two compounds, each consisting of two elements, are brought together, they may exchange partners. In his novel, two couples do exactly that. In a publisher's advance notice, which he wrote himself, he defended the novel against possible criticism that there is too great a difference between chemicals and people: "There is after all everywhere only *one* nature" (Hamburger Ausgabe 6: 621).

Goethe's short visit to Weimar became permanent when he assumed the responsibilities of a high official: "I came to Weimar most ignorant in all nature studies, and only the need to be able to give the duke practical advice with his manifold undertakings, building and landscape plans drove me to the study of nature" (*Goethes Gespräche*, conversation with Kanzler von Muller, 16 Mar. 1824). His scientific interests were of an astonishingly broad sweep, but it is well to limit attention for the moment to botany, where Buchholz gave the original impetus, to anatomy, and to geology. He was so successful in his new studies that, although he later characterized himself as "a self-taught beginner" (Hamburger Ausgabe 13: 16–17), he rapidly reached the stage of doing original research.

This progress can best be seen, perhaps, in his discovery, or rediscovery, of the human intermaxillary bone. Here he was influenced in part by his short-lived interest in Lavater's theory of physiognomy, according to which the facial features of any individual reveal his or her innate abilities and future career. Goethe soon saw the error, but for the second time a pseudoscience had stimulated him to study more fruitful fields. The face, of course, is shaped by bones of the skull, which is where Goethe began. The contemporary authorities in anatomy (Camper in the Netherlands and Blumenbach in Göttingen) held that the lack of this intermaxillary bone distinguished human beings from all other animals. Goethe intuitively hesitated to believe that nature acted in such an arbitrary fashion, and by using the technique of the series (which he developed into a useful tool and into the foundation for comparative anatomy), he compared all the mammalian skulls he could find, proceeding in the smallest steps possible from the mouse to the elephant. He checked his results by using a developmental series, beginning with the skulls of the embryo and going step by step through the development to end with the adult. Finally he checked with a third series, in which he arranged various abnormalities, culminating in the normal skull. The result was obvious: human beings *did* possess this bone; it was easy to overlook, since in the adult it had usually grown together with adjacent ones. It is of little importance that the great Vesalius (1516–64) had recognized it more than two centuries earlier in a half-forgotten work; Goethe's accuracy and method of study were confirmed.

His excited letter to Herder in which he announced the discovery is well-known (Weimarer Ausgabe, part 4, 6: 258), but more revealing is the letter of the same date (27 Mar. 1784) to Charlotte von Stein: "i have such pleasure [from it] that all my intestines are stirred." His intense visceral emotion derives from the discovery that nature follows similar, discoverable laws in its creations. And here again is not only a proof for him of the relation between religion and science but a proof that affected his own person, as had the alchemical potion. His interest was now spreading into all the sciences available to him; he was looking everywhere for further confirmation of the laws of nature (God) that he had so far discovered. His work with anatomy continued at irregular intervals, and the results were published in an essay of 1795, "Preliminary Outline of a General Introduction into *Comparative Anatomy*, Starting with Osteology" (Hamburger Ausgabe 13: 170–84). Goethe is here really founding the science of comparative anatomy.

Actually the first science to which he devoted close study was botany, as he reported later (1817) in his "Geschichte meines botanischen Studiums" and the very important "Verfolg" 'continuation' to it (Jubiläums Ausgabe 39: 296–328). Goethe had begun properly enough with the work of the great Swede Linnaeus, *Species plantarum* (1753), which he used as a handbook. It is difficult; it is in Latin and, being a taxonomy based on the plant's reproductive elements, it is complicated. Goethe soon saw, as had many others, that a simpler system was desirable, and he eventually set up a partial one of his own. He based it on the growth of the simple annual plant, which growth he conceived as consisting of alternate stages of expansion and contraction, emphasizing in the process polarity and contrast. The last stage consists in a *Steigerung* 'enhancement' of leaflike forms into the petals, stamens, and pistils of the flower. The final contraction is into the seed, thus completing one cycle and beginning another. To be noted here is the limited point of view: he does not mention trees, grasses, mosses, or lichens, and he ignores the roots. Nonetheless, his conceptual tools were important: expansion, contraction, polarity, contrast, and enhancement. It has been demonstrated that the seven stages that Goethe saw in the plant correspond almost exactly to the seven qualities in the nature of God that Jacob Boehme described in alchemical language (Gray, *Goethe* 81–82). Thus, despite Herder, alchemical and religious concepts were still alive in Goethe, and, more important, the link between science and religion remained for him fundamental.

Goethe then became involved in reactivating the worked-out mines near the town of Ilmenau, an enterprise that of course necessitated knowledge of geology and mineralogy. As he had in other scientific areas, he turned first to a contemporary authority, here Abraham Gottlob Werner, director of the mining academy at Freiberg in Saxony. There were two schools among contemporary geologists; vulcanists believed that volcanic forces had shaped the earth's surface; the neptunists were convinced that the slower processes involved in receding seas were the cause. Werner was a neptunist, whose gradual doctrine was more congenial to Goethe's nature than the sudden, cataclysmic, "revolutionary" vulcanism. In the years after the French Revolution, vulcanism became for the poet a synonym for political revolution.

Goethe's mineralogical studies were of lasting value to him. He learned to date strata through the enclosed fossils, he came to look on granite (erroneously) as the original type of rock, he observed weathering and exudation, and he understood that glaciers had contributed to surface phenomena, although he had little concept of the enormous extent of the glaciation. And here, too, one must recognize Goethe's errors: as a good neptunist he rejected the theory that the earth's surface had risen, fallen, folded, or cracked and faulted (Magnus 214). Most amusing is the conflict in the "Classical Walpurgis Night" of *Faust II*, where the vulcanist Anaxagoras competes with the neptunist Thales for the soul of the (alchemically produced) Homunculus. Here Anaxagoras, by means of a magic spell (line 7900) calls down a chunk of the moon to strike the earth in a cataclysm.

One must constantly emphasize the many-sidedness of Goethe's science. In the 1780s he even observed microscopic life. It was then the fashion to "infuse" a straw into a glass of water, let it stand for several days, then observe through a microscope the various one-celled life forms (called "infusoria") in the water. The poet's careful notes, complete with drawings, make it clear that he had observed *paramecia* and *vorticellae* and had recognized ciliary movement of the latter (Magnus 121). At about this time also falls his second and much more serious study of Spinoza. The reasons for this all-encompassing curiosity are important. When he had begun his concentrated scientific study, he was already 30 years old, a mature and world-famous artist. He was thus devoted to form, and was convinced that he could find a fundamental unity of forms in nature. He wrote to Charlotte von Stein about the essential form ". . . with which nature is always playing, so to speak, and playing brings forth manifold life. If I had time in this short space of life, so I venture I could extend it to all the realms of nature—to its entire realm" (10 July 1786).

The Italian journey of 1786–88 was an identity crisis for Goethe, from which he returned with much profit, not only artistically but also scientifically. He codified two new concepts, first a system of metamorphosis (Hamburger Ausgabe 13: 64–118) and second the conviction that nature followed similar laws in three apparently widely separated realms, the realm of natural science, that of art, and that concerning social groups (Jubiläums Ausgabe 49: 317–28). In 1790 he published an eighty-page pamphlet on the metamorphosis of plants, incorporating ideas that had long moved half-formed through his mind to assume final shape in Italy. He distinguished three types of metamorphosis: the progressive, or normal, by which leaves develop successively in the growth of a plant; the abnormal, or retrogressive, which marks the degeneration of a plant form (again Goethe studies the abnormal in order better to understand the normal); and last, the accidental metamorphosis that is caused by unusual climate or injury. He also distinguished (later) between successive and simultaneous metamorphoses—the first, seen in the transformations of successive leaf forms in the development of a plant, and the second, in the elements of a segmented worm, for instance, or the spinal column of an animal, where he saw each vertebra as metamorphosis of a general vertebra type. Here he felt that he had found a fundamental law of nature, which he expressed as "archetype and metamorphosis (thereof)." He applied this process also to the insects, which he studied with fascination in the 1790s. It is significant that he used the language of insect development

to describe the birth and growth of Euphorion (lines 9652–61) and the final
Steigerung of Faust in the last scene (11981–87).

Nature's use of similar laws with folk groups is harder to see but just as
important. In the already cited continuation (*Verfolg*) to his *History of My
Botanical Studies* (1817), he describes how these principles applied to other
areas than botany:

> In the course of two past years [in Italy] I had observed, collected,
> thought without interruption, sought to develop each of my abilities.
> I had learned to understand up to a certain point how the favored
> Greek nation had proceeded in order to develop the highest art in its
> own national circle, so that I could hope, bit by bit, to gain an overview
> of the whole and to prepare for myself a pure pleasure in art that would
> be free of prejudice. Further I believed I had discovered in nature by
> observation how it [nature] goes to work according to laws in order to
> bring forth a living image, as model for everything artistic. The third
> thing that had busied me was the customs of the peoples. To learn
> from them how, out of a combination of necessity and arbitrariness,
> of stimulus and will, of movement and resistance a third thing is pro-
> duced that is neither art nor nature but both at once, necessary and
> accidental, intentional and blind. I understand [by that] human soci-
> ety.   (Jubiläums Ausgabe 39: 317–18)

Therefore human history and folklore are a part of nature and hence, as
Goethe understood it, of science. I have already noted the poet's folklore
collections. The figure of Faust the savant who practices necromancy, is, of
course, out of folklore, as are Mephistopheles and his many minions. And,
as I will show, Goethe presents even Gretchen, at least in part, as a folk
figure. The importance of the basic folk unit, the family, its extended forms,
and finally *das Volk*, goes back to his work with Herder in Strassburg in
1771–72. In Italy he found significant corroboration. In Naples Filangieri
introduced him to Giambattisto Vico's *New Science about the History of the
Nations* (1725). This very learned study of the history of the Egyptian, Greek,
Hebrew, and Roman peoples from their beginnings is calculated to prove
that the power of God (for Goethe read nature) identified itself in the creative
human mind, as expressed in its social forms and institutions. On his return
to Rome, then, Goethe wrote an account of the Roman carnival, which is
in effect a glorification of the Roman folk. Later, in the *Campagne in Frankreich* (Hamburger Ausgabe 10: 188–363), which deals with the abortive
incursion of the Austro-Prussian allies into France in 1792, his sympathy
and understanding for the French *Volk* are clear. In *Faust I* the scene

"Outside the City Gate" is a fine folk scene, complete with folk songs. Philemon and Baucis in act 5 of part 2 are also, of course, folk characters. Furthermore, Goethe understood that folk superstitions contribute to the identification of a folk group. The "Walpurgis Night" of part 1 helps characterize Faust's (and Gretchen's) folk, while the "Classical Walpurgis Night" of part 2 does the same for the ancient Greek folk. Most important, however, is the folk strain in the characterization of Gretchen; Goethe is careful to make her typical of the simple people. She has no education or intellectual pretensions, and she is devout. Goethe uses songs extensively to characterize her, songs that are, in language and in spirit, essentially folk songs. This is true even of the gruesome lines the deranged girl sings in prison (4412–30), which Goethe based on a Low German folk song, "Das Lied vom Machandelboom," that he apparently found in Herder's folk-song collection.

About 1790 Goethe also began intense work with the theory of color. While his voluminous publications contain much that is of permanent value, such as the physiology of vision (artists of the Bauhaus school, Kandinsky and Klee, studied him with profit in the 1920s), they also contain fundamental errors, most notably his attempt to disprove Newton. What Goethe did was to impose the principles that he had discovered elsewhere onto the phenomena of light, where they fit poorly. Still, when his preconceived theories did not get in the way he proved himself a careful and accurate experimenter. For instance, he observed infrared radiation, although he refused to call it radiation (Artemis 16: 183). Needless to say the drama of color always fascinated him, as is shown in the first scene of *Faust II*, where at daybreak the drama of color emerges from darkness and he observes in the scene's famous final line, "Am farbigen Abglanz haben wir das Leben" 'It is in the colored reflection that life consists' (4727).

The weather was another lifelong interest, as the beginning of act 4 demonstrates. Here Faust sees female shapes in the clouds, first Helena, then —so much closer that it touches him—a cloud that symbolizes Gretchen. He sees the Helena form as a cumulus cloud, the Gretchen one as a cirrus, as he indicated in an outline that has survived (Hamburger Ausgabe 3: 609). With his artist's fascination with forms the poet had always observed cloud formations. In 1815 he learned of an essay on cloud shapes by the Englishman Luke Howard, whose terminology he adopted and whose achievement he celebrated with a series of poems (Hamburger Ausgabe 1: 349–52). He went further: he established a weather observatory near Weimar, and he wrote an outline for a projected doctrine on meteorology in 1825.

There is another fascinating scientific possibility in *Faust II*. The final fate of Homunculus makes the question unavoidable: to what extent did Goethe understand evolution? Homunculus's drive is to obtain a body to match his mind. Thales advises:

Give in to this praiseworthy desire
To begin creation from the beginning.
Be ready for quick activity,
There you'll move through eternal norms
Through thousands and thousands of forms
And there'll be time enough until you become a man.   (8321–26)

And Homunculus does finally smash his test tube against Galatea's shell boat and, as marine phosphorescence, pours himself into the sea. The "Classical Walpurgis Night" was put into final form between 1826 and 1830, about thirty years before Darwin's *Origin of Species!* The German popularizer of Darwin's theories, Ernest Haeckel, started a lasting scholarly argument by claiming that Goethe's work foreshadows Darwin, which others denied. Yet, if one understands evolution in the general sense that complex life forms developed out of simpler ones, then the theory has a long history before Darwin. Goethe apparently first came into contact with it in the work of the great French naturalist Buffon (1707–88), whose *Epoques de la nature* (1779) convinced Goethe even though its hypothesis was still unproven. In a letter to Merck he wrote, "I agree, and I won't permit anyone to say it was a hypothesis or a novel [i.e., imaginary]. . . . No one is to say anything detailed against him unless he can construct a larger and more coherent whole. At least it seems to me that the book is less hypothesis than the first chapter of Genesis" (7 Apr. 1780).

In 1790 Erasmus Darwin, grandfather of Charles, wrote a book, *Zoonomia*, in which he advances a similar hypothesis. Goethe was struck by it and arranged to have it translated into German. Finally, in a letter to C. H. Schlosser, the poet shows clearly that he was convinced that life began in the sea: "The important point, where the life, which first appeared in the waters, is drawn by light and dryness towards vegetation, by darkness and moisture towards animalization, is becoming clearer and clearer, and our knowledge is constantly being reinforced from inside out" (2 Dec. 1814).

One more aspect of *Faust II* needs to be noted—the figure of Euphorion, which represented Goethe's admiration for Byron. Like all of Europe, Goethe mourned Byron's dying at Missolunghi while engaged in supporting the Greek war of independence. The figure in the stage direction after line 9902, Goethe later told Eckermann (5 July 1827), was meant to be Byron. This knowledge gives a latest date for *Faust*, 1824, the year of Byron's death.

If readers are to grasp the importance of the links between *Faust I* and *Faust II*, they must understand the problem of time, of history. Part 1 seems to be set in the early sixteenth century. This was the period of the historical Faust, and the evocation of Luther in the translation of the Bible would indicate the same general period, as would the emperor, whom Goethe identifies in one outline as Maximilian (1459–1519). But the figure could also have been medieval, because the distribution of honors and responsibilities to members of the court in act 5 is a clear reference to Charles IV and his Golden Bull of 1356. Then the "Classical Walpurgis Night" takes place on an indefinite anniversary, although still in antiquity, of the battle of Pharsalus in 48 BC. The first scene of act 3 of part 2 occurs shortly after the fall of Troy, which in Goethe's day was calculated as 1200 BC. The second scene of the same act skips 2,400 years to AD 1200, since Faust's medieval castle is in the Peloponnesus, where ruins dating from the fourth Crusade (1202–04) can still be found. Act 5, with Faust's colony on the newly won seashore, recalls the worldwide European colonizations of the seventeenth and eighteenth centuries. Finally, Byron's death in 1824 brings the poem into the nineteenth century.

Faust, Mephistopheles, and Homunculus travel from central Europe to Greece on a cloak used as a flying carpet. What Goethe is doing in the entire work is to transport his readers backward and forward through time on a similar magic carpet—"Genug, den Poeten bindet keine Zeit" 'Enough, no time limits the poet' (7433). He wrote the following important words to Wilhelm von Humboldt on 22 October 1826:

> I have continued to work on it [Faust], but the drama could not be concluded except in the fullness of time, since it now plays its full three thousand years, from the fall of Troy to the capture of Missolunghi. One can take this also for a unity of time, in the higher sense; but the unities of place and of action are observed most exactly in the usual sense.   (Hamburger Ausgabe 3: 438)

This extraordinary assertion was repeated on the same day to his friend Sulpiz Boisserée and yet a third time in an outline for a letter to an unknown person at about the same time. Only rarely did Goethe repeat himself verbatim, and then only on the most important subjects. What he is saying here is that he intends Faust as a journey over highlights of European civilization. Its "unity" of time—classical Greece to the nineteenth century—says as much. The place is Europe, from Greece on the southeastern corner to the shore of the North Sea along the northwestern edge (Faust's reclaimed land—the Dutch and German coasts). He takes Herder's concept of the family folk (in Goethe's scientific language, the Volk as the largest metamorphosis of the Urform family) and extends it through time. Influenced then by Vico's concept Goethe adds something new—he gives literary form to the entire three-millennial sweep of a supranational civilization.

Such is an outline of the key importance of Goethe's science for Faust. A no less important role for science is to be observed in his other works. To cite only one instance: in all his narratives the central role of the collector-narrator has surprising ramifications for their form and meaning. A narrator is an artist, of course, and a collector a scientist, so the collector-narrator, like Goethe himself, plays both roles simultaneously.

For Goethe all of nature, including human beings and their works, which in turn most emphatically include history, art, and literature, are one huge entity. For the pantheist, the whole is a divine manifestation, and hence the study of nature, including all sciences, is the true theology. Goethe's immersion in science lasted throughout his life. In his mature years he spent as much time on scientific studies as he did on any other activity. During his life all the basic sciences were in an early stage of rapid growth. He witnessed the transformation of alchemy into chemistry and himself made valuable contributions to botany, geology, and anatomy, among others. In addition he was in close and lasting contact with the German, French, English, and Italian scientists who stood at the growing tip of their respective fields. Consequently the science of his day forms the background, the unobtrusive skeleton, as it were, of all his literary work.

Aesthetic Qualities

Stuart Atkins

Faust is one of the few modern works of literature rarely read simply as an expression of aestheticism, defined by Frederick P. W. McDowell as "the point of view that art is self-sufficient, need serve no ulterior purpose, and should not be judged by moral, political, or other non-aesthetic standards." *Faust* owes its wide readership to what it has to say about large themes like fate or the human condition and about special aspects of these themes, such as love, religious faith, and social concern (education, government, war, etc.). When topics such as genre and structure, classicism and Romanticism, or Goethe's use of language and poetic devices are introduced into discussions of *Faust*, they tend to serve exegetic or—especially when they concern rhetoric and versification—apologetic functions.

To know that Goethe, like Tennyson and Auden, enjoyed displaying formal virtuosity and expected it to afford many of his readers moments of almost "purely" aesthetic pleasure cannot prevent someone reading *Faust* for the first time from being bored by what will seem the longueurs of overfull statement and of inexcusable overelaboration of motifs tangential even to a work of its broad thematic scope. Few readers of part 1 will ever be persuaded that its "Walpurgis Night's Dream" serves a dramatic function that is proportionate to its length or that compensates adequately for the obscurity of most of its allusions. To know that it establishes the structural pattern of a double dream to be repeated in part 2, as "Classical Walpurgis Night" and the Helena act, adds nothing to its readability; if it must be read, it will surely be least forbidding if it is characterized as a sustained display of a kind of epigrammatic virtuosity that occurs, only in passing, elsewhere in the text—in part 1, for example, most notably in the "Auerbach's Tavern," "Witch's Kitchen," and "Walpurgis Night" scenes.

The long introductory masquerade that leads to the more obviously dramatic (and dramatically functional) masque of Faust-Plutus in the opening act of part 2 is another section of the text that presumes an audience or readership appreciative of formal virtuosity; whatever the relevance of its social, artistic, literary, and other motifs to the drama of Faust's aspirations and strivings, the passage affords aesthetic pleasure only as a very leisurely showpiece of a minor kind. To a considerable degree the same holds true for "Classical Walpurgis Night," a masque in which elements of pageant or masquerade (line 7795) are often developed more fully than either the immediate dramatic action or the effective elaboration of major *Faust* themes can plausibly justify. Even act 4, in which the dramatic action develops conventionally and, for the most part, rapidly, contains several passages of lyrical and rhetorical display at its beginning and, in its final scene, an unhurried parody of the tired rhetorical elegance and dramatic devices of late neoclassical drama.

Into act 3, somewhat shorter than *Oedipus at Colonus*, are crowded elements variously characteristic of classical, medieval, Renaissance-Baroque, and contemporary-"Romantic" poetry and drama. They function as economical exposition of the wealth of information needed to establish the character and identity not only of Helena and the other characters but also of the times and milieus of a dramatic action spanning three thousand years of history. With great virtuosity Goethe evokes different rhetorical manners: Greek pithiness (especially in stichomythic passages) and formulaic elegance (becoming overstatement in the choral odes), medieval and neoclassical preciosity, the self-conscious simplicity of the eighteenth century and after, the stylized realism of German classicism, and the insistent musicality of Romantic lyricism. This virtuosity is not, however, exclusively functional. Like architectural ornament, it provides discrete moments of aesthetic pleasure and has its counterpart in the set piece of Elizabethan drama (e.g., Mercutio's Queen Mab speech, Polonius's advice to Laertes, Hamlet's instructions to the players, or Jaques's "All the world's a stage"). Any student ready to read *Faust* should therefore be persuadable that, in a work longer than even the longest of Shakespeare's plays, a proportionally greater number of such set pieces may, like their Shakespearean equivalents, serve the important aesthetic function of providing pleasurable moments of rest in what, even without them, would not be a text assimilable in one uninterrupted reading or performance.

To demonstrate that Goethe uses rhetoric for intensification, to underscore moments of dramatic or thematic importance, and that his changes in style and tone signal shifts to new levels or spheres of experience is easy. To convince students that his use of rhetoric also has independent value as ornament was once a difficult task, when "rhetorical" was generally a term of opprobrium; but to current students even slightly familiar with linguistic and other forms of deconstruction the point may now be presented without immediate rejection. Moreover, since *Faust* is not a contemporary work and must be read with more than a modicum of knowledge of intellectual, literary, artistic, political, and social history, emphasis on the historical importance of rhetoric is unlikely to meet with total hostility, so long as the text is not simply exploited to teach classical rhetoric or one of its modern equivalents.

Some figures of speech need attention only if *Faust* is being read in German. Archaism and zeugma fall into the etymological class; lexical identification usually suffices for the former, while the contribution of the latter to economical concision and, occasionally, colloquial or comic effect will be obvious to students linguistically sophisticated enough to read literary German. Normally, the various figures of redundancy (e.g., pleonasm, anaphora) are kept in English translations, but of them only hendiadys and parallelism present difficulties. Since parallelism is a structuring principle throughout *Faust*—most obviously as the variation of motifs of part 1 in part 2 but also within each part and even within individual scenes—to point out its presence as a rhetorical figure contributes to heightened awareness of a central feature of the text.

Although chiasmus may seem a minor rhetorical flourish, a merely aesthetic ornament, it too deserves attention, since at certain critical points in *Faust* it determines the order in which motifs of repetition occur. (Taken in this extended sense, it can be used to clarify the complex structure of "Classical Walpurgis Night," with its reduplication of the pattern of paired appearances and disappearances used in simplest form in part 1 for the first scene in Marthe's garden.)

Enallage, antimeria, hypallage, synesis, and anacoluthon are figures that only the reader of the German text will normally encounter; except for one or two instances of the last of these, their occurrence will represent minor lexical or syntactic irregularities hardly noticed and rarely worth noticing. Grecisms and Latinisms, however, which traditional rhetoric also places in the same class as the foregoing figures of substitution, are important as signs of deliberate stylistic elevation: for example, in Faust's first scene they mark moments of emotional exaltation, and in part 2 (especially, of course, in act 3) they heighten the evocation of classical antiquity in a context of language already rich in allusion, elegant paraphrase, and such verbal transpositions as hyperbaton, anastrophe, prolepsis, hysteron proteron, tmesis, and, already mentioned, chiasmus.

Whereas several of the grammatical figures I have mentioned may today demand special attention if their presence and function in *Faust* are to be recognized, the rhetorical figures of old-fashioned poetics—simile, metaphor, metonymy, synecdoche, personification, apostrophe, hyperbole, climax, litotes, irony, epexegesis (often simply as more or less elegant variation), aposiopesis, allusion, and onomatopoeia—are so familiar, even to readers whose literary experience is limited to contemporary writing only, that it is often counterproductive to draw attention to them. (This is particularly true for irony; like humor, if stressed it merely seems heavy-handed.) The one exception to this generalization is allusion, which occurs in *Faust* in a greater variety of forms than even highly experienced readers normally expect to encounter in a single text: as direct or indirect mention of events and of literary, historical, and mythological figures; as diction, stylistic mannerisms, and verse forms that by evoking a given genre or its literary-historical period mark important changes in perspective; and as references to or descriptions of works of art that by virtue of theme, style, or intrinsic quality indicate that special importance is to be attached to a given motif or the context in which it occurs. Unfortunately, the aesthetic pleasure derived from recognizing an allusion is minimal when, like humor and irony, it requires explanation. But since Goethe probably did not expect any reader to possess the identical fund of knowledge from which he drew his myriad allusions, I find it pedagogically sound to ignore all allusions not important for following major dramatic developments and situations, even though one should never be surprised if asked whether a passage contains an allusion and what it might mean.

Since iconographic allusion often takes the form of pictorial description, it may simultaneously be aesthetic ornament (set piece) and functional rhetorical device. An example is Faust's description of his study after Wagner has left him in the opening scene of part 1; by evoking a host of paintings of scholars and alchemists in studies and laboratories already old-fashioned —what we would call "medieval"—when artists executed them, it reestablishes the sixteenth century iconographically as the time of a dramatic action that, while Wagner was present, had slipped forward into Goethe's Storm and Stress period. The important iconographic allusions in *Faust* have long since been identified—for example, the pictorial models for such scenes as "Witch's Kitchen," "Walpurgis Night," and "Faust's Interment"; for the tableau of Paris and Helen (see line 6509: "Endymion und Luna! wie gemalt!" 'A picture of Diana and Endymion!'), and for descriptions like Homunculus's vision of Leda and the swan and, at the very end of the drama, that by the doctor, Marianus, of the Virgin Enthroned. Nevertheless, there has often been insufficient emphasis on the fact that such descriptions may have a rhetorical or an ornamental function (or both), are not mere substitutes for stage sets—something nowhere more evident than in Mephistopheles's description of what he claims to see through a round or arched hell mouth: a four-cornered painting or engraving with perspective background that is meant only for the inner eye and that no stage designer could realize in the frame the stage directions call for (11644–53).

Helping students read *Faust* with maximum awareness of the aesthetic qualities that make it a unique literary achievement is an obligation that even the philosophically oriented teacher would do well to assume. Doing so will not only make the work mean more to those students reading it for the first time but may also prepare them for the discovery that, reread later, Goethe's tragedy will—like every truly great work of art or literature— always reveal new facets in proportion as its reader grows in knowledge and experience.

The Structure of *Faust*

Christoph E. Schweitzer

Over the years of teaching Goethe's *Faust* I have come to put more and more stress on various structural aspects of the work. I do this when teaching both parts of *Faust* or when teaching part 1 only. I find it advisable to keep students aware of the overall design since the length of *Faust* and its heterogeneous contents let one easily lose sight of that design.

In addition to the play's two parts, there are, at the beginning of part 1, three clearly marked introductory sections whose functions need to be pointed out. Structurally, each belongs to a different frame of reference. First, Goethe stresses the point that what we are about to see and hear or read is the author's poetic creation, the product of many years ("Dedication"). We move to a different level in the next scene ("Prelude in the Theater"). Here we listen in on a discussion involving a theater director, a merry person, and a poet on the work about to be presented. It becomes clear that the poet will put the matter in the form of a play in which there will be multiple points of view, including the serious and the humorous. There will also be something for the eye of the spectators. With the third introductory scene ("Prologue in Heaven") we have reached the level of the play proper. God, in traditional Christian guise, comes onto the stage and challenges Mephistopheles to try to lead Faust, whom God calls his servant, astray. The scene forms the point of departure for the contest between Mephistopheles and Faust and also between Mephistopheles and God. In the struggle, Mephistopheles unwittingly acts as part of God's plan: Mephistopheles will keep Faust forever striving.

God is again heard at the end of part 1 when the stage direction indicates that a voice from above announces that Gretchen is saved (4611). This means that it is possible for the divine to reach directly down to the human level. In "Mountain Gorges," at the end of the play, Faust's spirit is carried upwards toward the region of "Prologue in Heaven," thereby completing the circle to the "high" place of the beginning of the action proper. In "Mountain Gorges" there is no more space for Mephistopheles.

There are also many smaller units into which *Faust* can be divided. The first couple of scenes of the action help us understand the protagonist and his desperate state of mind, a situation that, as in Marlowe's *Doctor Faustus*, leads quite naturally to Mephistopheles's appearance. Mephistopheles can only arrange a wager, not the traditional exchange of his services in this world for a fixed number of years for those of Faust in hell for eternity. Neither participant realizes that the agreed-on contract is ultimately in harmony with God's plan for Faust. The wager also indicates Faust's independence with respect to Mephistopheles, thus making the antagonists equals. Finally, in the discussion of the terms of the wager, Faust's aim becomes clear: no longer does he seek to discover what holds the world together (382–83); rather he wants to experience the full range of human possibilities. Here, then, the direction of the work's action is indicated: love (Gretchen), conquest of legendary classical beauty (Helen of Troy), power (conquering the sea, ruling). Before the wager Faust had, of course, led the life of a scholar in search of truth, a life of contemplation (*vita contemplativa*) that now turns into one of action (*vita activa*) (see Mason, *Goethe's* Faust 141–48).

The next two scenes ("Auerbach's Tavern" and "Witch's Kitchen") are best considered as a transition to the work's most famous part, the Gretchen episode, which makes up the rest of *Faust I*. In a balladlike succession of scenes Goethe captures the intensity of first love that ends tragically. By balladlike I mean the representation of an action through short and emotionally packed scenes. Within this section, "Forest and Cave" forms the turning point leading to Gretchen's seduction. The sensual implications of "Walpurgis Night" are obvious, and one might point here to the structural contrast between this scene and Gretchen's singing while spinning. The function of "Walpurgis Night's Dream," however, is less obvious: the scene can safely be skipped—as it is in most productions—so long as it is made clear that it is another attempt on the part of Mephistopheles to distract Faust from the thought of Gretchen by trying to entertain him with an inane series of verses. Only if we remember the lack of relevance of these smooth verses can we fully appreciate in the next scene the raw force of the prose and the half-finished sentences in which Faust vents his rage at Mephistopheles.

While in part 1 Faust moves largely in a late medieval and early modern Christian world, part 2 leads us to Greek mythology. "Walpurgis Night" of part 1 takes place on the Brocken, the highest elevation in the Harz mountains in Germany, while the "Classical Walpurgis Night" of part 2 is located on the shores of the Aegean Sea. In other scenes of this part we find Faust and Mephistopheles at the court or on the territory of a late medieval emperor. In part 1 their place of action was primarily a small town to which they return for a brief visit in act 2. Thus, there are many structural contrasts but also many correspondences between the two parts. It is not possible to be exhaustive here. Some of the contrasts and correspondences should, though, be mentioned so that students will see the unity of *Faust*. Or, better still, students should be encouraged to discover on their own these as well as other structurally significant aspects of the play.

The brightness and optimism ("That life is ours by colorful refraction" [4727]) of the first scene of part 2 is reminiscent of the introductory scene of part 1, "Prologue in Heaven," and forms a contrast to the dark and confining study in which we first meet Faust. At the end of "Night" (part 1) Faust hears bells and the choral song of an Easter Mass and thus remembers his former faith: in the first scene of part 2 the rising sun's causing the iridescent play of a rainbow above a waterfall brings about Faust's renewed will to strive. Both scenes point to renewal and prefigure Faust's ultimate salvation. There are two more scenes in which Faust reflects in monologues on human existence, "Forest and Cave" in part 1 and "High Mountains" at the beginning of act 4 of part 2. An analysis of the four scenes will reveal that, within the structure of the work, they have the function of introducing a new section.

Act 1 of part 2 acquaints Faust—and the spectators—with the world of lavish frivolity and clever deception at the emperor's court, a world that forms a sharp contrast to the heartbreaking directness of Gretchen's last hours in prison. The masquerade, in turn, prepares us for the mythical world of the "Classical Walpurgis Night" and the phantasmagoria of the Helena act. While the court society is satisfied with the dumb show from Greek mythology, Faust must learn that the greatest beauty known to man cannot be touched without a thorough preparation for and immersion in the world to which Helena belongs. Act 2 forms the structural link to the union with her in act 3, which, in turn, forms the center of part 2. Here the marriage between the German Faust and Helena, the embodiment of classical beauty, is enacted. But she is less than real, that is, she is put on the stage by Mephistopheles as a product of Faust's creative ability, and thus is ephemeral. When Helena leaves the stage, she follows Faust and her son, who had vanished so quickly and who represents the self-destructive spirit of modern, that is, Romantic, poetry. Act 4 prepares Faust for his role as the powerful lord who in act 5 will rule over vast lands gained from the sea. As each previous experience, this too leads to ambiguous results. It is interesting to observe that in the end it is not the intellectual search for truth, or the conquest of the greatest imaginable beauty, or power that counts but Faust's love for Gretchen, who reappears in the final scene of *Faust*. Or, to put it more accurately, it is Gretchen's love for Faust that ultimately counts.

While keeping students aware of the overall structure of *Faust*, I also point to other structural devices, each of which can profitably be investigated at length. Here are a few suggestions.

Most noticeable is the alternation between scenes with bright light and those that show a dark stage. "Prologue in Heaven," "Outside the City Gate," and, in part 2, "Charming Landscape" and the very end come to mind as outstanding examples for scenes with much light. Then there are scenes like "Night" (part 1) and "Midnight" (act 5 of part 2) in which the very titles point to darkness. The alternation is also obvious in the sequence from "Dark Gallery" to "Brightly Lit Ballrooms" in act 1 of part 2. Many more examples for both types can be found; in them, light is associated with hope, positive meaning, salvation, while darkness points to despair, chaos, and damnation.

Related to the "bright" and "dark" significance is the contrast between "high" and "low" that I have already noted. "High" would normally be associated with light and clarity ("Prologue in Heaven"; the first and last scenes of part 2; the shining band of mist representing Gretchen, who, in drawing upward, pulls the best in Faust with her at the beginning of act 4, lines 10055–66, and thus anticipates the ending; and the bird imagery in general, as in lines 1090–99 and 4419–20), while "low" would point to darkness and obfuscated vision. A good example for the latter is "Auerbach's Tavern," really an underground drinking den, in which the revelers are as close to Mephistopheles's domain as one can be in this world. However, we must not apply such a symbolic interpretation to the "high"-"low" structural contrast or to any other such device mechanically. In "Walpurgis Night" witches and others have ridden upward only to meet in the impure, unenlightened world of demons and devils. Those who congregate have attempted to reach the higher elevations by the wrong means. "Dungeon" at the end of part 1 gives us a good example of how the relative location of characters is connected with meaning. Here Gretchen must occupy the highest place, near death and salvation, and Faust an intermediate position, between clarity and chaos, while Mephistopheles appears from down below (4601). Similarly, in the "Palace" scene of act 5 in part 2, Lynceus stands at the top of the building, Faust is below him, and Mephistopheles, with his three henchmen, approaches on the lowest level. The following scene, "Deep Night," specifies that Faust is on a balcony below Lynceus, who stands on a watchtower. A few scenes later, in "Entombment," we see the gaping mouth of hell reaching far into the earth.

In *Faust*, Goethe presents his argument to an imaginary spectator or reader. The "serious" and potentially tedious sections of the play are interrupted by the appearance of characters whose statements form variations, often in a humorous vein, on what has been said before their entrances. Such an alternation between serious and humorous perspectives is found throughout the play, beginning with the entrance of Wagner, who serves as the butt of Faust's critical remarks. Wagner, like Euphorion in the Helena act of part 2, shares many characteristics with Faust but also differs from him in significant aspects. Wagner's entrance in "Night" provides relief, even if only temporarily, not just to Faust, who has come to a dead end in his reaching out for superhuman knowledge, but also—and as importantly —to the spectator-reader. The obvious humor of the scene in which the bewildered freshman is "advised" by Mephistopheles disguised as Professor Faust again serves as a welcome change from the lengthy bargaining of the two principals. Mephistopheles and the student, now a Baccalaureus, square off again in part 2, act 2; in a hilarious series of pronouncements the Baccalaureus appropriates the universe to himself, putting Mephistopheles-

Faust down as obsolete. Structurally one can speak here of an echo of part 1; the humor of the earlier scene is intensified in the second. The Baccalaureus serves as a comic parallel to Faust, who was as presumptuous as this young graduate and know-it-all. In part 1 Mephistopheles dominated the conversation; in part 2 he has to take a back seat to the Baccalaureus. In general, the second part of *Faust* has as many humorous characters and scenes as the first, perhaps more. In part 1 we laugh at Marthe's all too obvious designs on Mephistopheles; in part 2 we laugh when we listen in on the courtly society commenting on the dumb show of Helena and Paris. Shortly before Faust bursts out, "Without her [Helena] [I] cannot live" (6559), the Savant remarks that he "rather trust[s] documentation" (6536) than what he witnesses. In the same vein we cannot help but laugh, or at least smile, when Wagner timidly asks Homunculus "And I?" (6987) when he wishes to join Homunculus—whom he believes to be his own creation —Mephistopheles, and Faust in their adventurous visit to the classical Walpurgis Night. Wagner is told that he had better stay home and tend to his scholarly pursuits. One more example must suffice: just before "Mountain Gorges," the final weighty scene, Goethe places the predominantly humorous "Entombment." We laugh at Mephistopheles's stupidity when his pederastic lust after the angels makes him lose sight of Faust's soul. Now we are ready to pay attention to the statements of the anchorites, to the various activities involving spirits in the afterlife, and to grace and love working the miracle of Faust's salvation.

It may also be instructive to look at the structure of "Dungeon" and "Mountain Gorges," the two smaller units that form the conclusions of parts 1 and 2 respectively. Before "Dungeon" we have seen Faust and Mephistopheles ride at great speed past the place where Gretchen is to be executed the next morning. In "Dungeon" physical motion has come to a stop, and Faust hesitates and hears Gretchen's rendition of a verse from the fairy tale "The Juniper Tree." In her slight but significant rewording of the verse Gretchen points to her hope of ultimate salvation—associated here with the flight of a bird, that is, with freedom and upward motion. One might also refer to the implied bird-soul equation. In the ensuing dialogue Faust remains bound by only one thought, that of Gretchen's physical salvation, while she herself passes through a number of emotional and spiritual stages, from fear of death and of hell to the feeling of closeness to her former beloved, who cannot reciprocate her embraces or kisses. Her recapitulation of the horrors of the last days before her imprisonment as the murderess of her own child and her anticipation of public execution make clear where she must turn: not to Faust and physical survival but to God and the guardian angels, who will protect her from the evil personified by Mephistopheles, who, she thinks, rises from below. The voice from above confirms what must by now be clear to everyone: Gretchen will be one of the saved. As to Faust, the ending pointedly leaves his fate open; he follows Mephistopheles to pursue further the elusive goal of the moment he would desire to turn into eternity.

The structure, then, of "Dungeon" offers multiple and fascinating aspects: "high" and "low" distribution of characters and points of reference; awareness of the past and coming to terms with it, understanding the present, upward direction on Gretchen's part; horizontal, possibly descending motion for Faust, who wants to flee with Gretchen and is taken away by Mephistopheles. The scene in general is a dark one; light comes in only when Mephistopheles appears, but his "morning" (4600) is not the light of hell but that willed by Gretchen's strong faith, which finds a physical equivalent in the ray of light that could accompany the voice from above.

The structural parallels as well as the contrasts between "Mountain Gorges" and "Dungeon" are numerous. Those between "Mountain Gorges" and the rest of the work are even more numerous. A few examples will have to do. "Mountain Gorges" is characterized by constant upward movement, obviously with positive connotation. Equally obvious is the increasing brightness of the scene, which starts in the lower regions, between mountains, and then lets us see with Dr. Marianus, located in the highest cell, the *Mater Gloriosa*, the Virgin Mary, soaring to heights of eternity. The true movement, though, in this scene, as it was in "Dungeon," is spiritual. In "Mountain Gorges" we first hear the voices of holy men who are still struggling to gain a pure faith while Pater Marianus has reached the clearest vision humanly attainable. Gretchen's prayer forms, of course, an easily detected echo of the one she recited in part 1 (3587–619). What was then pure anguish over her own fate has turned into rejoicing over the return of the beloved who is no longer bewildered. Equally important is the structural device of bringing together the spirit of Faust, who has lived as full a life as possible, with the blessed boys who died in birth at midnight, that is, without even the possibility of catching a glimpse of light. They constitute one more example of the many figures in act 5 who lead lives that form clear contrasts to Faust's own: the Wayfarer, Philemon and Baucis, Lynceus (carried over from act 3), and the holy anchorites. Through the interaction between Faust and the blessed boys and between the boys and Pater Seraphicus, Goethe establishes a type of compensatory justice whose primary concern, interestingly enough for the play's values, is for the earthly experiences the stillborn boys never had. In the case of Faust, by contrast, the flaking films life has covered him with have to be peeled off. At the end, Faust's salvation is made possible through feminine intercession, through Gretchen and the Virgin Mary, representing love and grace. Traditionally male figures, God and Mephistopheles, had initiated the action proper in

"Prologue in Heaven." Thus, the overall structural principle of a progression from the male to the female with multiple symbolic and philosophic implications becomes evident.

Finally, we must address, if ever so briefly, the structure of *Faust* and its designation by Goethe as a tragedy. The ending of the work clearly contradicts such a designation. However, the ending of "Outer Precinct of the Palace" does not. This scene is the last one to take place on the level of reality established in "Night" of part 1. At the conclusion of "Outer Precinct of the Palace" Mephistopheles seems to have triumphed. One must assume that Faust has been damned, that the play has, as the Director suggests in "Prelude in the Theater," proceeded "From Heaven through the World to Hell" (242). In the beginning of "Entombment" we even see the jaws of hell open. But the Poet of "Prelude in the Theater" goes beyond such a limited perspective and envisions principles for Gretchen and Faust that, as he shows in "Mountain Gorges," ultimately validate their lives.

APPROACHES TO TEACHING
FAUST: UNITS AND COURSES

Two Roads to *Faust*

Henry Hatfield

Having been fortunate enough to teach *Faust* in the original at Williams, Columbia, and Harvard and in translation in the Harvard Extension program, I have accumulated some experiences and suggestions that may be helpful. Doubly fortunate, I attended the *Faust* course given by Barker Fairley, a scholar of unsurpassed brilliance.

The drama seems to have fabulous vitality: it has survived moralistic, condemnatory, and ill-informed critics—one of whom described it as a *near-masterpiece*—and the worse handicap of bad teaching. Well presented, it is competitive, at the very least, with the finest products of modern literature. How then shall we present *Faust*?

Presentation implies facing the problem of length, the solution being largely though not entirely dependent on the literacy and maturity of various groups of students. In any case, the some nine hundred lines of the carnival could well be trimmed, as could the remarkably irrelevant scene "Walpurgis Night's Dream." This is no aspersion on our poet, who well knew that *Faust*, for all its richness, was not a classically rounded work of art. As for the abundant mythological and historical references, it may well be a genuine fringe benefit for the student innocent of such background to learn who Hercules, Ariel, Thales, and so on, were. Above all, students need to know, however roughly, the content of *Faust II*.

Whether in German or English, *Faust* can best be presented in a frame; of course the frame should be subordinated to the picture. Rather than rely on biographic material, the teacher might well use as background the tradition extending from the *Faustbuch* and Marlowe to Lessing's fragment, which revolutionized the treatment of the legend by daring to save Faust from hell. Two or three well-organized class hours should provide orientation. Cardinal points that should be raised for discussion at tactful intervals include the splendid if elusive combination of Enlightenment and Romanticism (Mephistopheles's Voltairean aspect, Homunculus's Romanticism), the cast of mixed characters (Gretchen is not all good nor Mephistopheles all bad—thus there can be an uncanny bond between Faust and his special devil), the literal and symbolic play of light and dark, the wealth of literary references and borrowings from Homer on, the role of irony, the shift from the traditional pact to the more flexible wager (would not Faust, had he stayed in his Gothick university, have betrayed his deepest convictions?).

This list of moot points could be much extended. Indeed, *Faust* is probably the only work that fulfills Friedrich Schlegel's call for a truly all-inclusive "progressive universal poetry." The play does indeed display an infinite variety. Aside from its human characters, we encounter angels, good and bad spirits from the holy to the obscene, the uncanny Mothers, existing out of time and space, the amoral Earth Spirit, and sheerly allegorical personages. Mephistopheles, drawn with numerous nuances, reminds us of an evil human being with certain attractive traits rather than of a stock devil. With its middle position between this world and the next, the Faust legend lent itself to such a variety of persons. Only Goethe fully exploited this abundance. In a manner as modern as that of *Ulysses*, the action of *Faust* ranges over Europe from Holland to the Alps to Arcadia and encompasses three thousand years. A similar diversity marks the metrics of the drama: we find *Knittelvers*, blank verse, terza rima, alexandrines, trimeters, and so on, along with one scene in prose. The tone ranges from the majesty of the archangels' song to the frightening threat of the *Dies irae* to Mephistopheles's scurrilities.

Undoubtedly, the most debatable question in *Faust* concerns the reasons for and the justice of the protagonist's salvation. Students of all ages and convictions argue intensely on this point. If they wish to discuss, as they often do, whether Faust is really a good man deserving of salvation, it is their right; the poem itself raises these questions. Going back to the wager, Faust's defenders point out that he has never sunk into slothful ease; therefore he has won. This is true, but it was "a damned nice [close] thing," to quote the Duke of Wellington, even though God himself, in the "Prologue in Heaven," has indicated that Faust, a basically good person, will be saved. It is also significant that he renounces magic at the end of his long life. He has, however, been involved in the death of seven persons. Generally he seems immune to the pangs of repentance. Summing up his situation, Goethe stated that Faust half wins, half loses the wager—"a damned nice thing"—but that "the Old Gentleman"—God—made use of his privilege to pardon the problematic hero. From another point of view, Faustian striving from below combined with Grace from above, emanating from the Virgin and the chastened Gretchen, to ensure the hero's salvation.

The moral action of the play proceeds on two levels, the theological and the secular. The God of the "Prologue in Heaven" genially proclaims that "a good man in his dark urgings" still knows the right way. Even in Faust's psyche the play of light and dark persists: God will "soon" (that is, at the end of Faust's long life) lead him into clarity. In God's hotly debated statement "Man errs as long as he strives," the Almighty is not suggesting that one should either err promiscuously or give up striving. It is rather that error, not a good in itself, is a necessary concomitant of striving, which is a good though not absolutely so.

Why did Goethe call a drama that closes triumphantly a tragedy? (Note that Faust is not an evil protagonist like Macbeth.) For one thing, Goethe could be quite arbitrary about the labels he applied to his works: thus he called his deeply tragic *Torquato Tasso* a play (*Schauspiel*). More important, around 1800 he and Schiller studied Aristotle's *Poetics* with energy and admiration. Here he read that tragedies need not conclude unhappily, though such an end is usual, but need a hero of stature, elevated language, catharsis, and an intellectual element, "thought." No doubt Goethe achieved catharsis in the Gretchen tragedy.

For a serious drama *Faust* contains a wealth of comedy. Mephistopheles is the master of a sharp, deflating wit, aimed mainly at Faust, whose own wit is often Mephistophelean. Thus when Faust's spells force this devil to emerge from his disguises, he remarks, "So that was the poodle's core." The amateur bawd Marthe could be said to "scare the hell" out of Mephistopheles when she hints that she might be interested in marrying him. For his part, he is almost genial in greeting the tiny spirits of his entourage. Parodying Faust, he remarks that while he is not omniscient, he does know a great deal. Similarly, Faust's pathetic assistant Wagner states that while he knows a great deal he would gladly know all. Toward the end, even puns occur.

In an ironic way, certain characters are unmasked. The brave soldier Valentine, once ostentatiously proud of his sister Gretchen, treats her viciously once it is known that she has "fallen"; the spirit of the scene "Cathedral" is rightly called evil, for he tortures Gretchen with pseudo-Christian reproaches while holding out no hope for forgiveness. The jolly bourgeoise Marthe is really the toughest of operators.

In a broad sense we come to see that in *Faust* evil as such is stupid. Mephistopheles's last speeches in part 2 show that he is not only defeated but crushed and disgraced, as is vividly illustrated by his partly comic, mainly repellent passion for the boy angels. Indeed, God's words in "Prologue in Heaven" are an infallible prophecy of the defeat of evil; Goethe's art makes us forget this. This is the most genial of great works.

A few words about the ending. Faust has long been fascinated by flying; now he is borne upward by angels. He has been assigned (how seriously?) to serve as a celestial tutor of a group of small boys who died prematurely. (Santayana well surmises that this occupation will not hold him for long.) He will, however, be reunited with Gretchen, who, with other repentant women, enjoys the special protection of the Virgin Mary. Since Goethe was not a devout Christian and Faust is still less one, indignant critics have queried the authenticity of this closing. In clarifying his intentions, Goethe stated that he used the "sharply outlined Christian-ecclesiastical figures" to avoid vagueness and that he had always envisaged the ideal in feminine form. One might add that as Gretchen in her need turned to the Virgin, Faust needs Mary's help also as the merciful giver of grace. At any rate the scene gives a strong sense of elevation, of peace, and of moral victory. The question of the poet's private beliefs is relatively unimportant. Goethe's works should be judged, like Shakespeare's, per se, even though Goethe himself called them "fragments of a great confession."

Goethe's *Faust*: Poetic Devices

Victor Lange

A poetic work is the result of two impulses—one, the spontaneous creative imagination, the other the given resources of language and the traditional organizing instruments of rhetoric, of genre and prosody, of rhythm, meter, and verse. Goethe's *Faust* is a supreme example of the successful fusion of these elements; inspiration and reflection are brought into play, sustained and made compelling through an impressive variety of literary devices, some conventional, however modified, some the result, solemn, playful, or ironic, of a remarkable instinct for specific purposes and intended effects. Genius and craftsmanship are in Goethe interdependent, and it is well to recognize the means by which the power as well as the complexity, the lyricism as well as the pathos of the tale of Faust are rendered.

It is evident from the beginning of this long work of some twelve thousand lines that its intellectual propositions are articulated in a design appropriate to the figures, incidents, and issues that enliven and elucidate the poem as a whole. Its fascinating but often disjointed plot projects the spiritual aspirations of a mind never satisfied with received wisdom, a Renaissance character with a modern critical intellect, impatient of the limitations of human experience, of time and space, of faith and knowledge, of love and power over others as well as the elements. In many of its details the plot draws on traditional features: it retells parts of the story of Dr. Johannes Faust (first published in 1587), which subsequently became the subject matter throughout Europe of chapbooks and Punch and Judy shows. In part 1 the misery and glory of this eccentric scholar are rendered in a series of theatrical scenes that illuminate Faust's reaching out for superhuman insight and power within an order of divine benevolence, made all the more compelling by the ever-provocative presence of Mephistopheles, that "son of chaos" yet one of the Lord's indispensable servants, the arch-questioner and tempter, who tries relentlessly to alienate Faust from an order, as Goethe sees it, at once natural and sacramental. This essentially biographical scheme provides the structure, more epic than dramatic in its evolving pace, of the first part.

Goethe worked throughout his later life on a sequel to this colorful and altogether realistic "morality" play, different in its intellectual and poetic intentions, more challenging and richer by far than part 1, and published (at his own request) only after his death. In this second part, Faust and Mephistopheles continue to appear intermittently as significant personages in a concatenation of five discrete acts; but they are now, like countless other figures, allegorical representatives: they have become the instruments of an elaborate unfolding of a cluster of ideas that illuminate the interplay of modern consciousness and the continuing presence of ancient values and myths. Faust and Mephistopheles together here test the exemplary classical and religious traditions, one represented by the elusive beauty of Helena, the other by the ultimate act of divine grace bestowed on the grand failure of Faust's life.

It stands to reason that these two parts of *Faust*, linked by the proposition of a human commitment to undaunted questioning and an intensely conscious participation in all realms of being, must differ in design and style. In part 1, Faust's recognition of ultimate human ignorance, his assertion of the defiant resources of the self in the face of an inscrutable universe, the fateful pact and the discovery of an unsuspected meaning in love—both envisaged in superhuman dimensions and both failing in the end—all lead, in a rapid series of colorful scenes, to Mephistopheles's triumph over Faust.

In the second part, Faust is less an intelligible dramatic person lending coherence to the progression of the action than the vehicle and "embodiment" of ideas, aspirations, and propositions in a vast panorama of symbolic action and discourse. The second part is not "realistic" but allegorical: each scene, each encounter or argument seems turned on itself, reflecting on its own range of possible meaning and thus meeting the expectations not so much of a "naive" as of a modern and critically self-conscious reader. This distinction must be kept clearly in mind if the various parts and facets of the poem are to be adequately understood. It is quite insufficient, perhaps even wrongheaded, to read *Faust* as a character drama, held together by the emotional makeup of one person and his private concerns; its coherence is not psychological but conceptual and, above all, poetic. If Goethe called the work as a whole a "tragedy," he was fully aware of the traditional associations of that term; but he cannot have had in mind the severe Aristotelian definition of that genre. The tragedy here enacted is an account of the characteristically modern experience, secular as well as religious, of a tension between aspiration and limitation, of the burden on our thinking of the compulsions of history and the vision of freedom, of the ineluctable constraints as well as the liberating resources of "nature." What makes Faust a tragic figure is his will to resolve these conflicting antitheses in speculations beyond the sanctions of belief and in actions that transgress social constraints. Neither the first nor the second part achieves an acceptable or even plausible resolution; these tensions are shown as inherent in any fully examined life and are, in this work of consummate poetry, demonstrated in all their complexity and through superbly imaginative figures, metaphors, and parables: "for all that passes is but refracted, the unattainable, here it is enacted, the indescribable here is given reality"—this is the elliptical conclusion formulated in the final Chorus Mysticus.

If the experience of this paradoxical coincidence of striving and resignation, of love and failure, of power and beauty, or of history transcending human dimensions is shown in its most radical implications, Goethe's procedures as a poet in turn employ and challenge the traditional forms of literary representation and invoke and modify them with incomparable subtlety. The abundance, throughout the poem, of intellectual or spiritual issues may, in some readers, blur a full awareness of the prodigious variety of offered poetic devices. Careful attention to the poet's calculated strategy seemed to Goethe of utmost importance: "You must not mind," he wrote to his friend von Knebel on 21 October 1821, "dissecting the poem in a thoroughly analytical manner; I know of no other way to move from a vague and general sort of admiration to one that is truly concrete."

Readers of *Faust*, in contrast to those of Dante or Shakespeare, must be struck by Goethe's ease in commanding a "natural" German idiom that even in the most elevated scenes is far from "poetic diction"; except for special effects, solemn or grotesque, the flavor of his language is achieved without recourse to speech unfamiliar to the literate reader. This, incidentally, is one of the reasons why translations of *Faust* so often seem stilted or uncomfortably lofty: they tend to give to Goethe's seemingly effortless statements a special "aura." Yet it is equally obvious that, in all his work, and, superbly, in the two parts of *Faust*, Goethe's figures reflect his unfailing sense for the color and tone of a phrase or a gesture: Faust's pathos is projected in strong, often pointedly extravagant emotional statements; Mephistopheles's ironic and deflating function is, with certain exceptions in the second part, made compelling by his coolly logical, at times satirical, often devastating manner of speech. Gretchen as well as, later, Helena are characterized by their distinctive syntax and imagery. Far from maintaining a single, integrated linguistic level—such as Dante's in the *Divine Comedy*—Goethe fashions each scene or phase of action in a language appropriate to the intended thrust. He employs a multitude of linguistic conventions, those of the academic world, the village, the imperial court, the legal profession, the language of religion and art, of medieval and classical oratory, of gossip and love, even of fashions in philosophical jargon.

The resonance of biblical borrowings and of technical, learned, or popular allusions cannot be missed. Mephistopheles's frequent use of French words is intended to suggest his supercilious and foppish manner. In the fantastic "Walpurgis Night" scene the language of witchcraft and perverted theology is meticulously borrowed from relevant sources; in Faust's attempt at translating the Gospel, in his conversations with Wagner, or in his guarded response to Gretchen's request for an unequivocal definition of his religious views, the problematical character of language is rendered as plainly as it is in that wonderfully comical scene in which Mephistopheles, before the ingenuous student, insists on the ambiguity and deviousness of speech. Goethe's inventiveness in modifying the familiar is forever engaging the attention of his audience or meeting and galvanizing their expectations. Especially in part 1 he employs folk motifs and folk songs, proverbial sayings and telling commonplaces: in "Auerbach's Tavern," where Mephistopheles offers the grotesque ballad of the flea, or in those scenes where Gretchen sings a simple but moving song, they establish a mood or stress the emotional charge of a dramatic situation—as much through rhythm as by what is said.

But the exuberant display of language in countless different ways is merely the texture of a piece whose pattern is organized and given variety and coherence by an inexhaustible wealth of rhythmical and metrical forms. Neither an inventor of forms (in the manner of the European Baroque poets) nor a creator of metrical schemes (like Klopstock), Goethe was nevertheless able in a singular fashion to infuse the repertoire of established verse forms, ancient or modern, with ever-astonishing fresh energy. The specific use of the various poetic devices, their functioning in a traditional system of prosody, was familiar enough to Goethe and his readers; some had the sanction of classical poets, others were derived from more modern models, such as the *Edda*, Dante, or Calderón. To identify and recognize these metrical conventions is to become aware of their remarkable impact on readers or listeners.

The difference in conception, scope, and style between the two parts becomes instantly palpable through the prevailing choices of meter and rhythm. The reader of the first part moves from the controlled elegiac eight-line stanzas of the "Dedication" to rhythms appropriate to the speakers of the "Prelude," from the grand four-beat chant of the archangels to Mephistopheles's first appearance, from his five-beat lines deferential to the Lord to the casual "madrigal verse," a meter common throughout the play—especially in the dialogues between Faust and Mephistopheles—in which stressed and unstressed syllables alternate in lines of varying length and beat. Faust's first monologue begins in so-called *Knittelvers*, a form popular in the fifteenth and sixteenth centuries, with four stresses and four to eleven syllables, the lines usually in rhyming pairs. This relaxed meter Goethe varies constantly: he places rhymes carefully, invariably to make a point; they urge forward and thus serve a distinct dramatic purpose. Unrhymed blank verse, so common in English and German eighteenth-century literature, is seldom employed.

Regular rhythms and madrigal, or "free," verse sustain the suspense in the first scenes, accented by the ecclesiastic, hymnic meter of the angelic choir and, in contrast, the dry, learned perorations of Faust's self-satisfied assistant, Wagner. These few examples of constantly shifting but meticulously crafted metrical patterns, of alternating rhymed and unrhymed lines, should demonstrate Goethe's skill in creating a lively world of decidedly popular appeal, the spheres of the scholar and of the lovely but conventional young woman, the progression from scholarly resignation to spiritual exaltation and passionate love, the seductive magic of Mephistopheles, the clashing temperaments of the chief actors—all this is told with an intense lyrical fervor, designed, above all, to engage our imagination and compassion.

The second part is, by contrast, directed at far more subtle sensibilities in the modern reader: the wide arches of its five acts, constructed in deliberate contrast to the quick succession of poignant scenes in part 1; the extraordinary array of figures and the immense horizon of its historical scope; the insistent succession of intellectual challenges—all require different formal features in structure, language, imagery, and rhythm. What is astounding from beginning to end is Goethe's command of prosody, of verse and stanza forms. The intricate iambic trimeters, the superbly chained triplets of the terza rima, and the alexandrine's antithetical six iambs, rhymed in pairs and often employed for symbolic or satirical purposes, make *Faust* the richest metrical achievement in Western literature. Goethe's systematic deployment of the forms of the past, with their infinite power of recollection and evocation, anticipates a procedure that modern artists have used impressively: T. S. Eliot's drawing on Spenserian language, Stravinsky's playing on Gesualdo and Pergolesi, Picasso's recovering of primitive and Hellenic styles.

The remarkable abundance of meter and verse forms is paralleled by the spectrum of dramatic forms: monologue and dialogue, disputation and swift action, lyrical effusion and recrimination follow each other; lofty and ironic scenes, paeans of praise and fierce abuse, realistic and highly mannered interludes, operatic passages and imaginative visions, lavish color and frugal linear design provide, especially in part 2, an unending succession of prospects. The "Classical Walpurgis Night," the climactic act of part 2, is in itself one of the most fascinating spectacles of any stage work, an inexhaustible panorama of attitudes, styles, and poetic configurations. While Goethe never seriously considered a stage performance of the first part, he envisaged a theatrical representation for the second; to realize the extraordinary dimensions and demands of such a performance has been possible only in recent years.

A poem of the magnitude and intricacy of *Faust* is ultimately held together by the force and coherence of its ideas and the means by which their range is given concreteness. Goethe himself often spoke of his "mirroring" technique, his conviction that the validity of a poetic production depends on the echoing of propositions and topoi, of motifs and images. To create and elaborate such correspondences in *Faust* was, over the many years of its composition, his chief concern; to develop and intensify their effectiveness meant that he had to transcend the foreground incidents of action or character. As we follow the topography of the two parts, we must, therefore, carefully note the recurrence of metaphors in their allusive play; indeed, of all poetic devices the web of symbolic imagery is the most important. Goethe's symbolic procedure does not aim so much at enriching the meaning of general experiences as at creating a literary system: the significance of a given image must here be derived from its immediate context or from the relation of one occurrence of the same symbol to another. Concepts such as power, illusion and reality, solitude and community, space and time offer us the themes of discourse, light and darkness, gold and granite, sun and moon, cave, hut and palace, cloud, flight, or veil; and countless other images represent chiffers that, by their recurrence in ever new perspectives, give substance to the implications and associations of given propositions. These images are something like leitmotivs that form a nexus of ever more striking references.

The concrete and individually memorable figures and encounters of the first part exert a universal emotional appeal; the mode of the second part is, in a narrower sense, not so much symbolic as allegorical. It offers scenes and personalities drawn from mythological or classical sources with a circumscribed aura of allusion, whose meaning and relevance must be understood and interpreted within the framework of particular convictions or concerns of Goethe and his age. Thus each character in the "Classical Walpurgis Night" or at the end of the final act requires our familiarity with established connotations. The allegorical form demands of the reader a far more intimate knowledge than is expected in the first part of the cultural accretions of each figure or situation. Mephistopheles here represents a manner of operation quite different from his earlier, negative role: the complexity of his modern and uncompromisingly analytical voice makes him, like Helena, that multifaceted embodiment of classical beauty, an allegorical character; and so are Homunculus, the emperor and his court, Euphorion, the four gray women, or the supreme ultimate interlocutor, Dr. Marianus. Part 2 presupposes not our immediate, almost instinctive, participation in the spectacular career of Faust but our readiness, with our intellects alert and with the burden of historical judgment as our guide, to reflect on the great sustaining themes of the poem, on the ceaseless creative interplay between ancient and modern, classical and romantic, objective and subjective, aesthetic and political alternatives and forms of life.

In Search of Goethe's *Faust*
from Without: A Dramatic Approach

Hart Wegner

Solche Mühe hat Gott den Menschen gegeben.
Dichtung und Wahrheit

The obstacles placed in the way of bringing *Faust* to the classroom seem at times insurmountable, because to most of our students the magic worlds of *Faust*—especially those of the second part—are alien territory. What once constituted the common language of the educated and even of those *being* educated—familiarity with the Bible, Greek and Roman mythology and history, classical and "modern" philosophy—is now missing. Instead, students often complain, "How can you expect this of us? We've never taken a course in mythology (or the Bible as literature, ancient philosophy, or medieval history)." The teaching of *Faust I and II* to a class of undergraduates during a single term becomes a forbidding task, because, by necessity, the body of explanations dwarfs and often smothers the works to be studied.

Having taught *Faust* on the undergraduate and graduate levels, in German, English, and comparative literature courses, I found a workable approach in the re-creation of *Faust* as imaginary theater, in the original meaning of the word *theater* as a place of seeing. In our classes the theatrical reality of *Faust*—the casting of characters, the scenery, the costuming, or the movement of the actors on stage—is often neglected in favor of the dialogue. But it is exactly this neglected visual environment of a production that greatly aids the understanding of these plays. Goethe himself acknowledged that theatrical productions provide valuable help in understanding the complex abstract thoughts of *Faust*. When Eckermann worried that *readers* of *Faust* would experience difficulties because the play contained "half a world history," Goethe replied that the theatrical performance would transform the abstract into the material and stressed the visual by using the expression "in die Augen fallen" (29 Jan. 1827; Artemis Ausgabe 24: 223. I cite the Artemis Ausgabe throughout). He also preferred communal viewing ("gemeinsames Anschauen") over solitary contemplation as a better means of comprehension of a work written for the many (letter to Knebel, 14 Nov. 1827; 21: 775).

One can argue that the second part of *Faust* "is no drama at all," as Erich Heller has done ("On Goethe's *Faust*" 134) or point out that Goethe himself was reluctant to have *Faust* performed on stage, as he stated in letters to Zelter and Rochlitz (28 Mar. and 29 Sept. 1829); and yet even the notoriously difficult part 2 was staged impressively by Gustav Gründgens in Hamburg, by Ernst Schröder in a stunning modern interpretation at the

87

Schiller-Theater in Berlin, and in six separate productions at the Vienna Burgtheater.

The communication to our students of Goethe's creative process, which he based on "impressions . . . of a sensual, animated, charming, varied, hundred-fold kind" (my translation), can be facilitated by bringing *Faust* to an imaginary stage in the classroom and thus to life (Eckermann, 6 May 1827).

First the conventions of the theater are introduced. Since students often lack contact with the legitimate theater it is both informative and stimulating to let them experience a real stage, to have them stand on those bare "boards that mean the world." They are told that this limited space has to be transformed into the palace of Menelaos, a shore of the Aegean Sea teeming with mythological creatures, a cathedral, an alchemist's laboratory, or a mountain top. The students worry initially that the action of part 2 cannot be reduced to the size of a stage, but once they ask, "How can we do it?" the interpretation of these two plays by staging can begin.

The introduction of the stagecrafts is accomplished through explanations of the different approaches to a proposed staging. First, standing on the empty stage as our class has done, the director assesses the stage in terms of the movement of the actors. For this space the set designer creates thumbnail sketches, then rough sketches, and finally paper models. Although the individual sets are not yet "designed," the class surveys the locales of *all* the scenes in parts 1 and 2, an exercise that reveals to the students the structure and the cosmic scope of the tragedies and informs their close reading of the text.

In order to re-create *Faust* on the stage of the imagination it is important to supply sufficient material. Students have suggested the woodcuts of Albrecht Dürer for the Gretchen episode and the paintings of Hieronymus Bosch for the Walpurgis Night scenes. One student suggested Greek vase paintings for part 2, and although they would not be appropriate for all the acts, this student has understood the classical nature of parts of the play: the clean lines, the solidity of bodies, and the simplicity of their depiction.

The set and costume design as well as the lighting may be modeled after Goethe's own sketches and the work of others, including the works of artists found in Goethe's Weimar collection. The lighting of our mind stage can recreate the air of mystery—the eeriness of light and shadow—in Delacroix's lithographs to part 1. The murkiness of the light illuminating the ruins of the tomb of Caecilia Metella in a drawing by an unknown English artist in Goethe's own collection illustrates the combined principles of northern and Mediterranean sensibilities informing part 2.

Then the costume designer and this class take recourse to reference books, such as Lucy Barton, *Historic Costume for the Stage*, or Douglas A. Russell,

Stage Costume Design: Theory, Technique, and Style, which provide a wide range of illustrations of Greek, Gothic, *Directoire*, and Romantic dress, aiding immeasurably in the visualization of the plays.

The casting of the major characters follows. An awareness of the continuity of certain characters enables the students to focus their attention, from the very beginning, on the relationship of Faust and Mephistopheles. The casting of Faust, the questing hero, usually presents no problem, while Mephistopheles needs to be understood quite clearly before he can be cast. Which actor known to the students would be capable of playing a convincing Mephistopheles? The "casting" of this part may have to be changed during the course of the reading, but the process of casting and recasting is not a waste of time but an essential exercise in the act of interpretation, leading to a careful examination of the dramatic characters.

Throughout the interpretation I continue to ask for descriptions of the characters' appearance. How do we *see* the Phorkyads, the Telchines, or the disgusting Lamiae? Goethe speaks of "mythological figures . . . that visually make the proper impression" (Eckermann, 24 Jan. 1830; 24: 389), and one can ask, "What impression do they make on you?" In order to bring a complex mythological being to the stage it is necessary to understand the meaning of this figure. Does the essence of the Phorkyads lie in their shared eye, kept in a box for safe keeping, or in their formlessness? How can you translate this amorphousness to the stage and why, in the first place, should such ugliness be shown in the theater? These questions are the lead-in to a discussion of Lessing's comments on the repulsive in art in *Laokoon* 25.

As the class creates the outer shell of *Faust* through the assembling of sketches, paintings, and reproductions of statuary and stage sets, music adds yet another dimension. Thirty-eight years after Mozart's death Goethe stated to Eckermann that Mozart should have composed the music to *Faust* "in the character of Don Juan" (12 Feb. 1829; 24: 313). Selections from Mozart's "dramma giocoso," played in class, can illuminate the humorous aspects this opera shares with *Faust*, although Shaw argued for a tragic interpretation of the opera. Berlioz's operatic adaptation adds to the class, but Mozart's music seems closer to the spirit of Goethe, especially as expressed in part 2.

I continue to ask, "How does she look? What does he do? Why is he wearing that?" Theater as a place to see aids my students' close reading of *Faust* by letting them see what Goethe wanted his audience to see. However difficult the reading and re-creation of *Faust* may be, it seems incompatible with the intent and scope of this work to omit scenes or acts and to exclude part 2 from study. Visually realized, even the difficult second act of part 2 becomes an exhilarating journey of exploration through the layers of civilization and creation, ranging from chaos to the purity of classical line.

The activities of stage director, set and costume designers, and actor are interpretative acts, different, to be sure, from those of the teacher of literature but illuminating nevertheless. The re-creation of the visual surface of the two *Faust* parts probes the varied layered meanings and does not confine itself to the surface at all. As Leonard A. Willoughby notes in his observation on yet another surface of *Faust*, the linguistic one, "a true artist hides those depths on the surface" (Hamlin 535).

Teaching Structural Unity in Goethe's *Faust* through Language Patterns

Garold N. Davis

Listening to students describe their first confrontations with Faust and the devil I have more than once thought they have confused Goethe's text with some ancient creation myth. They describe the matter as nebulous, without form, a chaotic complexity. The teacher's task, of course, is to see that the text eventually evolves into a cosmos. The very abundance of material and ideas makes it difficult for students coming to the text for the first time to see the important structural unity. Ironically, concentrating at first reading on structural unity is, in a certain sense, contrary to Goethe's own advice. In his oft-quoted conversation with Eckermann (6 May 1827) he advises the reader: "Just have the courage to give yourself over to the impressions, to let yourself be charmed, moved, elevated, yes, even instructed. Let yourself be filled with passion and courage to do something grand, but do not always imagine that all is in vain if it does not contain some abstract thought or idea" (my translation). The two approaches to *Faust* are not, of course, mutually exclusive. One can be charmed, moved, and elevated by the individual parts while observing the evolution of these parts into a unified whole. But an initial frustration with the immensity of material can encourage a premature tendency to search for a singular plot line and to dismiss any material that does not seem to pertain as either superfluous or, at best, interesting but unnecessary. This is the tendency that Goethe condemned. He said frequently enough that he created *Faust* to be a *symbolic* drama, and most recent scholarship is convincing that he intended each of the symbolic parts to make up a unified whole. I find Harold Jantz's book *The Form of Faust: The Work of Art and Its Intrinsic Structures* extremely useful in this regard, especially the second section, "Goethe's *Faust* Intrinsically."

One linguistic device Goethe employs that I have found helpful in making a cosmos of the text is his use of word patterns or echoes. These word patterns can be taught easily, regardless of the length of the course. They can be mentioned in a relatively short lecture series, they can be discussed at more length in a survey course, or they can be treated in considerable depth in a *Faust* course that covers an entire quarter or semester. If one has the leisure of a semester, I have found it rewarding to let the students search the text and discover many of these word patterns for themselves. Even a simple word echo can be most welcome to students when it helps them see the union of parts 1 and 2. Sometimes a single word can be at the heart of this echoing pattern, as in the following example.

After many struggles and much suffering, Faust finally realizes that the power of magic is artificial and that true creativity must proceed from natural laws. On the threshold of his confrontation with Frau Sorge, Faust takes the important step of renouncing magic:

> Könnt' ich, Magie von meinem Pfad entfernen,
> Die Zaubersprüche ganz und gar verlernen. . . .
>
> Could I but clear my path at every turning
> Of spells, all magic utterly unlearning. . . .
> (11404–05; trans. Arndt [Hamlin])

When dealing with this passage I direct the students' attention back to Faust's first hyperbolic monologue, in which he states his intention to seek life's meaning with the aid of magic: "Drum hab' ich mich der Magie ergeben . . ." 'So I resorted to Magic's art . . .' (377). The word *Magie* associates Faust's first dedication to magic with his final rejection of magic. Although very simple, this echoing pattern puts important parameters around Faust's first futile attempts to find a union with nature, and the word *Natur* extends the pattern: "Und wenn Natur dich unterweist . . ." 'In Nature's proper school enrolled . . .' (422). And: "Wo fass' ich dich, unendliche Natur?" 'How, boundless Nature, seize you in my clasp?' (455). This is then echoed by Faust's successful union with nature, which he achieves by rejecting magic:

> Könnt' ich Magie von meinem Pfad entfernen,
> Die Zaubersprüche ganz und gar verlernen,
> Stünd' ich, Natur, vor dir ein Mann allein,
> Da wär's der Mühe wert, ein Mensch zu sein.
>
> Could I but clear my path at every turning
> Of spells, all magic utterly unlearning;
> Were I but Man, with Nature for my frame,
> The name of human would be worth the claim.   (11404–07)

Another example of a slightly more complex pattern that ties part 1 to part 2 is the echoing pattern Goethe uses to indicate the transformation of Gretchen's despair in part 1 to her joy at the end of part 2. The first lines appear in the scene "By the City Wall," in which Gretchen addresses the *Mater Dolorosa*:

> Ach neige,
> Du Schmerzenreiche,
> Dein Antlitz gnädig meiner Not!

Incline,
Thou rich in grief, oh shine
Thy grace upon my wretchedness!   (3587–89)

Using a technique that has the terseness of lyric poetry, Goethe echoes this passage nearly 10,000 lines later as Gretchen, in her joy at Faust's apotheosis, addresses the *Mater Gloriosa*:

Neige, neige,
Du Ohnegleiche,
Du Strahlenreiche,
Dein Antlitz gnädig meinem Glück!

Incline
Thou past comparing,
Thou radiance bearing,
Thy grace upon my happiness.   (12069–72)

There are patterns that become much more complex.

The translation scene that begins "Im Anfang war das Wort!" 'In the beginning was the Word!' (1224) and ends "Im Anfang war die Tat!" 'In the beginning was the Deed!' (1237) is a matrix for a series of word patterns that run throughout the text. Some are a positive echo, expanding the meaning of the translation scene, while others are used (especially by Mephistopheles) as ironic or nihilistic comments on the scene. Here, for example, are a few of the *seventy-two* appearances of *das Wort*:

Für einen, der das Wort so sehr verachtet
For one so down on the word   (1328)

Doch ein Begriff muß bei dem Worte sein
Yet with each word there must a concept be   (1993)

Von einem Wort läßt sich kein Jota rauben
From words no jot or tittle can be wrested   (2000)

Erfinde dir des Rätsels heitres Wort
You earn yourself the riddle's merry key   (5542)

Durch magisch Wort sei die Vernunft gebunden
Let reason be restrained by magic word   (6416)

> Des Kaisers Wort ist groß
> The Emperor's word is great   (10927)

> Des Herrn Wort, es gibt allein Gewicht
> The master's word alone imparts his might   (11502)

> Worte, die wahren
> Message of verity   (11731)

Of course, not all appearances of *das Wort* indicate the presence of a unifying structural principle, but many do.

The translation scene also contains the words *der Sinn* 'thought,' *die Kraft* 'power,' and *die Tat* 'deed.' Where these four words are found closely knit into a context, the pattern created may help draw the entire passage into a unity with the translation scene. A computer-concordance to *Faust* (generated at the Humanities Research Center of Brigham Young University) reveals the following number of appearances: *Wort* 72, *Sinn* 90, *Kraft* 85, and *Tat* 38. These are among the most frequently appearing words in the drama, and students can gain considerable insight into the meaning of the "Logos" by identifying and discussing this pattern.

There are times when Goethe joins such word patterns in chains, each echoing word linked to another. One interesting example of this pattern occurs with the verb *gleichen* 'to be like.' The chain begins with Faust's claim to have been created in the image of God and, therefore, like (*gleich*) the Earth Spirit: "Ich bin's, bin Faust, bin deines*gleichen*!" 'No, I am Faust, your match, I am the same!'   (500). The words of the Earth Spirit refute this claim:

> Du *gleichst* dem Geist, den du begreifst,
> Nicht mir!

> Close to the wraith you comprehend,
> Not me!   (512–13)

This particular pattern is rather important since it can lead to an interesting interpretation of Faust's salvation. Faust is not like the Earth Spirit, because he does not comprehend him. Therefore, he is also not like the gods: "Den Göttern *gleich* ich nicht!" 'Not like the gods am I!' (652). The implication is, of course, that he could become like the gods if he could comprehend them. As the pattern continues, Mephistopheles parodies this desire to become like the gods when he himself takes on the appearance of the three

ugly Phorkyads, who share one eye and one tooth for seeing and eating.
They advise Mephistopheles on how to obtain this likeness:

> Drück du ein Auge zu, 's ist leicht geschehn,
> Laß alsofort den *einen* Raffzahn sehn,
> Und im Profil wirst du sogleich erreichen,
> Geschwisterlich vollkommen uns zu *gleichen*.

> Just close one eye, 'twill do it even so,
> Let forthwith but a single eye-tooth show,
> In profile then you will attain the semblance
> Of a perfected sisterly resemblance.   (8022–25)

Nereus continues this ridicule of humans who attempt to become like the
gods:

> Gebilde, strebsam, Götter zu erreichen,
> Und doch verdammt, sich immer selbst zu *gleichen*.

> Those artifacts, to godly likeness prone,
> Yet sentenced to be ever but their own.   (8096–97)

Skipping through the text (there are 130 appearances of *gleichen*, some
pertinent, many not), one finds Gretchen's words to the *Mater Gloriosa* at
Faust's apotheosis forge one of the final links in the chain of "comprehension
equals likeness." Faust, surrounded by the spirit choirs, is scarcely aware
of himself, is scarcely aware of the newness of life, because he is no longer
in contrast with his environment. He has become *like* the holy host surrounding him:

> Vom edlen Geisterchor umgeben,
> Wird sich der Neue kaum gewahr,
> Er ahnet kaum das frische Leben,
> So *gleicht* er schon der heiligen Schar.

> 'Mid spirit choirs fresh life commencing,
> The novice scarce regains his wit,
> The heavenly host but dimly sensing,
> Already he has merged with it.   (12084–87)

And this line, commenting on Faust's salvation as Faust becomes more like the gods through his final comprehension, is echoed once more in the words of the Chorus Mysticus:

> Alles Vergängliche
> Ist nur ein *Gleichnis*.

> All in transition
> Is but reflection.   (12104–05)

When teaching *Faust* in English the teacher is faced with the obvious problem that the echoing word is often not present in the translation. I have found it helpful to teach the German words with which we will be dealing and then to make frequent reference to "das heilige Original." I have mentioned *Wort, Sinn, Kraft, Tat, Magie, Natur,* and *gleichen*. Other frequently occurring words that I often teach students are *schaffen, Zauber, weben, Himmel, Erde, Blut, Brust, Auge, blicken,* and, especially, *ewig*.

Ewig will make a good concluding example, since it figures in the concluding statement of the drama:

> Das *Ewig*-Weibliche
> Zieht uns hinan.

> Woman Eternal
> Draw us on high.   (12110–11)

The most important passage echoing this statement on eternity to which the teacher should draw attention is Mephistopheles's line following Faust's death: "Ich liebte mir dafür das *Ewig*-Leere" 'The Ever-empty is what I prefer' (11603).

It is obvious that the "Ewig-Weibliche" of the Chorus Mysticus and Mephistopheles's "Ewig-Leere" form an echoing (and contrasting) pair, although this is less obvious in the English "Woman Eternal" and "Ever-Empty." One could easily deal with a simple word pattern in English such as this if it involved only two occurrences. When discussing the great overarching theme of time and eternity in *Faust*, however, it is of some importance to know that the word *ewig* occurs eighty-nine times in the text and often forms a part of the pattern leading to the "Ewig-Weibliche." Here, for example, are a few occurrences of *ewig* in the Walter Arndt (ed. Hamlin), George Madison Priest, and Bayard Taylor translations. Reading down the columns one can quickly see the problem in identifying the usages as echoing patterns.

Goethe	Arndt	Priest	Taylor
ewig regen (1380)	ever sanely	never reposing	actively eternal
Ewig-Unselige (8747)	forever deplorable	ever accursed	acurst, reprehensible
ewig leeren (9121)	eternally void	ever empty	eternally empty
ew'ge Schaffen (11598)	constant doing	perpetual creation	endlessly creating
Ewig-Leere (11603)	Ever-empty	Everlasting void	void forever
ewiger Glut (11646)	blaze infernal	eternal glow	endless glow
ew'ge Schande (11697)	shame eternal	endless shame	lasting shame
Ewigen Scharren (11733)	Heaven's company	hosts in verity	Eternal Hosts
ewiges Entzücken (11791)	delight of it all	eternally entrancing	everlasting rapture
ewig schaffend (11883)	all-creative	creative powers	aye creative
ewige Liebe (11964)	Eternal love	Eternal love	Eternal love
ewigen Reiche (12033)	realms undying	realms eternal	endless Eden
Ewig-Weibliche (12110)	Woman Eternal	Eternal-Womanly	Eternal-in-Woman

There are many paths to take through the complexities of Goethe's *Faust*, from the "Dedication" leading to the Chorus Mysticus. The linguistic patterns I have suggested here can be used as signposts to assure students they are still heading in the right direction.

The Individual, Nature, and *Faust*

Cam Walker

> In our narrow house of boards, bestride
> The whole creation, far and wide;
> Move thoughtfully, but fast as well,
> From heaven through the world to hell.
> *Faust* 239–42

Goethe's theater director would surely applaud the Honors 201–202 course at the College of William and Mary. Each year approximately one hundred students and seven or eight instructors undertake an ambitious intellectual journey from heaven through the world to hell (and back) in order to explore some of the formative ideas that have shaped Western society and culture from ancient times to the present. Examining a text a week, we move thoughtfully but, perforce, fast as well.

Cultural and Intellectual Traditions, to use its formal title, is a thematically organized Great Books course aimed primarily at sophomores. The focus first semester is on the human predicament in the natural world; in the spring the emphasis shifts to the individual and society. Within these broad divisions, we proceed more or less chronologically each term from the Greeks to the twentieth century. Our intention is not to offer a complete historical survey but to enable the students to see connections and influences and to assess the merit and significance of individual texts.

Indeed, the texts are the true teachers of the course. The instructors, drawn from a variety of disciplines, function mainly as discussion leaders and critics. Each of us meets with a group of ten to fifteen students twice a week. We supply background information and answer questions but never lecture. Public forums every Wednesday night bring visiting scholars, films, and an occasional concert to supplement the seminars.

Although *Faust* might logically be read either semester, we have found that it works particularly well in the fall, as Goethe raises and illuminates important questions about humanity and nature and the nature of humanity in the West. The course syllabus varies slightly from year to year, but *Faust* usually claims the eighth or ninth week of the term—after the students have read *Oedipus Rex*, the Book of Job, and *King Lear* and before they encounter *Beyond Good and Evil* and *Death in Venice*. Goethe's masterpiece is new to most of the students, but they quickly come to share Walter Kaufmann's judgment that *Faust* "is not only profound and inexhaustible but also readable, enjoyable, and fun" (4).

Kaufmann's dual-language edition, which includes part 1 and excerpts of part 2, is the assigned text. Although we instructors used Hamlin and Arndt's

Norton Critical Edition in our preparatory faculty seminars, we soon realized that neither we nor the students could hope to do justice to the entire play in two class periods. We also feared that the Norton edition's extensive critical apparatus would undermine our goal of encouraging the students to form their own opinions before consulting the commentators and critics. Finally, the German speakers among us preferred Kaufmann's translation.

Students in Honors 201 have several opportunities to write about and discuss *Faust* (and the other required texts). A two-page reaction paper, due at the beginning of each week, ensures careful reading and informed discussion. Students may and do tackle any question, theme, or issue that arises from the text; they often draw on previous readings and discussions as well. We rely heavily on these papers to spark debate and shape the classroom conversation. The students also prepare two longer essays—a five-to-seven-page effort at midterm and a final paper of ten to twelve pages. (*Faust* comes too late in the term for inclusion in the midsemester paper, but it figures prominently in many of the final essays.) Although there are no written examinations, I require students in my section to defend their final papers in twenty-minute oral examinations.

What William and Mary students like best about *Faust* are its wit, its modernity, its broad sweep, and Mephistopheles; what they like least is Faust's salvation at the end of part 2. Some even object to the saving of Gretchen in part 1. Their reaction papers approach the play from a number of different perspectives. In a typical semester, two or three essays compare the "Prologue in Heaven" with Job, one essay contrasts the blinding of Faust with that of Oedipus, and one, by a prospective English major, examines the symbolic uses of nature in *Faust* and *King Lear*. One or two speculate about the source of evil in Faust's world; another attempts to puzzle out the character of Mephistopheles. Several question whether *Faust* is a genuine tragedy. Using *Oedipus Rex* and *King Lear* as models, the authors of these papers usually conclude that it is not. They might agree with Marshall Berman that *Faust* is the first "tragedy of development" (40), for they are outraged by the casual destruction of Philemon and Baucis, but they cannot reconcile Faust's salvation with their understanding of the genre.

The issue of Faust's fate dominates the class discussions, though questions about the role of Care and the meaning of the "eternal feminine" also arise. No amount of talk about Goethe's humane tolerance or Faust's ceaseless activity satisfies the students; they remain unmoved both by the Lord's observation that "man errs as long as he will strive" (317) and the angels' declaration, "Who ever strives with all his power, / We are allowed to save" (11936–37). Children of the nuclear age, they are deeply suspicious of the Faustian strain in Western culture.

The Wednesday night forum provides a change of pace and genre with a showing of Joseph Losey's film *Don Giovanni*. Although opera buffs have criticized Losey's version of the Mozart classic as too cinematic, the students love it. (It is the first exposure to opera for many.) They find Don Giovanni's descent into hell much more satisfactory than Faust's ascent toward perfection.

A very different film that we have encouraged students to see on their own and that we may add to the course in the future, is Istvan Szabo's *Mephisto*. Although it incorporates only two short scenes from *Faust*, the movie reveals something of Goethe's dramatic power and underscores his importance for German theater. It is a useful corrective in a course that neglects Goethe the dramatist for Goethe the thinker, as Honors 201 tends to do.

At the end of their week with *Faust*, the students readily accept Cyrus Hamlin's contention that "whoever would hope to grasp the ultimate complexity of this work . . . must be prepared to devote years of effort to the endeavor" (374). Yet they are not discouraged. As we hurry to the end of the semester—if it's week ten, it must be Nietzsche—they continue to ponder Goethe's work. They draw parallels between Nietzsche and Faust, Gustave von Aschenbach and Faust, atomic scientists and Faust. Many re-read the play for their final paper. And on their course evaluations, most rate it one of their favorite works. Even if they don't think Faust should have been saved, they are glad to have made his acquaintance.

The Romantic Revolution

Margot A. Haberhern

Although many, if not most, of us whose training has been in literature and language would probably prefer to teach students who are majoring in our fields or at least in humanities or liberal arts, such a dream is not always consistent with reality. The Florida Institute of Technology is a moderate-size independent university located on Florida's Space Coast. Except for a few students who are working toward degrees in communications or humanities, most students have as a goal training in science or technology. They take humanities courses for two reasons: the engineering accrediting body requires a certain number, and students often welcome a change from their major fields.

Given this student population, we must design courses that are both substantive and palatable. One such course is The Romantic Revolution, a one-quarter junior-level interdisciplinary survey. While it concentrates on Romantic literature, it includes music and the visual arts. For the music, I use short taped selections; for the art, color slides from the art history collection. I try to use representative, colorful, and dramatic examples of art and music to illustrate and amplify the ideas expressed in the literature. Some pairings are quite obvious, such as Chateaubriand's *Atala* with Girodet-Trioson's *Burial of Atala*, and Goethe's *Faust* with Liszt's *Faust Symphony* or Gounod's opera. Others are thematically related, as a descriptive landscape passage by Wordsworth or Radcliffe with paintings by Cole, Constable, or Rosa, along with portions of Beethoven's Sixth Symphony, Smetana's *Moldau*, or Sibelius's *Finlandia*. The possibilities for coordinating art, literature, and music are almost endless, making the problem one not so much of what to include as of what to omit. No college term is long enough to make use of everything available.

For texts, I use paperbacks, mainly to keep the cost reasonable. Vaughan's *Romantic Art* is a comprehensive, thematically arranged survey that places art in a historical context. Thompson's *Romantic Gothic Tales* is a useful anthology for near the beginning of the term, to initiate fact-oriented, practical-minded students into the irrational, nonscientific realm. For Goethe's *Faust*, I use the Penguin edition of parts 1 and 2 (trans. Wayne). For a general anthology, I use one that I compiled myself, after finding no appropriate one in print. As several editors pointed out, Romantic literature is in the public domain, and the translated selections are brief enough to comply with copyright guidelines. Students are not required to do any outside reading, because it would be unrealistic in light of their workloads.

For my own preparation, in addition to the German text of *Faust*, I use the Norton Critical Edition (ed. Hamlin). The essays raise issues that can encourage class discussion, and the Arndt translation is good. (I prefer not to teach a work in translation with only one English version at hand.) Schenk's *The Mind of the European Romantics* and Praz's *The Romantic Agony* both provide good overviews, and there are countless additional books about the period. For music, Einstein's *Music in the Romantic Era* is quite thorough. Honour's *Romanticism* deals with art in a cultural context, and most art history survey texts give the period good coverage. Of particular interest here is Gage's *Goethe on Art*, a compilation of Goethe's formal and informal art criticism.

In an interdisciplinary survey of Romanticism, Goethe's *Faust* cannot play the starring role it may deserve. I usually spend the seventh week, and perhaps one session of the eighth week, on *Faust*. This scheduling gives students time to assimilate Romantic theories and ideas and to read all of part 1, a summary of part 2, and all of part 2, act 5. The timing also works well because it follows midterms and precedes the end-of-the-term crunch. Since I use an English translation and believe that any literature, poetry in particular, is closely tied to its sound, I read several passages in German, while the class follows the English text. Students seem to appreciate getting a sense of the aural rhythm and texture of the work along with its meaning. There are usually a few grins during the *Knittelvers* passages and some nods of understanding during others. Actually, hearing works as they were intended to be heard does enhance their accessibility; and Romanticism, as an exploration of experience, particularly benefits from the use of the original languages, so I read a few passages in the authors' native languages when possible.

As for class sessions, they are usually a combination of lecture, discussion, and explication where applicable. The unit on *Faust* begins with a review of the plot, then proceeds to the various scenes as illustrating the basic themes of Romanticism, such as the revival of the past and the use of myth, the Gothic and the dark side (including the occult and the Satanic), the importance of nature, the notion of innocence, and particularly the Romantic striving for total experience. We also track various characters to see how they and their roles fit into *Faust* and into Romanticism as a whole.

Because many students are familiar with Marlowe's *Doctor Faustus*, and perhaps William Golding's *The Spire*, some of the discussion focuses on overreachers and the similarities and differences between these two works and Goethe's *Faust*. Students find the contrasts between Goethe's and Marlowe's treatments of Faust and Mephistopheles very significant and also useful for showing differences between Renaissance and Romantic worldviews. Additionally, because the bulk of Romantic literature and art is rather serious, I find that Mephistopheles's playful wit provides a refreshing contrast, one that can illustrate a further aspect of the comprehensive range of Romantic expression.

As if the basic themes of Romanticism and a major Romantic work such as Goethe's *Faust* were not enough to cover in ten weeks, I use two additional themes as leitmotivs throughout the course. Since the movement was a rebellious one, primarily anticlassical, I deal with the classic and romantic —or Apollonian and Dionysian—dichotomy as representing currents that may rise or fall but never disappear. These opposing modes lead nicely into the persistence of Romanticism today and a consideration of how many of its ideas have meaningful application in our technological, ostensibly rational world.

In our humanities electives, we include a term paper. The topic I assign for this course is the persistence of Romanticism in contemporary culture. Students would often prefer that there be a list of suggested topics, but I am not a prescriptive teacher. I give them a few deliberately general suggestions and tell the class that it is up to them to find suitable topics, which they must submit for approval. The papers may be purely critical, but I recommend that students consult secondary sources when possible, for both information and style. For many in the group, this paper may be the only one they will write about literature or art, and secondary materials provide useful guidelines for style and organization. If the class is small enough, I have each student hand in an abstract of the paper, which I photocopy and distribute to the entire class. The last one or two sessions then are discussions of paper topics, providing a lively and synthesizing end to the course.

In addition to the paper, there are two equally weighted examinations, the midterm and the final, each one-quarter identification (author, title, and significance) and three-quarters essay. On the final exam, I include one or two identifications from *Faust* and one essay question, usually dealing with *Faust* as a major creative document of Romanticism. Essays on the final exam indicate that students have absorbed the ideas and the spirit of the period. Among the *Faust* answers, there are often points that there was no time to raise in class, so the work evidently engages students enough to have them think about the play at some length and in some depth. The impact of Goethe's *Faust* is gratifyingly large in proportion to the time allotted to it.

When these practical-minded students complete the course, they have become acquainted with *Faust* and a wide spectrum of other Romantic literature and have seen the art and heard the music of the period. They have learned to acknowledge the roles of imagination, intuition, and the Dionysian aspects of life and to understand their currency. Perhaps most important, these science and engineering students have come to realize that human nature can be neither totally explained and understood through science nor totally satisfied and served by technology.

"Linger a While . . .":
Faust in a World Literature Class

Patricia Marks

Instructors who choose to teach Goethe's *Faust* to nonmajors required to take a world literature class are likely to feel that they themselves are facing Mephistopheles, the spirit "that always denies." If ever a nihilistic force existed, it does so in a class with little background and less German, with an attenuated vocabulary, and with a knee-jerk distaste for poetry, no matter how dramatic. Added to the difficulty is the necessity of discussing a lengthy work in three or four class periods. Yet the wisdom of Goethe is itself an unmistakable call to action:

> Man finds relaxation too attractive—
> Too fond too soon of unconditional rest.   (99–100; trans. MacNeice)

Beginning with a number of ultimate (and perhaps unanswerable) questions about the nature of humanity, of reality, and of good and evil, then, I use dramatic reading, lecture, and discussion "to find the path that is fit and right" for the class I am teaching.

Given four fifty-five minute periods, I usually divide the reading into sections. For the first period, I discuss background material and the "Prologue in Heaven." For the second, students must read through Faust's translation of the Bible; for the third, through Valentine's death; and for the fourth, through Gretchen's imprisonment. In practice, the time frame is fluid, depending on the class discussion I can elicit. To be sure, my method is somewhat old-fashioned, relying as I do on the tried-and-true: dramatic reading, explication, and leading questions. I find for the most part that students who are bewildered by *Faust*'s complexity appreciate some amount of lecturing; those who are usually too timid to speak up sometimes find themselves in vociferous arguments over who killed Valentine and who is to blame for Gretchen's plight. Those arguments are, to my mind, the focus of the class, and they need careful preparation.

The works that precede *Faust* in volume 2 of *The Norton Anthology of World Masterpieces*, the text used for the second half of the world literature sequence, help to "socialize" the students to certain literary conventions, but in a negative way as far as Goethe's work is concerned. Dramatic conventions are introduced by such works as Molière's *Tartuffe* or Racine's *Phèdre* and poetic conventions by Pope's "Rape of the Lock" or excerpts from *An Essay on Man*; in addition, Voltaire and the Leibnizian background to *Candide* provide some understanding for Goethe's use of Mephistopheles as an incentive for action. On the whole, however, the eighteenth-century

frame of reference is useful primarily as a foil, for since many of the works
that precede *Faust* are models of plotting, they are inadequate to prepare
for the special structure of the play, a structure alien to students nurtured,
if at all, on formula romances and westerns. Without this "new" notion—
that character, not plot, may be the key to a work—the first phase of the
discussion, Faust's search not only for himself but for the "Exalted Spirit,"
is meaningless.

The questions Faust asks and the means he uses to find the answers—
repudiation of knowledge, magic, and, finally, attempted suicide—are part
of a larger death-rebirth pattern whose elements I encourage my students
to identify and add to a constantly changing list on the board. What finally
emerges is a mixture of ideas that begins with Faust's redemption from
suicide by the chorus of women and angels and goes on to the "Easter
Holiday" scene, in which we examine the social reformism and unconven-
tionality of

> Out of the dismal room in the slum,
> Out of each shop and factory prison,
> Out of the stuffiness of the garret,
> Out of the squash of the narrow streets,
> Out of the churches' reverend night—
> One and all have been raised to light.
> (86–91)

We find other examples in this and the preceding scene. I try to weave
students' skeletal suggestions into the emergent pattern. The observation
that Faust "feels better" after the angelic chorus that interrupts his suicide
effort I develop in at least two ways. First, I show that his renewal of feeling
comes from a reminder of his spontaneous identification with "Spirit's own
festival" in childhood, and, second, I explain that his rejuvenation inspires
him to translate the biblical line "In the beginning was the Word" as "In
the beginning was the Deed"—a process of translation that carries the suggestion of life coming from what is inanimate. A comparison with Wagner
is usually pertinent here. Students learn the meaning of "pedant" as we
discuss Wagner's interest in mastering words, not ideas. Here, as elsewhere,
I both suggest and try to elicit commonplace examples—Wagner's similarity
to someone who "crams" for an examination by memorizing words instead
of by understanding ideas, for instance.

Once Mephistopheles introduces himself as the inadequate devil that he
is, unable to get the "Something," the "brood of beasts and men" under
control, we examine the wager in order to relate it both to the prologue and

to Faust's death in part 2 and, ultimately, to the death-rebirth pattern. I introduce a summary of part 2, a necessity ever since Norton removed the second half of *Faust* from the anthology. I describe how Faust, like Moses looking into the promised land, longs to live in the utopia he creates and ask students to show how Faust's last act—using Mephistopheles's power to drain the swamp—fulfills the idea in the cosmic framework that "God loves an active man." We discuss the ways in which Faust's "free land," which incorporates the idea of striving, is different from other utopias, like Eldorado in *Candide*. The way Faust is active—albeit unconventionally— occupies much of the discussion as I emphasize certain points: that Faust is the one to offer a wager to Mephistopheles; that in the "Forest and Cave" scene (which, taken out of context, is a compendium of Romantic ideas the class is to meet in the next reading, Wordsworth), Faust is thankful for the devil, who prods him into action; that when Gretchen catechizes Faust, he calls Yahweh—the center of existence—every name but "God."

Convinced by such unconventionalities that Faust is indeed damned and usually ignoring, at this point, my summary of part 2, the class is generally ready to say that when Faust kills Valentine, "the devil made him do it." That comfortable analysis evaporates when someone inevitably remembers that it was initially the Lord in the prologue who gave Mephistopheles permission to tempt Faust. Most classes deal with the alarming hypothesis that God is to blame for Valentine's death either by suggesting a form of Manichaeanism (although not by that name) or by citing a fuzzy notion of omnipotence or omniscience. When faced with the absurdity of placing the blame for Gretchen's pregnancy either on Mephistopheles or on the Lord, the class is ready to understand Goethe's conception of human responsibility. Only two things remain: Faust's confrontation with Mephistopheles and Gretchen's refusal to leave prison.

The confrontation, which takes place after Walpurgis Night during the "Dreary Day–Open Field" scene, demonstrates the point about responsibility, a point that I make by asking a series of questions. If Mephistopheles—or, ultimately, God—is responsible for Gretchen's downfall, then why does Faust feel guilty at glimpsing Gretchen, bowed down by fetters and disfigured by the hangman's rope? Why should he force Mephistopheles to take him to the prison to release Gretchen? Indeed, the question raised by Mephistopheles—"Who was it plunged her into ruin? I or you?"—is a rewording of the question of responsibility that arises from Valentine's death. Again, in the "Dungeon" scene the class finds that Gretchen, whether sane or mad, holds herself to blame for her mother's and child's death; this object lesson sends us back to the prologue for a clarification of the idea that omniscience need not imply dictatorial power. Faust (and by implication Gretchen) has the free will to act and the responsibility for his actions.

The keystone in the analytical arch I build with the class's help is finally put in place in the last scene. Here, where the death-rebirth pattern is most manifest, the students must deal with why Gretchen sees Faust as the hangman, while he sees himself as a life bringer. Since the conflict is both exacerbated and explained by Gretchen's refusal to leave the prison, I ask them to explain the following passage:

> To have to beg, it is so pitiable
> And that with a conscience black as night!
> So pitiable to tramp through foreign lands—
> And in the end I must fall into their hands!   (146–49)

After the students understand that Gretchen faces death whether she leaves or stays, they are ready to deal with her horrified cry at Mephistopheles's appearance: "What does he want in the holy place?" (203). After someone in the class reviews the cosmic frame that begins *Faust*, I remind the students that a cosmic battleground—a "holy place"—may occur anywhere, even (or especially) in the prison, where, on the one hand, Mephistopheles and Faust urge Gretchen to leave and thereby gain a short span of physical life, while, on the other, her fear of "the spirit that always denies" prompts her to call on the "judgment of God." When the voice that says "Redeemed" drowns out Mephistopheles's judgment, the class is ready to volunteer the idea that Gretchen's choice of physical death is actually a choice of spiritual life; with some prompting, they may even suggest that her redemption depends on her decision to remain in prison to pay for her deeds.

In discussing *Faust*, I hope to leave my students thinking about a number of ideas, but primarily that one is, indeed, ultimately responsible for the choices one makes and the actions one undertakes. Since for Goethe omniscience does not imply determinism, except in the sense that one is part of the cosmic framework, no single path, and certainly not necessarily the one set by convention, is correct; it is action—striving—searching—that is more important than the given answers.

I like to think that using both conventional lecture and free discussion mirrors Gretchen's and Faust's approaches to life. Certainly I hold myself responsible for the success or the failure of my method.

Faust in a Great Books Course

George Newtown

I have taught Goethe's *Faust* in two variants of the Great Books course. One is Great Books as it is traditionally conceived, with a smorgasbord of famous primary texts of the Western world; the second is my own design for an honors section of a world literature course, which combines the study of literature and opera. Both variants are intended to give superior students an introduction to Western culture. Both are discussion courses with an optimum size of about a dozen students.

In my experience, the traditional Great Books course has been a team-taught effort (with as many as 9 faculty members over 14 weeks, in fields of literature, history, philosophy, science, and social science). The books are selected on the basis of both faculty and student interest and the willingness of faculty members to take them on. (We have not attempted to choose texts thematically, although a thematic selection may be desirable.) While the composition of the course can vary, *Faust* seems to endure as a component. The texts in one incarnation of the course included the Bible, *The Iliad*, *The Oresteia*, *The Symposium*, *Paradise Lost*, *King Lear*, *Faust*, Montesquieu's *The Persian Letters*, Playfair's *Illustrations of the Huttonian Theory of the Earth*, selected texts of Marx, Freud's *The Interpretation of Dreams*, Camus's *The Stranger*, Borges's *Labyrinths*, and C. P. Snow's *The Two Cultures*. Customarily, in one evening (3 hours) per week, we present one book in its entirety or in major excerpts. During the fourteen-week semester, each student serves as comoderator with a faculty member in the presentation of one of the books. Each student also writes three papers (two of 3–5 pages, one of 5–7 pages). We read *Faust* in the Kaufmann translation, which includes, in facing-page arrangement, the original German and versified English of all of part 1 and act 5 of part 2.

I have billed the honors world literature course as "The Grand Passions"; the texts for the course, which I have taught over a ten-week quarter, consist of major works of literature that have inspired major operas or works of musical theater. We have three class meetings (1 hour each) per week for discussion of the literature and one evening (3–4 hours) per week for listening to music. Goethe's *Faust* occupies five or six (daytime) class meetings in this course, with Gounod's *Faust* taking up one evening. Each student introduces one of the musical works (i.e., gives brief biographical background on the composer, speaks about the structure of the work, and makes preliminary comparisons between the musical work and its literary antecedent); each student also writes two short (3–5-page) papers. I use the following texts and musical selections:

Vergil, *The Aeneid*	Purcell, *Dido and Aeneas*
	Berlioz, *Les Troyens*

Gottfried, *Tristan*	Wagner, *Tristan und Isolde*
Shakespeare, *Romeo and Juliet*	Bernstein, *West Side Story*
Shakespeare, *Othello*	Verdi, *Otello*
Beaumarchais, *The Marriage of Figaro*	Mozart, *Le nozze di Figaro*
Goethe, *Faust*	Gounod, *Faust*
Mann, *Death in Venice*	Britten, *Death in Venice.*

Because both of these courses are honors sections with highly motivated students, I anticipate (and experience) little difficulty with the rather heavy reading assignments. Students choose their own paper topics, in consultation with the faculty; as might be expected, many of the papers are on comparative topics.

In introducing a number of the monuments of Western civilization, I cannot attempt to be exhaustive in the treatment of any particular text. Three (or even six) hours of class give barely enough time to suggest major themes in Goethe's *Faust*. Since the participants are all honors students, however, and since *Faust* deals with the search for universal knowledge and the discovery of the connection between knowledge and power, the discussion rather quickly becomes intense and wide-ranging. One of the subjects certain to be introduced is the issue of Faust's character and, in particular, the justification for his eventual salvation. Is insistent striving sufficient to ensure salvation? This question leads into discussion of moral action and the responsibility of gifted people to the societies in which they live and to the (perhaps less gifted) people who populate those societies. Are moral categories suspended for those who are superior to (more knowledgeable or more powerful than) the mass of humanity? What is the responsibility of someone who imagines an ideal that would be better than perceived reality? Two of the touchstones in the text for the discussion of Faust's responsibility to those around him are his seduction and abandonment of Gretchen in part 1 and the destruction of the old couple, Philemon and Baucis, in act 5 of part 2.

The discussion of the relation between Faust and Gretchen expands easily into examination of relations between men and women in general; again the text helps us focus this discussion as we try to understand the references at the end of part 2 to "the eternal feminine," which "leads us onward." Clearly, *Faust* is a male-centered myth, in which the woman's role is to aid the man in his striving. While we can hardly expect that Goethe present a "liberated" hero and heroine, more modern views of sexual equality encourage us to probe Goethe's ideas on the relation of the masculine and the feminine. It seems worthwhile to suggest that the "eternal feminine" can be an "internal feminine," through which masculine striving is softened by feminine "being"; in the complete human, an accepting love can make ambition less naked and more humane. If we follow this interpretation, the life crisis in *Faust* and the hero's struggle to transcend the apparent insignificance of life can apply as well to modern women as to modern men: we all share active and passive dimensions, both of which deserve to be developed if our lives are to attain full human significance.

Apart from the importance of Gretchen in a discussion of roles of men and women, her passionate love poetry in part 1 is worth examination in its own right. If time allows, I try to introduce a recording of Schubert's "Gretchen am Spinnrade" even in the traditional Great Books course (in which I do not otherwise program a musical component), after we have discussed Goethe's lyric. Schubert's suggestion of the breathless energy of the spinning wheel in the piano and his breaking off of the accompaniment after the climactic "kiss" reinforce the insights into the structure (the increasing palpitations as the beloved moves closer and the climax at his imagined touch) that we have articulated in the discussion. Schubert's repetition of part of the refrain at the end of his song can facilitate discussion of the nature of poetic refrains. The few minutes spent on Schubert's song can also reinforce a realization of the seminal importance of *Faust* in Western culture. In the honors world literature course, in which we listen to Gounod's *Faust*, I also like to examine the "King in Thule" lyric that Goethe has Gretchen sing just before she discovers the box of jewelry in her bedroom and to point out the simplicity and angularity of the folk melody that precedes the famous "Jewel Song" in Gounod's opera; in that moment of transition in the music, from simplicity to pyrotechnic filagree, it becomes clear that Gretchen has changed in her essential nature and cannot return to a state of innocence. In this way, even without discussion of the technical elements of the music, the musical treatments of the lyrics can help elucidate Goethe's text.

One aspect that I feel obliged to introduce (perhaps pedantically) is the importance of humor in the work. Students seem especially unaware of the humor when they read *Faust* (as they do in these Great Books courses) in translation. Some of the scenes in which the humor is clearest and most engaging are the interview with the student in Faust's study, the parodied lovemaking between Mephistopheles and Marthe that parallels the courting of Faust and Gretchen in the garden, and the quasi-seduction of the devil when he is distracted by the succulent backsides of the *putti* who spirit Faust's soul away into heaven.

I may also introduce the question of the "tragedy" of the work, especially as *Faust* usually follows tragedies of the Greeks or Shakespeare. Goethe, after all, did call his drama a tragedy. If we have included *The Divine Comedy* among the Great Books of the syllabus, most students will see Goethe's drama as a "comedy" in the Dantean sense, since *Faust*, like the *Comedy*, ends in salvation; as long as they are asked to consider only Faust himself, students can dismiss the question of tragedy rather quickly. The increased focus on Gretchen in Gounod's opera can suggest tragic dimensions in her role in the literary work as well. Especially full of pathos and dramatic power are the *Mater Dolorosa* lyric and the final scene of act 1, in which Gretchen is so crazed with grief that she cannot recognize Faust even as a potential savior. In this way, a discussion of *Faust* can add complexities to the concept of genre that the Great Books course introduces.

We seldom have time for more than a few words about Goethe's biography or the transformations in the literary biography of his hero. Both areas of investigation seem worth mentioning, however, in order to suggest to the bright students in the Great Books course that they have not "dealt with" Goethe and *Faust* merely because they have read parts of the drama in translation and have discussed them for a few hours. A Great Books course should imply a wealth of knowledge beyond our acquaintance and suggest a lifetime of reading to help us strive to transcend our ignorance.

Teaching *Faust* with Art:
The Delacroix Lithographs

Richard Erich Schade

The artist-poet Goethe held Eugène Delacroix's seventeen lithograph illustrations (1828) to *Faust* in high esteem. "There is one remarkable thing about this: that an artist has made himself familiar with the original conception of the work [*Faust*] to such a degree that he has seized all the original gloom, and has accompanied an unruly, restless hero with an equal unruliness in his drawing" (Gage 242). First, Goethe's laudatory assessment is valuable in that it reveals the poet's perception of the drama's protagonist as "unruly" and "restless," his own play as gloomy. Furthermore, that Delacroix captured just these qualities is all the more revealing, as the artist came to know *Faust* initially through a London stage adaptation (Stewart 124–25) and later in French translation (Trapp 144). Finally, Delacroix's use of the earlier series of *Faust* illustrations by Peter von Cornelius, Moritz von Retzsch, and Ferdinand Ruscheweyh (all completed in 1826 [Neubert]), German artists schooled on John Flaxman's then-popular historicizing style, would have been reason enough for Goethe to reject Delacroix's work, for the poet held Flaxman to be "the idol of all *dilettanti*" (Gage 222) and von Cornelius to be little more than a facile stylist (Gage 235). These factors notwithstanding, Goethe praised the work of the French lithographer and therein lies the particular validity and acceptability of teaching *Faust I* through Delacroix's prints. It is an interpretive approach keyed to the significant interrelationship of text and its visual representation.

The few substantive studies on Delacroix's revolutionary series (Hofer, Jamot, Mitchell, Trapp) are instructive. They provide invaluable art historical backgrounds that the textual interpreter need take into account, though classroom pedagogy calls first for a balanced consideration of both text and graphics, for a step-by-step technique using only one print, that keyed to the line "Ho, grinning hollow skull, well you may leer" (664).

Contextual Description. The lithograph *Night: Faust in His Study* is the second print of the series. It is immediately preceded by an angularly muscular Mephistopheles swimming through the night air; it precedes Faust and Wagner seated conversing beyond the city walls on their *Osterspaziergang*. The progression of the three prints both introduces central figures and establishes significant tensions: Mephistopheles is all vital power suspended above a dim cityscape, Faust's body—in contrast—slumps lifelessly in the dark confinement of his study, and in the third print Wagner's animated gestures and expression emphasize Faust's markedly uninterested lassitude. Viewed in the context of the series, then, Faust shares none of the others' physical or intellectual energy.

Pictorial Description. Faust stands in the center midground of the lithograph. He is in flowing academic robes, garb imparting an undifferentiated, nonphysical quality to the body. His arms hang in inaction, as do his hands. The right leg, bent at the knee, is propped against a chair; it supports the weight of the entire body. The downward gaze from darkened eye sockets is fixed on the skull. He is thinking the words, not uttering them.

The immediate foreground is a textured floor. The heavy wooden chair on which Faust leans is solid, and an overstuffed pillow droops from between its cupped armrests. The table, covered with a coarsely woven cloth, extends wall-like into the close space. On it, two heavy volumes lie flat, on them the skull. Other books lean. The jawless death head is thus center-staged between Faust's body and the partially upright books.

Above the skull hangs a tallow lamp; only one of its four flames flares against a dark background wall. The meager light is diffused unevenly throughout the midground. To the left and above Faust is a bracket-supported shelf, on which stands a bottle (the poison). Behind Faust, but still in the lighted midground, is a chair with sagging backrest; behind it, a darkened background area separated from the midground by a vertical room corner. Its velvet darkness is broken only by a round-paned window admitting little more than a translucent glow.

Pictorial Interpretation. The predominant axes are either vertical or horizontal (no diagonals), and the viewer is confronted with three solid planes (floor, table, wall). The total impact is one of static crowdedness. The central figure is hemmed in by objects from all sides—Faust is confined. Furthermore, the chairs—furniture intended for inaction—either sag or cup the robed body, and the flaccid pillow lying on the one seems an extension of Faust, the robed body an extension of the pillow. Scanty artificial light illuminates the scene, lending it a quality of uncontrasted heaviness. In sum, the visual effect suggests physical inaction, psychic resignation, and a melancholy inwardness so appropriate to the textual line illustrated.

Textual-Representational Correspondences. Though these observations cannot but be informed by a preknowledge of the text, the correspondence in details requires specification. Indeed, it is key to textual evaluation, for such a comparative exercise increases the student's awareness of those subtle textual significances often overlooked in a first reading of the scene illustrated.

While the lithograph illustrates a particular moment, it also points beyond the immediate temporal context to that of the scene as such ("Night"). There Faust communicates with himself, that is, he unsuccessfully interacts alone and in semidarkness with various signs (Flax 183–203), before turning— after Wagner's brief interruption—in abject inconclusiveness to confrontation with the skull, the sign of mortality. His thoughts preceding the line refer to a high wall, to narrow and cluttered space, later, to a dim lamp, whose soot blackens manuscripts. These physical props, accurately depicted by Delacroix, visually reinforce literary significances. The student confronted by text and lithograph understands both, each by means of the other.

The focus of the comments has been on the second lithograph, one especially germane to a demonstration of method, for it defines the drama's protagonist. Of the subsequent illustrations, twelve include Faust. Never is he alone again; indeed, only Mephistopheles and Gretchen receive similar attention: she sits despondently next to an idle spinning wheel, "When he is fled, / My soul is dead" (3378–79). Other depictions of Faust in his study show a more active figure. He rises from his chair to challenge Mephistopheles (print 5). He observes with curious interest as the naive freshman is given the devilish runaround (print 6). In both illustrations the physical surroundings reflect Faust's condition. The cluttered shelves indicate the range of his intellect but also his vulnerability—two skulls and a miniature skeleton share his space (print 5). Where Mephistopheles dominates the action (print 6), Faust peers forth from behind a parted curtain, as if supplanted in influence. It is evident even without further detail that Delacroix's lithographs inform the flow of Goethe's text, are informed by the drama.

This interpretive approach to *Faust* maintains its pedagogic usefulness for the entire text and for the historical context. The melancholy Faust in his study is related to a tradition extending back at least to Albrecht Dürer. Even a cursory examination of Dürer's master engraving *St. Jerome in His Study* yields historic perspectives helpful to the proper assessment of both Goethe's and Delacroix's creative statements.

Dürer's print (1514) portrays the saint seated behind a table, engrossed in writing. The most learned of the Latin church fathers seems hedged in the corner by walls and bench, yet he is spiritually unconfined. Light from a pleasant bank of windows streams into the closed space, reflecting brightly from the tabletop, lighting the intricate wood grain of the ceiling panels. The reminders of human mortality—hourglass and skull—though present, are nonconfrontational: the skull leers at the print's viewer, not at the scholar-saint, protected as he is by the crucifix. Other details familiar from the Delacroix lithograph—pillows, books, shelves—define the space as one of ordered peace, of repose: even the dog and the lion, the emblematic beasts of Jerome, doze. The saint's inactive quietude is creatively inward, a radiant, self-contained spirituality.

Faust, as great a pursuer of universal wisdom as Jerome, is, thus, represented in a manner significantly informed by iconographic tradition. Delacroix adjusts the quality of the attributes to define the complex darkness of Faust's psyche. Just as Jerome's certainty of belief fills the inner space, so does Faust's brooding uncertainty manifest itself in Delacroix's lithograph.

St. Jerome, the model of medieval *vita contemplativa*, is supplanted by Delacroix's representative of problematic modernity. At the last, then, the lithograph defines the historical position of the *Faust* text as a statement on the human condition of Goethe's day.

My teaching of *Faust* with the aid of the Delacroix lithographs is embedded in an undergraduate special-topics course entitled Art and Literature in Germany. I deal with all the texts differently, whether they be emblematically structured Baroque poetry (Schoolfield); Grimmelshausen's lively picaresque novels *Courage* (Speier; Schade, "*Courasche*-Frontispiece") and *Springinsfeld* (Hiller and Osborne; Schade, "Junge Soldaten"), with their cryptic frontispieces; *Faust*; Trakl's expressionistically colorful imagery; or Günter Grass's novels (Schade, "Poet and Artist"). Yet the sequence of descriptions I outline above maintains its usefulness in the classroom. Typically, individual students are assigned the specific subsections for classroom presentation, a method that catalyzes an inordinate degree of participation. Horace's *ut pictura poesis* may be the academic motto of such a course; the commonsense "a picture is worth a thousand words" proves, however, to describe the results generated by the teaching of literary texts with the help of art.

APPROACHES TO TEACHING *FAUST* AND THE FAUST LEGEND: UNITS AND COURSES

Faust and Freshman Humanities

Larry K. Uffelman

Honors Humanities II is the second course in a two-semester sequence required of all freshmen admitted to the honors program. Consequently, the course enrolls a select group of students representing different majors. Although all students enrolled in the honors program have been specially selected, none of them has read widely. The humanities sequence was established to acquaint freshman honors students with basic texts and to show relations among the humanities by crossing disciplinary lines. The sequence is chronological, with Humanities II beginning in the Renaissance and ending in the twentieth century. It does, nevertheless, permit thematic grouping of materials.

In this context, the Faust story is a natural. It provides opportunities for cross-disciplinary work, for teaching students to read carefully, and for introducing them to timeless themes. The Faust materials are therefore valuable in themselves and also because they lead into the other work of the course. In this essay, I describe what I do with the Faust materials in my humanities course. You must imagine me throughout using audiovisual aids and ending each class period by suggesting study questions to direct the students' preparation.

We begin by reading excerpts from *The History of the Damnable Life and Deserved Death of Doctor John Faustus* (1592), a translation into English of the anonymous *Historia von D. Iohan Faustus* (1587), conveniently reprinted in the Signet Classics edition of Christopher Marlowe's *Doctor Faustus*. Reading these excerpts familiarizes my students with the elements of the story as it existed during the Renaissance. Students note that, according to this version of the story, Faustus seeks assistance from Mephistopheles in return for twenty-four years of service and that Faustus becomes a reprobate whose character deteriorates until he dies and who believes he can not be saved. We consider that the universe portrayed in this version of the story punishes overreachers. In this universe, Faustus gets what he deserves. Readers are warned by his example and by the narrational tone not to imitate Faustus but to be satisfied with their place in the natural order.

Once the students have a working knowledge of the elements of the story and have discussed several of its philosophical implications, we read Marlowe's *Doctor Faustus*. To impress on my students that *Doctor Faustus* is a play, I provide the standard lectures on the Elizabethan theater, call attention to how one might stage certain scenes, and assign parts for reading aloud. In our discussions, we observe that the basic plot pattern is the same in Marlowe's play as in the chapbook but that Marlowe's dramatic presentation emphasizes certain points.

For example, students invariably remark that bringing Faustus forward as a visible character speaking lofty blank verse heightens their sense of his greatness. They believe he becomes almost admirable, although deluded and fatally arrogant about his intellectual prowess. Likewise, we discuss Marlowe's portrait of the degeneration of the great man from one who, at the beginning of the play, would defy God to one who, by the end, would welcome self-annihilation as an escape from hell. We note Marlowe's emphasis on Faustus's pride reinforced by fear as the sin that persuades Faustus that God will not save him: in effect, Faustus is condemned by his proud assertion that his sin is greater than God's will to save. In a final comparison, we observe that in Marlowe's play, as in the chapbook, the rules of the universe are stern. In both works, Faustus gets what he deserves. In Marlowe's play, however, we note a change: Faustus seems awesome in his damnation, as if something potentially great has been lost in his fall.

Moving from Marlowe's play to Goethe's, I ask my students to identify the changes Goethe made in the story and to consider their effect on its meaning. My students usually find Goethe's play difficult; focusing their reading in this way helps them. We read all of part 1 and act 5 of part 2 in the Norton Critical Edition, edited by Cyrus Hamlin.

We begin by discussing the philosophical import of the "Prologue in Heaven." We note, for instance, that in Goethe's prologue God approves of Mephistopheles's temptation of Faust. Whereas the chapbook and Marlowe portray a universe in which Mephistopheles vies freely for Faust's soul, Goethe suggests that Mephistopheles works within permitted limits, ironically serving God. Goethe, if not Marlowe, views life, the universe, as whole. We observe, further, that Goethe's universe is more "open" than Marlowe's. It accepts error as a part of life but subordinates it to ceaseless striving, out of which come creative action and eventually, for Faust at least, a beatific vision.

We examine Goethe's portrait of Mephistopheles as an ironic courtier, a wit, and a rogue, but one who is bound to lose Faust's soul because he cannot comprehend Faust's aspirations. We explore this idea most fully when we consider Faust's and Mephistopheles's differing regard for Gretchen.

At this point in our study, I mention that Goethe's addition of Gretchen to the Faust story is his most significant change in it. I also urge my students to remain alert to literary portrayals of women in texts to come: *Candide*, *Pride and Prejudice*, *Madame Bovary*, *Lucia di Lammermoor*, and *The Awakening*. In short, I use Goethe's treatment of the Gretchen story to establish the basis for later discussions of other works. To establish this new theme and to show the importance of the Gretchen story in determining the philosophical direction of Goethe's play, I ask my students to compare the role assigned to women by Marlowe and by Goethe.

We note that in Marlowe's play, as in its source, women scarcely exist. They are, in fact, devils in woman's guise brought forward by Mephistopheles to frighten Faustus from his wish to marry or, as in the case of Helen of Troy, to seduce him into having sex with an incubus. Although Goethe accepts elements of this story, he distinguishes between Mephistopheles and Faust on this point. For Mephistopheles, Gretchen is a fleshly delight whom he can use to lure Faust to his doom. Mephistopheles, however, cannot understand love, a transcendental value in Goethe's play. As a result, Mephistopheles helps Faust reduce Gretchen, ironically serving God's purpose by bringing to Faust a being he can love. For Faust, Gretchen is initially an object of lust, but she becomes an object of love. Goethe makes her a victim whose innocence arouses the audience's sympathy and transforms her into a symbol of the "eternal feminine," whose virtue draws Faust to redemption. Although Gretchen is, in one sense, a traditional nineteenth-century fallen woman, Goethe's philosophy ultimately saves her from that fate.

In moving from our discussions of Goethe's *Faust* to Gounod's opera, my students move into territory only partly familiar to them. By this time, they are acquainted with three versions of the Faust story. Classical music, however, is to them a thing unknown, and opera is its bizarrest form. They are convinced before they hear a note they will not like it. I spend two class periods on Gounod's *Faust* in order to introduce my students to opera through material with which they are familiar and to suggest the continuing theatrical vitality of the Faust story. Occasionally I win a convert.

I open with a lecture-discussion on how Gounod and his librettists, Jules Barbier and Michel Carré, turned the first part of Goethe's play into a performable opera. I point out, for example, the reduction in the number of supernatural beings and the conflation of characters and incidents. I emphasize Gounod's virtual elimination of philosophical matter and his focus on the Faust-Marguerite story. In addition, I note that the complicated aspirations of Marlowe's and Goethe's Faust are simplified by Gounod to a struggle between lust ("A moi les plaisirs, les jeunes maîtresses") and self-denying love ("Salut demeure chaste et pure"). Finally, I observe that the story of Marguerite becomes for Gounod one of innocence betrayed, tormented, and redeemed (Budden 5).

After having set the stage, so to speak, I hand out English translations of the sections of the opera that I play in class. I bring in photographs of stage sets and costumes, and I try in my nonmusician's way to help the class listen to recorded selections by pointing out elementary ways the music complements the story. For instance, I suggest that as Faust, alone in his chamber, contemplates suicide, the accompanying tremulous orchestral chords dramatize the sense of threat. I point out that whereas Goethe interrupts Faust's suicidal despair with a youthful choir, Gounod presents the innocent choral voices. I mention that the tenor's leaps from middle or low notes to notes in the upper register, especially in such arias as "Salut demeure," enhance the poetic language and accentuate the character's romantic appeal. They do this, I suggest, by representing musically Faust's transformation from old man (low notes) to young man (high notes) as well as by emphasizing his earth-born desire for the physically and spiritually "chaste and pure" Marguerite. I observe that the music that surrounds Faust's vision of Marguerite at the spinning wheel suggests innocence as unaccompanied words cannot. Finally, I call the students' attention to the hymnlike conclusion of the opera and the focus on a sanctified Marguerite, assurance that tormented innocence has been redeemed. For Goethe, there is more to come, but for Gounod, Barbier, and Carré, Marguerite is, more simply, a nineteenth-century fallen innocent whose redemption is celebrated by a triumphal closing hymn.

The students' lessons on the Faust materials end when the curtain falls at the conclusion of Gounod's opera. But our consideration of ideas and themes raised by those materials continues. When we read *Candide*, for example, we consider Cunégonde a sort of feminine principle that drives the protagonist across continents to wed her at last, but only after she has lost her beauty and become a hag. Likewise, as we read *Pride and Prejudice*, *Madame Bovary*, and *The Awakening* and as we listen to selections from *Lucia di Lammermoor*, we consider woman as a central character and explore the ways literary characters are shown struggling to realize themselves in the worlds where their authors have placed them.

Beginning Honors Humanities II with a study of the Faust legend helps me meet several goals. First, it allows me to cross disciplinary lines naturally; second, it allows me to follow a single story across national boundaries. More importantly, though, it shows my students how a legend is redefined to express enduring human concerns. I sometimes close the study facetiously by reminding the students that George Abbott and Douglass Wallop, the authors of the Adler-Ross musical *Damn Yankees*, found the kernel of their story in the Faust legend. In that musical, a middle-aged salesman makes a pact with the devil: in return for the salesman's soul, the devil promises to renew the salesman's youth and transform him into an unbeatable baseball player who will lead the Washington Senators in a pennant race against the New York Yankees. With a happy ending that includes the defeat of both the devil and the Yankees, the show demonstrates its fidelity not only to the Goethean (rather than the Marlovian) tradition but to Broadway's musical comedy tradition as well.

The Many Lives of Dr. Faust:
An Interdisciplinary Television Course

Roslyn Abt Schindler

In 1975, the University Studies/Weekend College Program (US/WCP), a nontraditional interdisciplinary adult education program leading to the Bachelor of General Studies degree and housed in the College of Lifelong Learning at Wayne State University, originated a unique television course on Goethe's *Faust* and the Faust legend. Created as a course within one quarter of the interdisciplinary humanities year in the program's integrated curriculum, *The Many Lives of Dr. Faust* consists of fifty-five thirty-minute programs designed for students who have no knowledge of German and no background in the Faust legend, the centuries the legend spans, or the overall European perspective. The course's main objective is to examine the Faust legend as a universal theme and experience in Western culture: the legend is placed in historical and cultural perspective and viewed across national boundaries throughout the ages. Students are introduced to the historical, mythological, scientific, literary-aesthetic, philosophical, psychological, and cultural dimensions of the legend—in essence, to all aspects of the human condition as revealed in the Faust legend from the sixteenth through the twentieth centuries. The course includes lectures and discussions in class; dramatic readings; a puppet play; three major and several minor films; about a thousand reproductions of engravings, paintings, letters, and woodcuts; and excerpts from operas and other musical compositions.

Designed and developed by US/WCP humanities faculty, the Faust course is, nevertheless, the primary responsibility of one of its members, Eric Bockstael. He serves as the series host and has edited two of the four required texts: the anthology, *The Lives of Dr. Faust*, and the study guide (coedited with Sarah Evans), *The Lives of Dr. Faust: Television Study Guide*.

The anthology, correlating closely with most of the television segments, consists of historical documents and sources, biographical and bibliographical information, literary readings, libretti, and critical essays. The material attempts to enhance the student's understanding of the legend and, in turn, of Goethe's *Faust* by providing necessary background and source information as well as the stimulus for comparison and contrast with other works of literature, music, film, and visual art:

Introduction: Ancient and Modern Versions of the Faust Myth
1. Faust and His Time: The Renaissance, Humanism, and the Reformation in Germany
2. The Historical Faust
3. The English Faust book: *The Historie of the Damnable Life and Deserved Death of Doctor John Faustus*

121

4. The Concept of the Devil and the Myth of the Pact in Literature prior to Goethe
5. Marlowe's *Doctor Faustus*: A Study in Conventions
6. The Popular Fausts: The Puppet Play of D. Faust, *The Just Judgment of God Shew'd upon D. John Faustus*, The Folk Ballad
7. Goethe's *Faust* in Music: A Scene-by-Scene Outline of the Goethe, Berlioz, and Gounod *Faust* Settings—plus a Collated Guide to the Three Texts
8. Early American Fausts: "The Birthmark," "Ethan Brand" (excerpts), *Moby-Dick* (excerpts)
9. Faust in the Twentieth Century: "The Progress of Faust," *My Faust* (excerpts), Faust in Film: A Modern Medium for a Traditional Legend
10. Legend and Myth

Prepared as a supplement to the television course, the study guide serves as a pedagogical tool and as a syllabus. Following the above sequence, which includes reviews, major terms and concepts, questions, and required readings, students read the guide before and after each program to gain the maximum advantage from its structure and content.

The main literary readings in the course are Christopher Marlowe's *The Tragical History of the Life and Death of Doctor Faustus* and Johann Wolfgang von Goethe's *Faust* in translation (all of part 1 and part 2, act 5). Goethe's work especially occupies a central position of importance: studied as a masterpiece of thought and imaginative literature, it is set in relief against and compared and contrasted with sources, other literary interpretations, and nonliterary interpretations in music, film, and the visual arts. The Norton Critical Edition of Goethe's *Faust*, translated by Walter Arndt and edited by Cyrus Hamlin, is a particularly good choice for this course: it contains both parts within one volume, valuable notes and commentary, background and reference works, and a fine critical apparatus that complements the material in the Bockstael anthology.

The Faust course directly addresses three key issues involved in teaching Goethe's *Faust*, especially to an uninitiated audience: the historical background, development, and sources; the predominant themes and their contemporary relevance; and the universal significance of the Faust theme.

The course proceeds chronologically through four centuries and divides thematically into seven related units: (1) the historical context of the myth and the primitive Faust legends, (2) Marlowe's *Doctor Faustus*, (3) Faust and the folk culture of the seventeenth and eighteenth centuries, (4) Goethe's *Faust*, (5) Faust in art and music after Goethe, (6) Faust in America, and (7) twentieth-century Faust (Bockstael and Evans v). Experts participate in each section. Television permits the presentation of a wide range of knowledge and talent to enhance the student's enjoyment and learning.

After a general introduction to the eternal fascination with the Faust legend and possible reasons for it, the course considers the truth and fiction of Faust, based on historical documents (letters, city records, chronicles, sermons, Luther's *Tischreden*, etc.) as well as the first literary formalization of the legend by Johann Spiess. Discussion then turns to the concept of the devil and the myth of the pact in literature before Goethe, with particular focus on the Theophilus legend. Following Marlowe's *Doctor Faustus* (four programs, including a dramatic reading) and an examination of Faust as a popular legend in folk books, folk dramas, folktales, ballads, and puppet plays is "Goethe—A Genius in His Time," the subject of two programs, which prepare students for the subsequent analysis of *Faust I* (eight programs), including the film of Gustav Gründgen's 1959 stage production of Goethe's *Faust*. *Faust II* is examined much more briefly: students are offered a written summary (Bockstael and Evans 50–56) as well as a short discussion in program 26 about the relation between part 1 and part 2; Goethe's experimentation in part 2 with new artistic forms, styles, and methods of perception; and Faust's involvement in a dynamic journey and process that ultimately lends "an optimistic and redemptive view to the end of the drama" (Bockstael and Evans 49).

"Goethe's *Faust* and the Arts" (four programs) explores visual illustrations from copper-plate etchings to the works of Eugène Delacroix. "Goethe's *Faust* in Music" (four programs) is exemplified by two outstanding compositions, Hector Berlioz's *The Damnation of Faust* and Charles Gounod's *Faust*, as well as by additional interpretations by Franz Liszt, Ludwig van Beethoven, Franz Schubert, Robert Schumann, Richard Wagner, and others.

The course subsequently shifts to discussions of early American interpretations of the legend by Nathaniel Hawthorne ("The Birthmark" and "Ethan Brand") and Herman Melville (*Moby-Dick*). These programs emphasize the similarities as well as the cultural differences in the New World treatments of the legend.

"Faust in the Twentieth Century," which concludes the series, is introduced with Karl Shapiro's poem "The Progress of Faust" and an excerpt from Paul Valéry's play *Mon Faust*. Thomas Mann's *Doctor Faustus*, although not required reading, is treated by way of written summary (Bockstael and Evans 91–94) and discussion (program 40). Two particularly representative full-length films, F. W. Murnau's *Faust* and René Clair's *The Beauty of the Devil*, continue exploration of the twentieth-century Faust. The program "Faust and the World Wars" is an inquiry into the political and ideological reasons for the eventual rejection of Faust by the end of World War II:

> He was taken as a representative of ambition leading to evil, destructive ends. . . . World War II created doubts about Western man's ambition and the moral responsibility of a pursuit of knowledge. . . . [Faust] came to represent all the bad instincts and evil genius of the German soul, and the Faustian figure was condemned or at least demystified. (Bockstael and Evans 103–04)

The song "Sympathy for the Devil" by the Rolling Stones characterizes, finally, the post–World War II generations and especially the counterculture generation of the 1960s: "Images of chaos and a ruptured and disjointed world characterize the generation that sympathizes with the devil, yet wishes to restrain evil" (Bockstael and Evans 113).

The last four programs summarize and review, in discussions among faculty and students, the major issues, themes, concepts, and works presented in the series. Many issues are raised that cannot be addressed conclusively, among them the relevance of the Faust myth in today's world. In the final analysis, "[e]ach human being must weigh [the] desire for improvement and knowledge against the risk of their destructive force. One must determine one's own ultimate values" (Bockstael and Evans 119).

The Many Lives of Dr. Faust overcomes one of the major difficulties of literary interpretation in the traditional classroom: the lack of opportunity to view the work(s) as part of a cultural tradition and chronological continuum. The course offers an ongoing balance among the arts, within history, and across national boundaries, indeed continents. Interdisciplinary relations are constantly drawn; cultural, historical, and aesthetic similarities and differences are systematically reviewed and highlighted. In addition to ample opportunity for questions and intensive discussion with the classroom instructor, there are continuous checks on the student's comprehension of individual programs and completion of assignments through various forms of oral and written work: weekly quizzes primarily on program content, one major essay examination to explore broader concepts and development, and one major analytical research paper (students have a choice of topics) or creative project (students are encouraged, for example, to write their own plays, short stories, or poems on the Faust theme or to create visual-art projects—all with written commentaries, progress logs, and analyses).

This interdisciplinary television course has significant value for undergraduates of all majors. General education students are exposed to great works of literature and the other arts and discuss major issues in Western intellectual history. General humanities or interdisciplinary students acquire a wide range of perspectives that they may transfer to other learning. For language and literature majors, the course offers a strong foundation in literary analysis within a meaningful cultural and historical framework.

As a major mass medium in our society, television has vital, rich possibilities for the future of education, not as a substitute for the classroom but as a complementary mode of instruction. Educational institutions can use this medium not only to make education flexible and accessible for the growing population of adult learners but also to enrich education for learners of all ages.

The Faustian Theme in European Literature, Painting, and Music

Edith Potter

The Faust play, although reported by Gottsched in 1730 to have finally been laid to rest (Smeed 113), has instead proved unusually alive, undergoing periodic rejuvenations, transformations, and adaptations, its topic developing into one of the great themes in world literature. In both my Faust courses—Goethe's Faust and the Faust Legend, given in German, and The Faustian Theme in European Literature, given in English—one of my objectives is to have students realize that there is a long-standing tradition of legends dealing with human striving for supernatural powers. They also learn about the Faust tradition before Goethe, thus enabling them to appreciate how this theme evolved from crude beginnings to Goethe's masterpiece, which, in turn, set off an endless line of imitations, continuations, and new interpretations. For the sake of clarity, let me first discuss aspects unique to the German literature course, Goethe's Faust and the Faust Legend, before turning to the comparative literature course with its different aims and assumptions.

We devote not more than the first two weeks to a discussion of the legends, the historical Faust, and the *Spiessbuch* on Faust and its later versions, so that students may start to read Goethe's *Faust* as soon as possible. Palmer and More's *The Sources of the Faust Tradition* is indispensable for a knowledge of the forerunners of *Faust*. It enables students to get to know the Magus and Theophilus legends and to read the English version of the *Spiessbuch* and experience the tone and thrust of this early Faust treatment (Palmer and More 7–77, 134–236). Those few able to read the old German type are encouraged to try to read excerpts of the *Spiessbuch* in the original German.

Palmer and More also briefly discuss the later versions—Widman (1599), Pfitzer (1674), and *Der Christlich Meynende* (1725), whose condensed account is the foundation of the later chapbooks sold at fairs and probably known to Goethe—as well as translations of the evidence we have for the Faust story's developing into popular stage and puppet plays (129–33, 237–69). This is a good time to introduce the many contemporary woodcut illustrations to contrast the crude popular conception of Faust and the devil with Goethe's sophisticated pair (Wegner, illus. 1–13). Also useful at this point is a tape of Ferruccio Busoni's opera *Doktor Faustus*, inspired by one of the puppet plays.

Before starting Goethe's *Faust*, students read Lessing's *17. Literaturbrief* containing his Faust fragment. From Goethe's *Faust* I always have part 1, except the "Intermezzo," read in its entirety. Of part 2, I always omit sections of act 1 ("Spacious Hall," "Pleasance") and act 2 ("Classical Walpurgis Night," except "Rocky Inlets of the Aegean Sea") and most of act 4 (except for lines

10039–233 and "The Rival Emperor's Tent"), summarizing their content. Depending on the students, more cuts are sometimes necessary. The format of each class section consists of discussions, regular student reports, and oral reading of lyrical and significant passages so that the students may experience the magic of Goethe's language. Students, accustomed to reading silently, learn that poetry involves not only the mind but the senses as well, imparting stimuli through sounds, images, and ideas. Even in the English-conducted Faustian Theme course I read the "Dedication," the opening monologue, and the lyrics aloud in German to give students the experience of hearing *Faust* in its original language. Dramatizing suitable scenes provides an additional opportunity to involve and stimulate the students more fully as well as to enliven the class.

Goethe's *Faust* with its panoramic view of human existence is particularly well suited for a discussion of many issues, historic as well as contemporary. The cosmic frame of the "Prologue in Heaven" addresses issues involving the human condition and free will; the "Prelude in the Theater" deals with, among other things, creativity and eighteenth-century theater audiences. Part 1 with its Sturm and Drang elements offers an opportunity to explain the anti-Enlightenment stance of the Stürmer and Dränger, their criticism of the treatment of the unwed mother, their attitude toward genius and feeling, and their unconventional religious views. The opening as well as the Earth Spirit scene are concerned with the limitations of human knowledge and Goethe's view of nature. Comic relief is provided by the university and student satire and by Mephistopheles, who adds a light touch to many a somber scene with his ever-present witticisms, ironies, sarcasm, and sophistication. This partial list of possible discussion topics can easily be extended. As the Director says in the "Prelude in the Theater," "Wer vieles bringt, wird manchem etwas bringen" 'Who brings a lot, brings bits for everyone' (97; Hamlin ed.). The many aspects of Faust enable students from various disciplines, such as literature, history, science, economics, psychology, philosophy, to identify with Faust on a personal level. They also realize the complexity of such modern issues as the artificial creation of life, the manipulation of money, the question of guilt, social and community planning, forced labor, and the generation gap, to mention only a few. This wealth of issues should not, however, let us overlook to treat *Faust* first and foremost as a poetic creation, a *Gesamtkunstwerk*, written in a style and form that defies all categorization.

The Faustian Theme in European Literature course offers difficulties of organization and selection because of the overwhelming number of works dealing with Faust after Goethe's *Faust. Ein Fragment* was published in 1790. I have decided to make Goethe's *Faust* the focal point of the course. No other figure in all Faust literature is equal to Goethe's Faust, with his complex qualities, his range of noble aspirations, as well as his less lofty drives. He *is* the man both of the sixteenth and of the eighteenth century, and, with his modern social projects, he anticipates our own time. In his searching and striving he is clearly the Renaissance and the Romantic hero combined, and he opens up the horizons of the modern world. Finally, what other Faust can boast a companion of the caliber of Goethe's Mephistopheles?

Dealing with the pre-Goethean Fausts, I follow the plan of my Faust course in German but add Calderón's *El mágico prodigioso*, with its magus legend theme, and Marlowe's *Doctor Faustus*. That only a few years after the *Spiessbuch* a master playwright like Marlowe shaped the Faust story into a drama of true artistic merit is a blessing not only for the development of the Faust tradition but also for our students, who welcome early in the course a shift from necessary background reading to the enjoyment of reading great literature.

Choosing representative works for the post-Goethean period is much more problematic. Comparative principles, differences and similarities, national and universal traits, ironic counterpoints and prefigurations have to be kept in mind. To prevent the chronological sequence from becoming monotonous, I emphasize milestones in Faust treatments and point from the very beginning to crosscurrents and interconnections in the vast web of the literature. This approach assures coherence and structure. For comparative purposes I include at least one representative work from different national literatures, such as Byron's *Manfred*, Valéry's *Mon Faust*, and Lunatscharski's *Faust and the City* or possibly Bulgakov's *The Master and Margarita*. Depending on the class, I might add Imre Madách's *The Tragedy of Man* in J. C. W. Horne's translation. I even invite students to participate in the creative process of the class by asking them to suggest works with Faust themes from their own readings or their own cultures; the results are often excellent.

From among the German Sturm and Drang Faust treatments, I compare Klinger's thought-provoking Faust to Maler Müller's Faust, who strives only for power, wealth, and sensuous gratifications. Students read the many late-eighteenth- and nineteenth-century German Fausts, which show the impact of Goethe's work, in either German or English, depending on the students' backgrounds, and then write short classroom reports. Students want to know whether given authors depended on Goethe's depiction or not and whether they may even have parodied it. There are Fausts of many moods: despairing or solitude-seeking Fausts in Lenz's and Grillparzer's short fragments; pessimistic, brooding, and skeptical Fausts in Chamisso, Platen, and Lenau; a frivolous dancing Faust tempted by a Mephistophela in Heine; and the colorful and feisty Faust in Arnim's *Die Kronenwächter*. Grabbe's *Don Juan and Faust*, influenced by Byron's *Manfred*, shows the ingenius although unsuccessful attempt to combine two archetypal characters in one drama.

Whereas Goethe's Faust has universal dimensions, twentieth-century Fausts are often a mirror of their times. Lunatscharski's is an optimistic socialist Faust; Valéry's points to the chaos to come with the new machine age; Bulgakov's seeks freedom. There is an American Faust (John Hersey's *Too Far To Walk*) and a resigned Irish Faust (Lawrence Durrell's *An Irish Faust*), but the most profound and controversial is the hero of Thomas Mann's *Doktor Faustus*, which concludes the reading list for the course.

Although Faust stories have appeared since Mann's, his *Doktor Faustus* provides a good counterbalance and contrast to Goethe's *Faust* and an opportunity to finish with a significant, powerful work. It completes the cycle, so to speak, since Thomas Mann goes back to the *Spiessbuch* for his plot and language. Students will sense the stark contrast between Mann's archaic language and his twentieth-century setting, narrative techniques that achieve a dual time perspective. In choosing for his Faust figure an artist with Nietzschean features, a twelve-tone composer at that, and in giving music the prominent place in his novel, Mann brings a new, albeit controversial, dimension to Faust literature. The class should discuss the differences and interrelations—not necessarily the influences—among all the readings. In addition, the class should examine the evolution of Faust and of the devil from old-fashioned and traditional characters to sophisticated and psychologically oriented ones; this examination ties the readings together and suggests possible trends.

Thomas Mann's *Doktor Faustus* also provides a convenient transition to Faust in music—and in art. Indeed, I incorporate music and art in the course throughout the semester. I place tapes of musical settings on reserve in the laboratory and require students to listen to them and to include their listening experiences in discussions and reports. I also place Faust illustrations on reserve and refer to them throughout the course. Toward the end of the semester, I devote one meeting to playing characteristic excerpts from musical scores and one to showing slides. The musical interpretations and art illustrations also allow me to comment on the different artistic styles of various periods.

Students note again the international scope of the Faust theme as they listen to different interpretations by famous composers: Wagner wrote a *Faust* overture early in his career; Berlioz depicted the demonic aspects in his *Damnation of Faust*; Schumann selected themes congenial to his personality, endowing those themes with sublimely beautiful music. Liszt chose Faust, Gretchen, and Mephistopheles for character studies in his *Faust Symphony*, composing music, as Humphrey Searle observed, as daring and modern as Faust himself: "The opening theme of the *Faust Symphony* includes all the notes of the chromatic scale, and in several passages in the work the tonality is suspended altogether" (11: 35). Gounod saw in Faust not the seeker of knowledge but only the romantic lover. Arrigo Boito selected Mephistopheles, not Faust, as the focal point of his opera *Mefistofele*. Ferruccio Busoni's *Doktor Faustus*, undeservedly absent from the present opera repertoire, is composed in a musical style far ahead of its time. Hanns Eisler, who went back for his libretto to old sources too, never composed the music. (For suggested recordings of these works, see the list of works cited.)

Any discussion of Faust compositions must include references to Goethe's plan for the role that music would play in his *Faust* as well as to his persistent but eventually frustrated efforts to have *Faust* set to music. He finally realized that only Mozart could have written appropriate music (Eckermann, 11 Feb. 1829).

Illustrations are even more numerous than musical interpretations, but many are not easily available. Fortunately, Wolfgang Wegner's *Die Faustdarstellung vom 16. Jahrhundert bis zur Gegenwart*, with its informative text, reproduces a fairly good selection, including some illustrations not readily found; but Wegner's work is limited and gives no idea of the many artists that were inspired by Goethe's *Faust*. For that we need Franz Neubert, *Vom Doctor Faustus zu Goethes Faust*, long out of print, and Max von Boehn's informative illustrated introduction to the *Faust* edition of 1924 in the Askanischer Verlag, also no longer available.

In my art session I restrict myself to a small but representative selection of old and nineteenth-century pictorial presentations of *Faust*, in order to have enough time left for the many excellent illustrations created in the twentieth century, which demonstrate to students how timely the Faust theme is. I make sure, however, to include Goethe's own sketches, the three Kaulbach engravings (*Gretchen* [*Kirchgang*], *Gretchen* [*Mater Dolorosa*], and *Helena* [Faust]), and the two Delacroix illustrations Goethe praised so highly (*Auerbach's Tavern* and *Faust and Mephistopheles Charging by the Gallows-tree*). I am fortunate to be able to show students a typical nineteenth-century deluxe edition, the first part of *Faust* as illustrated by Engelbert Seibertz and published by Cotta in 1854. Listed below are suggested illustrations for a slide presentation:

1. Examples of woodcuts from the pre-Goethean era, selected from Neubert and Wegner.
2. Title page of the *Spiessbuch* of *Faust*, 1587 (Neubert 31).
3. Title woodcut that accompanied the 1631 edition of Marlowe's *Doctor Faustus* (Wegner, illus. 6).
4. Matham, Adrian. *Mephistopheles Brings Helena to Faust.* (Wegner 7).
5. Rembrandt. *Der Magier*, now called *Dr. Faustus* (Wegner 8).

6. Goethe. *Erscheinung des Erdgeistes*. (If possible, also some examples from the remaining six Goethe sketches for *Faust*.)
7. Cornelius, Peter. Selected drawings, including his *Faust and Mephistopheles Galloping along on Black Horses*, in order to compare it with the Delacroix etching (Wegner 39–41).
8. Retzch, Moritz. Selected drawings. (Wegner presents four, 42–43, 60–61.)
9. Ramboux, J. A. *Gretchen in Prison* (Neubert 94).
10. Neureuther, Eugen. Marginal drawings for songs from *Faust* (Neubert 140–41).
11. Kaulbach, Wilhelm von. *Goethe-Gallerie*. Three drawings from *Faust*: *Gretchen* (*Kirchgang*), *Gretchen* (*Mater Dolorosa*), *Helena* (Faust) (Neubert 173).
12. Hosemann, Karl. *Mephistopheles and Marthe* (Neubert 176).
13. Konewka, Paul. Silhouettes from *Faust* (Neubert 200–06).
14. Delacroix, Eugène. *Auerbach's Tavern, Faust and Mephistopheles Charging by the Gallows-tree*, and possibly also the cathedral scene, *Gretchen and the Evil Spirit* (Wegner 56).

The above suggestions do not include the twentieth century. Excellent examples can be selected from Detlev Lüders, *Goethe in der Kunst des 20. Jahrhunderts*, the exhibition catalog of the Freie Deutsche Hochstift. It gives an excellent selection of the great number of famous artists that illustrated *Faust*. The edition of *Faust II* with illustrations by Max Beckmann is also still in print. For useful secondary literature on art and music, consult, in addition to the works cited above, Fähnrich; Hubert; Kehrli; Mahal, *Faust-Museum Knittlingen* and *Mephistos Metamorphosen*; Schuh; Schult; Sternfeld; Tudor; and Wankmüller and Zeise.

The course is immensely enriched by the integration of music and art as well as theater and film—including, if possible, screenings of selected films (e.g., the silent *Faust: Eine deutsche Volkssage*, the Hamburg production *Faust I*, and the Richard Burton–Elizabeth Taylor *Doctor Faustus*). It helps students gain a memorable impression of the far-reaching significance and impact of the Faust theme.

Faust in Literature and Music

Carsten E. Seecamp

The single-semester course on the Faust legend in literature and music is offered by the German department with the aim of attracting new students from outside the traditional German program. Although the course retains a German component for majors, it is taught in English and cross-listed by the English department. Furthermore, it is offered as a split-level course (second and third year) to enable us to reach the greatest number of students.

All students take the midterm and final examinations, consisting of identification and essay questions. For upper-division students, and English and German majors in particular, greater class participation, more outside readings, as well as a research paper are expected. Wherever feasible, specific needs and interests are met through individually structured assignments. Therefore, in describing the course, I limit myself to aspects forming the common core for the entire class.

The texts used are Christopher Marlowe's *Doctor Faustus*, edited by Sylvan Barnet (included is an abbreviated version of the English translation of the original *Faustbuch*), Peter Salm's translation of Goethe's *Faust, Part I* (dual-language edition), Philip Wayne's translation of part 2, and James William Kelly's *The Faust Legend in Music*. In addition to a section on the musical analysis of various works and a listing of nearly thirty pages of musical compositions inspired by the Faust legend, Kelly's book provides a valuable framework for background material from the Faust legend in antiquity to Spengler and his concept *of the faustische Mensch* as the symbol and exponent of Western civilization.

My approach to the course is comparative. I welcome and expect uninhibited discussion, and I urge students to think creatively, rather than to seek definitive answers, about the interrelations in culture and the realm of ideas. Thus, for example, the class begins by examining religion and the extent to which it is likely to welcome or condemn human striving for knowledge and wisdom. Three striking contrasts can be drawn using the Old Testament and Greek and Nordic mythologies.

To generate discussion, I ask the students to consider the Genesis account of the creation from the viewpoint of the snake. Is it not paradoxical to punish Adam and Eve for an act committed while they are obviously still unable to differentiate between good and evil? Were human beings really meant to remain forever in blissful ignorance, unquestioningly obedient to Yahweh? I introduce the concept of *demon est deus inversus* as offering possible answers. Later, in the discussion of *Faust*, students see that Goethe's concept of good and evil, albeit not identical, is no less paradoxical.

For a discussion of the Prometheus myth in the context of Greek religion, I rely on Walter F. Otto's classic work, *The Homeric Gods*. Our subsequent treatment of Goethe's "Prometheus" poem in the context of his *Weltanschauung* reveals significant shared beliefs. (There is, for example, no place for dogma or contradiction to human experience since no part of life is without the divine.)

In discussing the peculiarities of Germanic mythology, we note that time and fate stand above the gods and that principles of honor govern the behavior of the gods, as well as of mortals. Thus, in contrast to the Book of Genesis, the gods themselves, not human beings, commit the original sin. More pertinent, however, is the fact that Odin, the god of wisdom, is not wise from the outset but, like Goethe's Faust, acquires his wisdom only gradually and not without sacrifice. In addition to the obvious Faust motif, I stress the concept of "becoming" (with reference to Nietzsche's characterization of the German soul), thus laying the groundwork for later analysis of Busoni's unique version of the Faust legend.

After this general introduction, the course becomes more focused as we refer to the texts and examine the Faust legend in antiquity and then quickly move on to the historical Faust figure and the *Faustbuch* of Johann Spiess. Discussion centers on the turbulent age, which, like our own, produces revolutionary changes and readily creates myths around a central historical figure. I ask students to draw parallels between the two periods (information explosion, conflict of ideologies, strong interest in the occult, discovery of new worlds, etc.) and to name the twentieth-century figure around whom the process of mythogenesis continues to produce a massive body of literature. That figure, of course, is Hitler, as is shown by the spate of novels and films in the vein of Ira Levin's *The Boys from Brazil*. On an artistic level, one cannot leave unmentioned Hans-Jürgen Syberberg's recent epic *Hitler: A Film from Germany*.

In treating Marlowe's *Doctor Faustus*, I emphasize the extent to which it shows the influence of the English translation of the *Faustbuch* and reflects the pride in intellect that marked the Renaissance. In contrast, Lessing's *Faust*, of which only a small fragment is extant, could not possibly retain the moralizing and trappings of Christianity still found in Marlowe's work. I translate the few short scenes for the class and show how Lessing's Faust embodies the ideals of the Enlightenment. Because he cannot be damned, he figures as an important forerunner for Goethe's Faust, whose damnation would be equally inconceivable. I am very fond of Lessing (who is totally unknown to the students), and I spend considerable time on his contributions to the Enlightenment before introducing other major cultural figures (Herder, Winckelmann, Schiller, etc.) of the Age of Goethe.

As for Goethe, he is in many ways unapproachable for a modern public because his legacy is heterogeneous in the extreme and seems to lack an inherent sense of harmony. Instead of overburdening the students with factual information about his life, I let them approach him directly through his works. I have discovered the *Farbenlehre* to be an ideal vehicle for making Goethe more accessible since it can demonstrate the organic coherence of his *Weltanschauung*.

I omit physical and chemical colors from discussion of Goethe's color theory. I restrict myself to those colors that, according to Goethe, are created through a combination of light and darkness. (A spinning disk divided into black and white segments *will* produce, albeit only subjectively, the colors of the spectrum.) The philosophical underpinnings of the theory are found throughout *Faust*, and the entire poem can be interpreted from the standpoint of Goethe's scientific treatise. (The Lord is light, Mephistopheles represents darkness, and Faust stands in the middle, the world of color.) Goethe reconciles the polarities inherent in Christianity, where they are basically antagonistic toward each other, into an optimistic and dynamic whole much along the lines of Leibniz's concept that imperfection is needed for the greater perfection of the whole. All the important concepts basic to understanding Goethe's *Weltanschauung* and his *Faust* can be derived from the color theory: harmony, duality, polarity, evolution, diversity, compromise between relativism and absolutism, and so on.

In teaching *Faust I*, I initially stress careful textual analysis of the *Gelehrtentragödie*. We read sections aloud, especially when I wish to illustrate Mephistopheles's marvelous sense of humor or to show that he is quite a likeable rascal and not at all diabolical. I point out the numerous comparisons with Marlowe's work (both Fausts' tendencies toward hyperbole, the use of music, etc.). I cover the remainder of part 1 rather quickly. Similarly, I find that part 2, with its rich mythological reference and imaginative speculation, can be adequately covered in a relatively short period, providing one does not get bogged down in too many side excursions from the main themes. At the end of *Faust II*, the German majors are given the opportunity to show the rest of the class the extent to which a translation is an interpretation. I give them five different translations of the last eight lines of the poem, and to a person they are capable of appreciating the enormous liberties taken by some of the translators.

The first time I taught the course, I covered the material strictly in historical sequence and did not discuss or play any musical works inspired by the Faust legend until we had covered the whole play. Subsequently, however, I have opted to introduce music at appropriate moments in the text. The "Prologue in Heaven," for example, has only one musical setting available, that by Boito. I play that section of *Mefistofele* immediately after covering the Goethe text. I then ask the students to what extent the music might fulfill Goethe's own wishes in light of his comments on Mozart. Does the libretto remain true to the spirit of the original or does it violate it? (One might bear in mind Zelter's comment that Berlioz's *Eight Scenes from Faust* is a fragment of an abortion resulting from a hideous incest!) In later sections of *Faust* one can, of course, play several musical settings of the same scenes and compare their effectiveness (Gounod, Boito, Schumann). Purely instrumental works such as Wagner's *Faust Overture* are best left as listening assignments. I play only the last sections (the closing lines of part 2) of Mahler's Eighth Symphony and Liszt's *Faust Symphony* and compare them with Schumann's setting of the same text. I assign the complete works for outside listening.

We do not discuss Busoni's opera *Doktor Faust* until after the completion of *Faust II* and a brief introduction to the philosophy of Schopenhauer. A fascinating treatment of the Faust figure, the work uniquely blends the original puppet play, Goethean influences, and Schopenhauer's idea of the will as the immortal element of life and thus avoids the traditional alternatives of redemption and condemnation for Faust.

The semester ends with a very broad discussion of two of the more obvious examples of Faust literature after Goethe: Thomas Mann's novel *Doctor Faustus: The Life of the German Composer Adrian Leverkühn, as Told by a Friend* and Klaus Mann's novel *Mephisto*. They are ideal choices since they add new dimensions to the Faust motif and yet return full circle to the original concept of the Faust figure who makes a pact with the devil.

One note of caution: the success of the course will be greatly enhanced or diminished by the quality of the sound equipment used in class. Operatic recordings especially need the benefit of a good stereo system if the students are to overcome their misconceptions and their almost natural aversion to opera.

Taming the Dragon: Or, How to Render *Faust* Congenial to Undergraduates

Frank S. Lambasa

According to an apocryphal Chinese anecdote, when the great teacher of the Celestial Kingdom, Confucius, came to pay his respects to the legendary founder of Taoism, Lao Tzu, he compared him—because of Lao Tzu's paradoxical, visionary, and isomorphic teachings—to the elusive, enigmatic dragon, which transforms itself whenever one thinks one has grasped it. This sinuous, coiling mythical beast continues to fascinate the Chinese creative mind and appears in manifold shapes and forms from the earliest periods of Chinese life, art, and literature down to the present time.

To me, the myth of *Faust* is equally fascinating to the Western mind, and in its numerous mythical and artistic transformations—of which Goethe's creation is only the most majestic example—it stands comparison with the emblem that has become the sign of Chinese imperial might. Are both the myth of the dragon and the myth of *Faust* inaccessible except to initiates?

Let me show how I try to make *Faust* a bit more understandable, more congenial to an average undergraduate student.

Stressing the Universality of the Faustian Theme in the West. Western civilization possesses only a handful of mythic themes on which popular dreams and aspirations, intellectual imagination and ambitions are centered in such a way as to render them timeless and capable of reinvention and reinterpretation. The German critic Hans Egon Holthusen names five such mythical themes: Oedipus, Hamlet, Don Quixote, Don Juan, and Faust (364). The importance of the Faustian myth is affirmed by an Irish novelist, John Banville, who says:

> The most enduring and pervasive myth of the postclassical world is that of Faust, the tragical doctor who sold his soul to the Devil in return for power and knowledge. There seems to be hardly a poet, novelist or playwright (with the exception, strangely perhaps, of Shakespeare) who has not treated the theme in some form or other.

In my course The Faustian Theme, Goethe's *Faust* naturally plays a pivotal role. I stress the idea of the manifoldness, the great significance of the myth as an ever-present motif in Western arts and, in one way or another, in Western science, politics, ethics, and religion. When I first meet with my students I emphasize this idea of universality by startling them into the realization that we are all potential Faust figures. I pose the following question: "Has anyone of you ever said, 'I'd give anything to get . . .' or 'I'd give anything to pass this exam' or 'I'd give anything to be like . . .'?" Invariably, at least a couple of students respond in the affirmative, and to the amusement and amazement of the rest of the class, I call them Fausts.

Then I pass around a number of newspaper clips (mostly but not exclusively from the *New York Times*) and magazine cutouts that touch on the theme. These give students additional proof of the relevance and vitality of the Faustian myth. Since students from various fields take the course, I find clips that connect with almost every field, whether business ("The Corporate Faust," an essay by William Safire), computer science ("Socrates, Faust, Univac," a review by Paul Delany of *Turing's Man*, and Christopher Lehmann-Haupt's review of the same book), atomic physics (John Leonard's review of a biography of Edward Teller), politics and movies (a Ray Milland movie described in the *New York Times* television listings as "Faustian politics. Strange but compelling drama."), or even rock and roll ("Faust and Acid Rock in Film by Williams," a review by Ian Dove).

Once the universality of the theme is established, I quickly develop the general evolution of the Faustian concept from a damnable act of selling one's soul to the devil, through the laudable quest for intellectual growth, knowledge, and mastery over nature, to the idea of "Faustian bargain." I give a brief explanation of the contributions of Oswald Spengler, Georg Lukács, and others to the ideological development of the Faustian notion. At the end of the first class, I ask the students to trace the meaning of the word *Faustian* in various dictionaries and encyclopedias and to report their findings in the following class.

In further lectures I raise the problem of temptation and evil and the timeless struggle between the world of darkness and the world of light, and I explain the religious origins in Babylonian and Persian beliefs. The class gets particularly animated when we touch on the subjects of witchcraft, satanism, and magic. Many young people seem entranced by these topics (witness the many Hollywood movies) and like to talk about them. I link the quest for the philosophers' stone and the fountain of youth of medieval alchemists to astrological pseudoscience (another interest of the class), and to the use of arcane symbols and formulas. Finally we come to the conjuring of demonic forces and the bidding them—for the price of one's soul—to aid the magus in the pursuit of the absolute.

Continuously mindful of the theme's universality, I introduce various Faustian figures (from Simon Magus to Paracelsus), all of them preparing the way for discussion of the historical Faust, George Sabellicus, around whom most of the medieval tales crystallize. Students become fascinated by the way inflamed popular fantasy transformed a marketplace trickster and charlatan into a magician in league with the devil. I explain why the legend of a man dealing with the satanic prince, Mephistopheles, became so powerful that it spread all over sixteenth-century Europe, fanned, on the one hand, by the Renaissance vision of unlimited human potentiality and, on the other, by the iconoclastic and at times fanatical zeal of the Reformation, with its obsession with the devil and sin. Soon Poland, whose famous University of Cracow supposedly conferred a degree in magic, produced its native Faust in *Pan Twardowski*, while Holland, France, and England contented themselves at first with translations and adaptations of Spiess's folk book about the notorious necromancer Dr. Faustus.

I highlight the rapid transformation of the fifteenth- and sixteenth-century world with an account of Gutenberg's invention of the printing press and the role played by Johann Fust. I enumerate the voyages of discovery and the ways Copernicus and Kepler changed views of heaven and earth (I use the television film *The Planets*), while Luther altered attitudes about the church, salvation, the devil, and the Bible. Finally, I recount the highlights of Spiess's "Damnable Life of Dr. J. Faustus."

Literary Transformation and Peregrination of the Theme. I devote one to two lectures to the transformation of Spiess's pedestrian and hortatory tale into Marlowe's rich Elizabethan poetic drama. A comparison of Marlowe's verses with Spiess's heavy prose underlines Marlowe's masterful conversion of a mere dabbler in black arts, an example of un-Protestant wickedness, into a tragic figure of hubristic defiance who bemoans his cruel destiny and trembles in metaphysical terror. From Marlowe's great drama, we trace the further peregrination of the Faustian figure back to Germany: English comedians, the puppet plays, various versions of the *Faust* book, and finally Faust's resurrection by Lessing as a figure of the German Enlightenment. The Storm and Stress rebellion against a stuffy aristocratic society (we cast a side-glance at the sixties in the United States) turns this Faust of the Age of Reason into a demonic adventurer of eighteenth-century Germany.

Goethe's Faust. I use slides (taken from Hoyer's *Goethe's Life in Pictures*) to present the exuberant life of an authentic genius, the last of the fabled *uomi universali*, whose monumental achievements in many spheres of endeavor are crowned by his *Faust*.

How does one approach such an intricate and complex work? Even its genre eschews easy categorization. Is it a drama? Is it an epic? The dilemma arises from an effort to avoid ambiguity, especially since students, particularly undergraduates, expect firm and fast definitions and often get lost when confronted with imprecise labels. If *Faust* is introduced as an epic, an aura of grandiloquent heroic posturing is evoked in the minds of students, who, in the present day of antiheroes, immediately prejudge it as tedious and arduous. Call it a drama, or a tragedy, which is its proper subtitle, and you have to justify long expository monologues, epic descriptions and digressions, various amorphous interludes (Oberon and Titania, to name one), and the general inconclusiveness of Faust's fate (tragedy with a hero saved?). Yet tragedy is still the preferred term, since *Faust* is a truly "modern" internal, psychological drama in which the external action is only half as important as the tragic psychological tension faced by a paradigmatic human being who surmounts a series of existential crises at considerable sacrifice. It is a universal human drama in which inner striving is directed toward renewal of an almost misspent life, toward reimmersion into the small world of everyday human joy and pain, surrender to passion and love instead of isolation in the dry scholarly pursuit of abstract parchment wisdom, and finally mastery of all of one's resources to achieve—albeit with the help of an evil force— the transcendent vision of a grandiose plan involving humanity at large.

To survey the work's range and total structure, I distribute handouts that chart *Faust*'s symmetry. Taking the cue from the line "Two souls, alas, are dwelling in my breast" (1112), I group the scenes around two main axes: one of philosophical contemplation and reflection and the other of action. While this division is not an absolute one, and a great many scenes could be arranged under either heading, it helps clarify a key aspect of *Faust*. Students easily grasp this division, the binary mode, especially computer students.

The idea of Faust as man of action is obliquely introduced by the Lord in the "Prologue in Heaven" (340), unmistakenly reinforced in the "translation scene" (1225–37), and fully developed in the scenes comprising both "the small world" and "the large world" and ending in "Great Outer Precinct of the Palace," with its vision of the exemplary life of action (11573–86). The contemplative axis is introduced in the "Dedication" poem, touched on in the "Prelude in the Theater," then fully unfolded in the opening scene of *Faust* ("Night") and continued intermittently throughout both parts, ending with "Midnight." The scenes of composite nature, that is, containing both contemplative and action elements, are in part 1: "Prelude in the Theater" (Director and Clown), "Study" (Mephistopheles and Student), and "Rejuvenation."

Another division I map out for students contrasts supernatural and realistic action. I also show the parallels between certain scenes ("Walpurgis Night" and the "Classical Walpurgis Night," Mephistopheles and Student, and Mephistopheles and Baccalaureus, etc.).

Since the aim of the course is to approach *Faust* as a whole rather than to dissect it into lifeless pieces, I present it in such a way that the class does not lose itself in small details. While giving proper due to every segment of part 1, I find some portions less poetic or less relevant to the dramatic development of the whole (e.g., "Walpurgis Night's Dream"), and I skip these or touch on them only lightly. To allow students to see Goethe in a worldly-wise mood standing somewhat apart from his creation, I point out his irony and sarcasm with respect to academia, the church, and society, as well as his magnificent humor (e.g., Mephistopheles's dialogue with the freshman).

While the elegiac tone of the "Dedication," with its evocation of lost youth, makes the student aware of the long span of time (60 years) Goethe spent on his *Faust* and "The Prelude in the Theater," with its exotic source in Sanskrit drama (Kalidasa's *Shakuntala*), lends an idea about the place of theater in eighteenth-century Germany, one must explain the confrontation between the Lord and Mephistopheles in the "Prologue in Heaven." The Job-like wager not only sets in motion the earthly drama of Faust the seeker but transposes it to the cosmic plane by justifying the existence of evil in the world in terms of Goethe's philosophy.

Prepared in this way, students more easily grasp Faust's restlessness and dissatisfaction, his lament for a life spent in vain pursuit of the secrets of the universe, and even his turning to magic to achieve a kind of breakthrough toward the absolute. I point out that *Faust* is, for the most part, an internalized drama, in which the external world exists to give the tragic struggle its appropriate concreteness. Goethe's vivid depiction of this concrete world surrounding Faust ranges in chromatic richness through all possible colors of the spectrum (I note Goethe's preoccupation with color theory): from the most somber, dark hues of the Gothic chamber—appropriated by the Reformation for secular, scholarly use—to the colorful folk festival of the Easter parade. Through pictures, slides, and etchings I give students visual impressions of the dank wine cellars, the small town markets and narrow alleys, the open fields, the mountains of Brocken, the late-medieval dungeon. I point out the timeless characters and prototypes: the caricature of an academic scholar in Wagner; the motley group of burghers, maids, old women, peasants, soldiers, apprentices, students, and city girls in their finery before the town gates; the mooching student idlers of Auerbach's Tavern; the scheming widow Marthe; the upright and prissy soldier Valentine; and, in the midst of all of these, the innocent, trusting Gretchen. They are all masterfully delineated in the first part of *Faust*, as the pleasure-loving court aristocrats are in the second.

When we talk about Faust's depression, his suicide attempt, the pact with Mephistopheles, and rejuvenation, students recognize the many human anxieties, cravings, and ritualizations that are invoked. This appeal to even their limited experience of life makes *Faust* understandable to students as the deeply human work that it is.

The students' favorite reading, however—aside from the Mephistopheles-Student vignette—is the tragic story of Gretchen. After I have explained the world in which she lives, they empathize with her initial modesty, her awakened curiosity, her trusting surrender to love, then her feeling of abandonment, her heartrending anguish, and ultimately her final terror. I point out that every aspiring actress in Germany coveted the role of Gretchen as a vehicle for displaying the gamut of human emotions and thus proving her artistry. It is much harder to explain Faust's character and his role in the tragic end of Gretchen and so many others. At this stage of students' intellectual development, when moral indignation is readily targeted toward the outside, students are not prone to exculpate Faust's sensual appetites, his unsavory degradation with Mephistopheles, or his arrogant superman egotism just because he nurtures a darkling Promethean aspiration and pronounces in rhapsodic terms a distant vision of human beings who will conquer "freedom and life each day anew!" (11575). All of one's literary as well as practical knowledge and experience of life have to be mustered and conveyed in such a way that students obtain, through their microcosmic concerns and cares, a much larger picture of the macrocosmic "Faustian" optimism of Goethe!

The final part of the semester, dedicated to Faust figures after Goethe, may often turn out to be an anticlimax. The students' appetite for broader knowledge of the Faustian theme, however, can then be reinforced by initiation into Thomas Mann's *Doctor Faustus*, which, in the words of Erich Heller, brings "the literary history of Dr. Faustus to a conclusion that is definitive in its perversity: the Devil is now the giver of a soul" (Bates 192).

But that is the concern of another teaching task!

Ivan Turgenev's "Faust": A Realist's Transformation of the Gretchen Tragedy

Werner Hoffmeister

A discussion of Goethe's *Faust* can take place in a variety of academic contexts. Goethe's work may form the subject of an entire seminar; it may be one among several works discussed in a course devoted to Goethe or to the *Goethezeit* or to European Romanticism or to the literary evolution of the Faust myth; it may be part of a course on Great Books or on the history of ideas or on major myths in Western civilization. But no matter what the specific course contents and objectives may be, a classroom approach to Goethe's *Faust* ought not to limit itself to an explication of the play's intrinsic ideas and values. Rather, any approach should at some point confront the play's historicity, should in some way locate the work in literary and intellectual history, on the one hand relate it to Goethe's predecessors—in particular to the *Volksbuch* and to Christopher Marlowe's tragedy—and on the other hand make students aware of its enormous impact on nineteenth- and twentieth-century literature, up to Mikhail Bulgakov, Paul Valéry, Thomas Mann, Hanns Eisler, Lawrence Durrell, Michel Butor, and Volker Braun. Goethe's *Faust* superbly exemplifies the way in which significant literary works act on one another in a perpetual process of reception, transformation, and intertextual allusion.

A comparative literature course on variations of the Faust theme in world literature from the sixteenth to the twentieth century, with Goethe's play occupying a central position, provides a particularly suitable format not only for elucidating the uniqueness of Goethe's creation but also for demonstrating the historical dynamics of re-creation and transformation, the richness of the *Wirkungsgeschichte* characteristic of the Faust myth. In the context of such a course, a discussion of Ivan Turgenev's "Faust: A Story in Nine Letters" (1856) can help convey a sense of what happened to the Faust myth in the post-Romantic era and, particularly, how Goethe's drama was received and perceived in the Age of Realism. The decisive issue is that of historical change, and it implies questions such as these: could the aspirations of the Romantic-idealistic imagination be sustained and affirmed in an age that underwent a rapidly increasing process of secularization and compartmentalization of values in all spheres of life? could the metaphysical thrust of Goethe's drama of quest still be credibly assimilated by a literature that was increasingly preoccupied with the social and psychological facets of secular reality?

By the middle of the nineteenth century, when Turgenev wrote his epistolary novella, the Faust theme had been received and appropriated by the educated middle and leisure classes. Goethe's *Faust* had become part of the literary canon in Russia as elsewhere, a source of edification, a vehicle of intellectual refinement and self-cultivation. Turgenev's novella deals with two leisure-class readers of Goethe's play and the effects of a shared reading on the protagonists; it accentuates the affective qualities of *Faust* and ties the human events within the tale directly to the literary experience. Fictional characters as readers are not uncommon in world literature: Don Quixote is absorbed in chivalric romance; Werther is enthralled by Homer, Ossian, and Klopstock; Wilhelm Meister studies *Hamlet*; Thomas Buddenbrook finds metaphysical comfort in Schopenhauer. Among the works in which fictional characters appear as readers, Turgenev's tale stands out as a singularly effective dramatization of the impact that a specific work of great literature has on the lives of its readers. Turgenev endows art's power over life with profound ambiguity. On the one hand, the reading experience involves an educational process of illumination and liberation; on the other hand, it results in disaster and death for the female protagonist.

Turgenev's assimilation of Goethe's *Faust* works on two different intertextual levels. On one level, the German play, as a literary artifact, is made the central agent and stimulus in the love relationship that develops between the narrator, the squire Pavel Alexandrovitch, and Vera Nikolaevna, a neighboring landowner's young wife. On another level, the entire love story between them is presented as a distant echo of the Gretchen tragedy, as a transposition of the Faust-Gretchen story into an altogether different milieu, with a different set of social and psychological determinants. Turgenev's tale fundamentally retains the crucial components of Gretchen's tragedy as a story of passion and seduction, of liberation from and transgression of a moral code, of agonizing guilt and ensuing mental-physical breakdown. And as in Goethe's play, the male partner's identity, despite self-accusations, remains whole and unimpaired: "Vera perished, while I was untouched" (Turgenev 221).

In Turgenev's transformation of the Goethean components, the process of seduction is sublimated into an aesthetic experience. The shared reading of Goethe's *Faust*, in which Pavel plays the role of the teacher and Vera that of the student, facilitates their intellectual and emotional rapprochement. Since Vera's mother kept her innocent with regard to works of the imagination, "invented works," Vera is now able to undergo a process of emotional as well as aesthetic-literary maturation and liberation. She frees her imagination from the constraints imposed by her mother; she grows from a childlike being with an emotional tabula rasa into a woman with the capacity for love. The aesthetic experience has a profound, vitalizing effect on her; it sets free repressed erotic energies within her and propels her into a state of precarious adulthood. The hazardous freedom she has attained finds expression in her daring confession of love to Pavel and in their exchange of a single kiss. This is the decisive step into the realm of the illicit; it conflicts sharply with the values of her upbringing and creates havoc in her emotional life.

The fundamental similarity between Gretchen's and Vera's behavior consists in their transgression of a maternal code of morality. Gretchen's mother, an embodiment of conventional sexual mores, represents an obstacle to the consummation of love; Gretchen's passion for Faust leads Gretchen to become an instrument in her mother's death. Vera's mother, Madame Eltsov, tries to protect Vera against emotional conflicts by making her abstain from reading any books that might affect her imagination and emotions. Since a history of destructive passion runs in the family, Madame Eltsov is "afraid of those secret forces on which life rests and which rarely, but so suddenly, break out" (Turgenev 166–67). The mother-daughter relationship in Turgenev's story is one of emotional and erotic repression. When "those secret forces on which life rests" do break out in Vera's life, they clash irreconcilably with the internalized dictates of maternal morality, the end result being her mental and physical collapse before any consummation of love can occur. In Freudian terms we might say that the *Ich* ("ego") is destroyed because it is no longer capable of negotiating and harmonizing the conflict between the libidinous forces of the *Es* ("id") and the demands of the maternal *Über-Ich* ("superego").

Similar to Gretchen's hallucinations in the dungeon scene, Vera's two visions of her mother are representations of her feelings of guilt and shame. Turgenev employs quasi-supernatural incidents as correlatives of psychic disturbance. The mother appears to Vera in ghostlike fashion, "as if to reclaim her both from poetry and illicit passion" (Schapiro 112). Pavel speaks of the "incomprehensible intervention of the dead in the affairs of the living" (Turgenev 220), but the reader may well perceive the fatal intervention as coming from Vera's subconscious, the seat of the power that her dead mother holds over her. On her deathbed, Vera deliriously "raved about *Faust* and her mother, whom she sometimes called Martha, sometimes Gretchen's mother" (Turgenev 220). This is another echo of Gretchen's delirious fantasizing in the dungeon scene; more significantly, however, Turgenev here permits us insight into the most profound effects the *Faust* readings have had on Vera: she sees herself as Gretchen; her mother, Gretchen's mother, and Martha merge into a collective image of maternal guardians. Paradoxically, then, the same work that set in motion a process of emancipation of the senses and emotions in Vera has also reinforced her fear of, and respect for, maternal authority. It may be appropriate to say that Turgenev's novella deals with "the potentially malign influence of artistic literature upon the minds of people unprepared to cope with it" (Moser 15); but it seems fair to add the complementary observation that it also deals with the potentially malign influence of excessive maternal authority.

Turgenev's transposition of the Gretchen tragedy is presented as a drama enacted primarily in Vera's mind. The male protagonist's participation in this drama is limited. While Pavel is instrumental in bringing about Vera's emotional turmoil, his awareness of her crisis is slight. While we may understand his infatuation with her, it is hard to discern any strong personal qualities in him that would cause Vera to fall in love with him. His interaction with her is channeled primarily through the literary experience of reading *Faust*. Pavel's conduct manifests a dubious encroachment of aesthetic consciousness on life.

While Vera must be perceived as a genuine reembodiment of Goethe's Gretchen, Pavel can hardly be considered a reincarnation of the Faust figure, as some critics claim he is (see Bem 366–67; Kopelew 126). He does not possess Faust's expansiveness, energy, and drive to know, to love, to create, to experience the totality of life. A subtle but profound authorial irony runs through the self-portrait that Pavel conveys in his letters to his friend, an irony that makes him a mock reproduction of the Faust figure. Pavel is a well-educated member of the leisure class, the landed gentry, and he is endowed with refined tastes, imagination, and aesthetic sensitivity. But approaching forty, he has found no purpose or fulfillment in life, neither vocation nor human attachment. When he returns to his dilapidated country estate after an absence of nine years, he feels that life has passed him by; he resigns himself to a solitary existence, gives himself up to unproductive musing and reminiscing, and suffers from apathy and melancholy. It is in this state of dejection and ennui, when "one is too lazy for thought, but not too lazy for musing" (Turgenev 156), that Pavel turns to his library for comfort and falls upon the favorite book of his student days. Pavel's rekindled enthusiasm for *Faust*, conditioned by the emptiness and tedium of his present life, implies a nostalgic yearning for the romantic idealism of his youth. His literary state of mind, which he transfers to Vera, is a surrogate for what he has missed in actual life (Turgenev 159, 204).

Essentially, Pavel belongs to the class of "superfluous men" portrayed by Turgenev in several of his works, most notably in "The Diary of a Superfluous Man" (1850). They represent a type of antihero whose principal traits are social ineffectiveness, lack of energy and purpose, and egotism. The "superfluous man" is a distinctly un-Faustian figure, characteristic of an era in European life and literature in which the aspirations of the Romantic-idealistic imagination are no longer tenable. The realist Turgenev writes a story that is an acknowledgment of historical change. Social awareness and psychological analysis replace the thematics of metaphysical quest. Turgenev's tale, which has rightly been called "a work of great beauty and artistry" (Schapiro 112), exemplifies Hegel's historical dialectic of *Aufhebung* as both preservation and annulment of the past. Through an intricate network of thematic, structural, and textural references, Turgenev pays tribute to, and preserves our memory of, Goethe's creation. By substituting a nineteenth-century antihero for the questing figure, however, he negates the very substance of the Faust legend. There are still *Faust* readers in this story, but there is no longer a Faust.

The Devil in *Faust* and in World Literature

Laurence M. Porter

In wide-ranging classes on the devil in literature, I start by learning what the students already know. I devote the first session to having them write down their own definitions of key concepts. Ten or eleven is a comfortable maximum for fifty minutes. In a course whose centerpiece is Goethe's *Faust* I might ask the students to define the terms *myth, devil, prayer, grace, salvation, worldliness, temptation, sin, damnation, pact,* and *satire.* To check which allusions will be recognized, I ask students to list the books, plays, operas, movies, television programs, and comic strips they remember as featuring the devil. I refer them to the *Catholic Encyclopedia* and to *Hastings' Encyclopedia of Religion and Ethics* for authoritative discussions of theological terms. I keep the student definitions until the end of the term and use them to plan discussions (see below).

During the second session we discuss the nature of myth. Here G. S. Kirk offers the best orientation for the instructor. According to him, myth operates, commemorates, or speculates. Literary myths speculate by using dramatic action to explore phenomena beyond ordinary human experience —our origins and destiny, the supernatural order. Authors generate drama by personifying clashing motives. Goethe was strikingly original as a myth-maker. "The virtuosity, scope, and bold irreverence toward tradition of Part Two of *Faust* has been recognized as anticipating and rivalling a pioneering 'modern' work like Joyce's *Ulysses*" (Feldman and Richardson 260). Goethe's deities are Dionysian, embodying power rather than morality. *Faust* rejects the reductiveness of monomyth: pagan and Christian worlds autonomously coexist (260–63).

I use the third session to explain the concept of a typology (a system of classification based on salient differences). Students devise their own typologies of possible myths involving relationships between two or three of the following: human beings, God, and the devil. One could suggest some organizing criteria: who wins or loses? who helps or opposes whom? who changes, and how? what is at stake? how lucid are the characters? what are their attitudes toward one another? what is the author's attitude toward them and toward events? I point out that the outcome of a story implies the author's attitude.

During the fourth session we discuss the students' typologies and integrate them with mine. In summing up, for example, I might explain that a strict monotheistic system perceives a radical binary opposition between good and evil. Since evil is weaker *eo ipso*, the struggle can have only two outcomes. Either evil is expelled (exile, damnation, annihilation) or absorbed (enslavement, redemption, atonement—one can allude to Origen's heterodox speculations concerning the salvation of the devil). Christian thought makes possible eight rather than two mythic configurations by introducing the complications of deception (of human beings by the devil) and self-deception (by human beings or by the devil). Thus the weaker party can believe itself superior or capable of achieving superiority. For examples of self-deluding devils, see *Faust*, Milton, C. S. Lewis's *The Screwtape Letters*, or Spanish drama of the Golden Age; for examples of self-deluding human beings, see *Faust*, Milton, Matthew Lewis's *The Monk*, C. S. Lewis's *The Great Divorce*, or Charles Williams's *Descent into Hell*.

The eight resulting situations are (1) Fall—God expels human being or devil; (2) Revolt—a human being or devil erroneously believes it can expel (which includes existing independently of) God; (3) Redemption—God absorbs human being or devil (examples of the latter are uncommon; see Victor Hugo's *Contemplations* and *La fin de Satan*); (4) Epiphany—the true God becomes manifest, absorbing a previously dominant false god (see Hugo's "Le satyre" from *La légende des siècles*, Charles Williams's *The War in Heaven*, or C. S. Lewis's *That Hideous Strength*); (5) Satire—the devil expels the human being (i.e., renders a hypocritical society powerless by unmasking it); (6) Ordeal (*tentatio probationis*)—a human being, with or without overt divine aid, resists and expels the devil (the pseudepigraphical *Books of Adam and Eve*, Martin Luther, Flaubert's *Temptation of Saint Anthony*, C. S. Lewis's *The Screwtape Letters*. Dostoevsky innovates in *The Brothers Karamazov* by depicting Father Ferapont's ordeals as self-aggrandizing delusions); (7) Seduction (*tentatio subversionis*)—the devil absorbs a human being; and (8) Pact—the devil erroneously believes that he absorbs (i.e., controls) God, or humans that they control the devil. Revolt or Pact must be resolved by Fall or Redemption.

Such reductive schemata are merely provisional heuristic devices serving to provoke reflection and to illuminate the originality of masterpieces like *Faust*. For the fifth session, students hand in lists of the scenes from *Faust I* that correspond to the mythic situations listed above, with two or three sentences of commentary on each. A week later, they do the same for *Faust II*. Such an approach helps beginning students by deemphasizing the more topical, allusive parts of the work, while guiding readers along the main story line. A sampling of potential discussions follows.

Pact. In the "Prologue in Heaven" Mephistopheles proposes a wager to God, believing he is binding God to a competition the devil will win. But God, who brought up Faust's name in the first place, foreknows that Mephistopheles will serve as a redemptive instrument. Noteworthy after the Book of Job is that God consents to speak to this devil at all. Goethe's originality consists in assimilating Mephistopheles to the natural order as part of the cosmological vision of *concordia discors* rather than expelling him as a superstition (Enlightenment thought) or as a principle of nonbeing (Catholic thought).

Redemption. "Night."

Pact. "Study" (two scenes). Faust mistakenly believes he can harness the devil's energies to realize his own visions. He does not yet understand that his ideal aspirations are incommensurate with the material theater the devil offers to fulfill them in. This original motif of a human being dissatisfied with the imaginative resources of the devil he has conjured up is echoed in Grabbe's *Don Juan and Faust.*

Satire. "Study" (second scene: Mephistopheles and the Student). Throughout the term, I introduce discussions of the students' initial definitions as the occasion arises. About three-fifths of students associate satire with humor and about two-fifths with an attack, but few invoke both concepts together. For initial clarification, I use examples from the "Prelude in the Theater" to distinguish polemic (attack; lines 59–62, 104–07) from burlesque (humor directed at the audience; 111–28) and satire (attack plus humor; 271–92). I have students ask themselves what is being attacked, and how. In later satiric scenes, I find it useful to explain the problem of topicality—allusions to persons, movements, and events contemporary to Goethe that prevent satire from being fully appreciated by following generations (the mysterious tag names in "Auerbach's Tavern," the dense tissue of literary and philosophical allusions in the "Walpurgis Night"). Topicality weakens the structure of a literary work, since ordinarily it is not introduced by a main character, and it does not move the plot. Students, incidentally, usually know few examples of satire in world literature. I find it helpful, therefore, to come prepared with some—Petronius, Swift, Fielding, Quevedo, Cervantes, Velez de Guevara, Le Sage, Vonnegut, Mikhail Bulgakov, *M.A.S.H.*, *All in the Family*, and current films and television series.

Seduction. During the Gretchen episode, the devil lures the lovers to fornication, manslaughter, and infanticide. At the conclusion of this scene I spend a session having students listen to Berlioz's or Gounod's *Faust* to illustrate how naturally Seduction leads promptly to Fall. I contrast this movement with Seduction leading to Redemption through divine intervention in the medieval miracle plays. Goethe employs the latter pattern but innovates by postponing it throughout part 2.

Satire. During the ascent of the Brocken, Faust is impelled by the same delusion that governed him at the beginning—presumption to absolute knowledge. He wants to interview Satan and learn his secrets. Satan's secret is that he has no secrets. Faust fails to learn this because his quest once again is trivialized when he is diverted into sexual experience.

Redemption. "Dungeon." Goethe's originality consists in making the idealized female, whom part 2 transforms from goal to guide, into a sinner rather than depicting a superhuman beloved in the manner of Dante or Petrarch.

During discussions of part 2 I bring out the role reversals that make the devil a target of satire in the mythic and then in the individual sphere.

Throughout the "Classical Walpurgis Night" he no longer calls into question the status of other myths; his own status is questioned. And during the return journey in "High Mountains" (act 4), Faust becomes the *eiron* to Mephistopheles's *alazon*. He refuses to allow the devil to debase his vision again. Faust remains materially dependent on the devil to the end, but he has become imaginatively independent. With the "Entombment" scene Faust and the devil move in opposite directions, toward Fall and Redemption. Here Goethe innovates by showing the devil attracted to good, but for inappropriate reasons (homosexual lust) determined by the limitations of his materialistic vision. Here I refer to student definitions of "worldliness." Nearly all students associate this term with cosmopolitanism but hardly any with the religious sense (physical rather than metaphysical, secular, of this world rather than the next). It is important to show how the two meanings of worldliness coincide in Mephistopheles. Despite his magical powers, experience has not broadened him spiritually. But it does broaden Faust, preparing his salvation.

The mainstays of my reading lists are either *Paradise Lost, Faust I and II*, and Bulgakov's *The Master and Margarita* (for a course on the devil in literature) or else Marlowe, *Faust*, Grabbe, and Thomas Mann's *Doctor Faustus* (for a course on the Faust myth). To help the students generalize about myths, however, it is essential throughout the term to enlarge their experience more expeditiously than assigned reading does. In one fifty-minute session it is possible to play recorded selections (with texts) from such devil stories as the Adler-Ross musical *Damn Yankees* or Douglas Moore's folk opera *The Devil and Daniel Webster*, based on the story by Stephen Vincent Benét. With many students taking part, dramatic readings of such texts as Marlowe, Flaubert, Klopstock's *The Messiah*, or Archibald MacLeish's *J. B.* can readily be tailored to fit one class period. And when the budget permits, one can rent such relatively inexpensive films as *Rosemary's Baby*, Bergman's *The Devil's Eye* (a reworking of the Don Juan legend, situated in hell), and Cocteau's *Orphée*. Thus the students encounter twice the number of devil stories they ordinarily can read during a term, while their reading time remains free for difficult, rewarding texts like Goethe's *Faust*.

To conclude, I sketch a historical perspective. There are two main strands of devil myths. One, the satiric, is nearly timeless. Since the ninth century, European authors have made hells to punish their enemies. In the second, eschatological tradition, Christianity centered mythic speculation on a devil who could rebel against a benevolent God. He was either fearful (in the apocryphal *Gospel of Nicodemus* or the Anglo-Saxon *Christ and Satan*), treacherous (*The Books of Adam and Eve*), or blindly aggressive (the Anglo-Saxon *Genesis B*). Later, Thomism discouraged dramatizations of the devil because it saw no fundamental opposition between God and creation. Evil derived from corruption, not from nature, and such corruption was never absolute. But after the Reformation, Protestant literature reflected the Augustinian perspective: nature was irremediably depraved. An active devil embodied this depravity. And human beings' spiritual struggles in this life became all-important once the Catholics' merciful compromise of purgatory had been rejected. From a psychological viewpoint, the Protestant pressure for perfection and the disquieting experience of rebelling against the Church Universal revived the literary devil as an unacknowledged unworthy self or as an exemplary antiself, repository for repressed self-doubts. Thus contaminated by human psychology, the post-Reformation devil evolved in two directions: to become either a figment of the human imagination or a humanlike creature who could be redeemed. Milton originated these developments with the first mimetic Satan in literature—a figure who possesses contrasting traits and also evolves. His complexity, however, remains sterile. Only divine revelation can guide the creaturely mind in *Paradise Lost*.

In contrast, the Enlightenment theism of Goethe's *Faust* glorifies mental venture. The mind earns salvation through persistent response to challenge, which is incarnate in the devil. He exists in a broad social context, speaking with others and considered real by them both on earth and in heaven. After *Faust*, Flaubert's *The Temptation of Saint Anthony* depicts a devil who is real only to the saint, while Dostoevsky's *The Brothers Karamazov* presents a devil unreal even to the person to whom he appears (Ivan). The devil's ontological status becomes increasingly tenuous in nineteenth-century literature. In the alternate development, inherited from Origen, Hugo depicts a devil who reforms and ultimately, in the eyes of God, becomes indistinguishable from Christ; Anatole France's devil in *The Revolt of the Angels* (1914) is even morally superior to a tyrannical God.

The wars, nuclear weapons, and genocide of the twentieth century have made it difficult to sustain subjective, optimistic views of evil like those of Goethe, Flaubert, and Hugo. After 1918 the literary devil was restored to his traditional Augustinian role as devourer and principle of nonbeing. He lost his anthropomorphic aspects and came instead to be represented by metaphors of fire, homosexuality, disease, death, and decay (compare Bernanos's *Diary of a Country Priest* to his *Monsieur Ouine*). In the most ambitious of such portrayals, Thomas Mann's *Doctor Faustus*, the Ancients' concept of *furor poeticus* is transformed into the notion that artistic inspiration can result from a neurosyphilitic infection. By equating this disease with demonic possession, Mann adds the mythic overtones, in which the composer Leverkühn represents variously the suffering Christ, the legendary Faustus of the 1587 chapbook, and the German people caught up in the pernicious euphoria of fascism. This morally ambiguous figure supersedes Goethe's hero and Marlowe's knave (Vickery 69).

PARTICIPANTS IN SURVEY
OF GOETHE INSTRUCTORS

The following scholars and teachers of Goethe generously agreed to participate in the survey of approaches to teaching *Faust* that preceded preparation of this volume. Without their invaluable assistance and support, the volume simply would not have been possible.

Stuart Atkins, University of California, Santa Barbara; David Ball, Smith College; Eric A. Blackall, Cornell University; Edith Blicksilver, Georgia Institute of Technology; Albert M. K. Blume, Bucknell University; Frank L. Borchardt, Duke University; Jane K. Brown, University of Colorado, Boulder; E. M. Chick, Williams College; Garold N. Davis, Brigham Young University; John Duffy, Tufts University; Hans Eichner, University of Toronto; John Fitzell, Rutgers University; Neil M. Flax, University of Michigan, Dearborn; Lilian R. Furst, University of North Carolina, Chapel Hill; Ailene S. Goodman, Washington, DC; Doris Starr Guilloton, New York University; Margot A. Haberhern, Florida Institute of Technology; Carl Hammer, Jr., Texas Tech University; Kathleen Harris, Toronto, Ontario; Henry Hatfield, Harvard University; G. H. Hertling, University of Washington; Werner Hoffmeister, Dartmouth College; Herbert H. Jackson, Memorial University of Newfoundland; Ruth-Ellen Boetcher Joeres, University of Minnesota, Twin Cities; Steven G. Kellman, University of Texas, San Antonio; Bettina Knapp, Hunter College and Graduate Center, City University of New York; John Kulas, St. John's University (Minnesota); Frank S. Lambasa, Hofstra University; Victor Lange, Princeton University; Leta Jane Lewis, California State University, Fresno; Patricia Marks, Valdosta State College; John A. McCarthy, University of Pennsylvania; James McIntosh, University of Michigan, Ann Arbor; Margaret McKenzie, Vassar College; George Newtown, Deep Springs College; Charles E. Passage, Brooklyn College, City University of New York; Laurence M. Porter, Michigan State University; Edith Potter, Scripps College; Ernst Rose, New York University; Victor Anthony Rudowski, Clemson University; Isolde Salisbury, Landespolizeischule, Niedersachsen (West Germany); Richard Erich Schade, University of Cincinnati; Roslyn Abt Schindler, Wayne State University; Henry Schneider III, Gettysburg College; Christoph E. Schweitzer, University of North Carolina, Chapel Hill; Carsten E. Seecamp, University of Colorado, Denver; A. G. Steer, University of Georgia; Larry K. Uffelman, Mansfield State College; Christiane Ullmann, Mt. Allison University; Hans R. Vaget, Smith College; Karl H. Van D'Elden, Hamline University; Cam Walker, College of William and Mary; Hart Wegner, University of Nevada, Las Vegas

WORKS CONSULTED

Books and Articles

Abrams, Meyer Howard. *Natural Supernaturalism: Tradition and Revolution in Romantic Literature.* New York: Norton, 1971.

Adams, H. P. *Life and Writings of Giambattista Vico.* New York: Russell, 1970.

Andrews, William. *Goethe's Key to* Faust: *A Scientific Basis for Religion and Morality.* Port Washington: Kennikat, 1968.

Angelloz, Joseph François. *Goethe.* 1949. Trans. R. H. Blackley. New York: Orion, 1958.

Atkins, Stuart. *The Age of Goethe: An Anthology of German Literature.* Boston: Houghton, 1969.

————. "The Evaluation of Romanticism in Goethe's *Faust.*" *Journal of English and Germanic Philology* 54 (1955): 9–38.

————, ed. and trans. *Faust I and II.* By Johann Wolfgang von Goethe. Goethe in English. Boston: Suhrkamp, 1984.

————. "Goethe, Calderón, and *Faust: Der Tragödie zweiter Teil.*" *Germanic Review* 28 (1953): 83–98.

————. *Goethe's* Faust: *A Literary Analysis.* Cambridge: Harvard UP, 1958.

————. "Motif in Literature: The Faust Theme." *Dictionary of the History of Ideas.* 1973 ed. 3: 244–53.

Badelt, Otto. *Das Rechts- und Staatsdenken Goethes.* Diss. U Köln, 1956. Bonn: Schriften zur Rechtslehre und Politik, 1966.

Banville, John. Rev. of *Letter to Lord Liszt,* by Martin Walser. *New York Times Book Review* 15 Sept. 1985: 11–12.

Barton, Lucy. *Historic Costume for the Stage.* 1935. Boston: Baker, 1956.

Bates, Paul A., ed. Faust: *Sources, Works, Criticism.* New York: Harcourt, 1968.

Bem, A. "Faust bei Turgenev." *Germanoslavica* 2 (1932–33): 359–68.

Bergsten, Gunilla. *Thomas Mann's* Doctor Faustus: *The Sources and Structures of the Novel.* Trans. Krishna Winston. Chicago: U of Chicago P, 1969.

Bergstraesser, Arnold. *Goethe's Image of Man and Society.* Chicago: Regnery, 1949.

————, ed. *Goethe and the Modern Age: The International Convocation at Aspen, Colorado, 1949.* Chicago: Regnery, 1950.

Berman, Marshall. *All That Is Solid Melts into Air: The Experience of Modernity.* New York: Simon, 1982.

Beutler, Ernst. *Essays um Goethe.* 1941. 2 vols. 4th ed. Wiesbaden: Dieterich, 1948.

————. Faust *und* Urfaust. 1939. 3rd ed. Leipzig: Dieterich, 1951.

Bielschowsky, Albert. *Goethe: Sein Leben und seine Werke.* 1896–1904. 2 vols. München: Beck, 1908.

———. *The Life of Goethe.* Trans. William A. Cooper. 3 vols. New York: Putnam, 1909.

Blackall, Eric A. *The Emergence of German as a Literary Language, 1700–1775.* Cambridge: Cambridge UP, 1959.

———. *Goethe and the Novel.* Ithaca: Cornell UP, 1976.

Bockstael, Eric, ed. *The Lives of Dr. Faust.* Detroit: U Studies/Weekend College Prog., C of Lifelong Learning, Wayne State U, 1976.

Bockstael, Eric, and Sarah Evans, eds. *The Lives of Dr. Faust: Television Study Guide.* Detroit: To Educate the People Consortium, 1982.

Boehn, Max von. "Faust und die Kunst." *Faust.* By Johann Wolfgang von Goethe. Berlin: Askanischer, 1924. 1–220.

Boerner, Peter, ed. *Faust: Eine Tragödie: Erster und zweiter Teil.* By Johann Wolfgang von Goethe. München: Deutscher Taschenbuch, 1977.

Brown, Jane K. *Goethe's* Faust: *The German Tragedy.* Ithaca: Cornell UP, 1986.

Brown, Marshall. *The Shape of German Romanticism.* Ithaca: Cornell UP, 1979.

Bruford, Walter Horace. *Culture and Society in Classical Weimar: 1775–1806.* London: Cambridge UP, 1962.

———. *Germany in the Eighteenth Century: The Social Background of the Literary Revival.* Cambridge: Cambridge UP, 1935.

Bryce, James Viscount. *The Holy Roman Empire.* Rev. ed. London: Macmillan, 1950.

Bub, Douglas F. "*Faust* 2248: 'So ein lieb Ding.'" *South Atlantic Bulletin* 34.4 (1969): 11–12.

Buchwald, Reinhard. *Führer durch Goethes Faustdichtung: Erklärung des Werkes und Geschichte seiner Entstehung.* 6th ed. Stuttgart: Kroner, 1961.

Budden, Julian. "Gounod's *Faust* over the Years." Libretto. *Faust.* By Charles Gounod. Cond. Georges Prêtre. Capitol Records, 1979. 5.

Bulfinch, Thomas. *Mythology: The Age of Fable, the Age of Chivalry, Legends of Charlemagne.* 1855–63. New York: Modern Library, 1934.

Bulgakov, Mikhail A. *The Master and Margarita.* Trans. Michael Glenny. New York: Harper, 1967.

Burger, Heinz Otto, ed. *Begriffsbestimmung der Klassik und des Klassischen.* Wege der Forschung 210. Darmstadt: Wissenschaftliche, 1972.

Burton, Clare. *Subordination: Feminism and Social Theory.* Winchester: Allen, 1985.

Butler, Eliza Marian. *Goethe and Byron: Analysis of a Passion.* Nottingham: Nottingham U, 1949.

———. *The Fortunes of Faust.* Cambridge: Cambridge UP, 1952.

———. *Myth of the Magus.* 1948. Westport: Hyperion, 1979.

Carlyle, Thomas. *Essays on Goethe.* London: Cassell, 1888.

Cassirer, Ernst. *Rousseau, Kant, and Goethe.* Princeton: Princeton UP, 1945.

Chiarini, Paolo, and Walter Dietze, eds. *Deutsche Klassik und Revolution: Texte eines literaturwissenschaftlichen Kolloquiums*. Rome: Ateneo, 1981.

Cottrell, Alan P. *Goethe's* Faust: *Seven Essays*. Chapel Hill: U of North Carolina P, 1976.

Croce, Benedetto. *Goethe*. New York: Knopf, 1923.

Curtius, Ernst Robert. *European Literature and the Latin Middle Ages*. Trans. Willard Trask. New York: Bollingen-Pantheon, 1953.

———. "Klassik." *Europäische Literatur und lateinisches Mittelalter*. 2nd ed. Berne: Francke, 1954. 253–76. Rpt. in Burger 17–33.

Dabezies, André. *Visages de Faust au XXᵉ siècle: Littérature, idéologie et mythe*. Paris: PUF, 1967.

Davidson, Thomas. *The Philosophy of Goethe's* Faust. Ed. Charles M. Bakewell. New York: Haskell, 1969.

Delany, Paul. "Socrates, Faust, Univac." Rev. of *Turing's Man*, by J. David Bolter. *New York Times Book Review* 18 Mar. 1984: 13.

Dieckmann, Liselotte. *Goethe's* Faust: *A Critical Reading*. Landmarks in Literature. Englewood Cliffs: Prentice, 1972.

———. *Johann Wolfgang Goethe*. New York: Twayne, 1974.

Diener, Gottfried. *Fausts Weg zu Helena: Urphänomen und Archetypus*. Stuttgart: Klett, 1961.

Dove, Ian. "The Pop Life: Faust and Acid Rock in Film by Williams." *New York Times* 25 Jan. 1973: L20.

Durrani, Osman. *Faust and the Bible*. Bern: Lang, 1977.

Eckermann, Johann Peter. *Gespräche mit Goethe*. Ed. Fritz Bergemann. Wiesbaden: Insel, 1955.

———. *Gespräche mit Goethe*. Ed. Ernst Merian-Genast. 2 vols. Basel: Birkhäuser, 1945.

Einstein, Alfred. *Music in the Romantic Era*. New York: Norton, 1947.

Emerson, Ralph Waldo. *Representative Men*. 1850. Boston: Houghton, 1883.

Emrich, Wilhelm. *Die Symbolik von* Faust II: *Sinn und Versformen*. 4th ed. Wiesbaden: Athenaion, 1978.

Enright, Dennis Joseph. *Commentary on Goethe's* Faust. Norfolk: New Directions, 1949.

Fähnrich, Hermann. "Goethes Musikanschauung in seiner Fausttragödie—Die Erfüllung und Vollendung seiner Opernreform." *Goethe, N. F. des Jahrbuchs der Goethe Gesellschaft* 25 (1963): 250–63.

Fairley, Barker, trans. *Faust*. By Johann Wolfgang von Goethe. Toronto: U of Toronto P, 1970.

———. *Goethe as Revealed in His Poetry*. Chicago: U of Chicago P, 1932.

———. *Goethe's* Faust: *Six Essays*. 1953. Oxford: Oxford UP, 1965.

———. *A Study of Goethe*. 1947. Oxford: Oxford UP, 1961.

Fausto-Sterling, Anne. *Myths of Gender: Biological Theories about Women and Men*. New York: Basic, 1985.

Feldman, Burton, and Robert D. Richardson, eds. *The Rise of Modern Mythology, 1680–1860*. Bloomington: Indiana UP, 1972.

Fischer, Paul. *Goethe-Wortschatz: Ein sprachgeschichtliches Wörterbuch zu Goethes sämtlichen Werken*. Leipzig: Rohmkopf, 1929.

Flax, Neil M. "The Presence of the Sign in Goethe's *Faust*." *PMLA* 98 (1983): 183–203.

Franz, Erich. *Mensch und Dämon: Goethes* Faust *als menschliche Tragödie*. Tübingen: Niemeyer, 1953.

Friedenthal, Richard. *Goethe: His Life and Times*. 1963. Cleveland: World, 1965.

———. *Goethe: Sein Leben und seine Zeit*. München: Piper, 1963.

Friedrich, Theodor, and L. J. Scheithauer. *Kommentar zu Goethes* Faust: *Mit einem* Faust-Wörterbuch *und einer* Faust-Bibliographie. Stuttgart: Reclam, 1960.

Frye, Northrop. *Anatomy of Criticism: Four Essays*. 1957. Princeton: Princeton UP, 1971.

———. *A Study of English Romanticism*. New York: Random, 1968.

Fuerst, Norbert. *The Pentalogy of Goethe's* Faust. Bloomington: Indiana UP, 1950.

Furst, Lilian R. "The Man of Sensibility and the Woman of Sense." *Jahrbuch für Internationale Germanistik* 14 (1983): 13–26.

Gage, John, ed. *Goethe on Art*. Berkeley: U of California P, 1980.

Gajek, B., and F. Gotting, eds. *Goethes Leben und Werk in Daten und Bildern*. Wiesbaden: Insel, 1966.

Geissler, Horst Wolfram, ed. *Gestaltungen des Faust: Die bedeutendsten werke der Faustdichtung seit 1587*. München: Parcus, 1927.

Gerhard, Melitta. *Leben im Gesetz: Fünf Goethe-Aufsätze*. Bern: Francke, 1966.

Gillies, Alexander. *Goethe's* Faust: *An Interpretation*. 1951. Oxford: Oxford UP, 1957.

Goethe, Johann Wolfgang von. *Dichtung und Wahrheit*. Ed. Wolfgang Stammler. München: Hanser, 1949.

———. *Faust: Der Tragödie erster und zweiter Teil*. 2 vols. Leipzig: Reclam, 1982.

———. *Faust: Der Tragödie zweiter Teil, mit den 143 Federzeichnungen von Max Beckmann*. München: Prestel, 1970.

———. *Gedenkausgabe der Werke, Briefe und Gespräche*. Artemis Ausgabe. 24 vols. Zürich: Artemis, 1954. 2nd ed., 1964.

———. *Goethes Gespräche*. 5 vols. Leipzig: Biedermann, 1909–11.

———. *Maximen und Reflexionen*. Vol. 12 of *Werke*. Hamburger Ausgabe. Hamburg: Wegner, 1953.

———. *Poetry and Truth*. Trans. Minna Steele Smith. Ed. Karl Breul. London: Bell, 1930.

———. *Samtliche Werke*. Jubiläums Ausgabe. 40 vols. Stuttgart: Cotta, 1902–12.

———. *Werke*. Ed. Erich Trunz. Hamburger Ausgabe. 11th ed. 14 vols. München: Beck, 1981.

————. *Werke. Hg. im Auftrage der Grossherzogin Sophie von Sachsen.* Weimarer Ausgabe. 143 vols. Weimar: Bohlau, 1887–1919.

Goethe-Jahrbuch. [Several variant titles since 1880.] Weimar: Goethe-Gesellschaft, 1880–.

Graves, Robert. *The Greek Myths.* 2 vols. Baltimore: Penguin, 1955.

Gray, Ronald. "Faust's Divided Nature." *Goethe's* Faust Part One: *Essays in Criticism.* Ed. John B. Vickery and J'nan Sellery. Belmont: Wadsworth, 1969. 102–11.

————. *Goethe the Alchemist.* Cambridge: Cambridge UP, 1952.

Haight, Anne Lyon, ed. *Hroswitha of Gandersheim: Her Life, Times, and Works, and a Comprehensive Bibliography.* New York: Hroswitha Club, 1965.

Haile, Harry Gerald, ed. and trans. *The History of Doctor Johann Faustus.* Urbana: U of Illinois P, 1965.

————. *Invitation to Goethe's* Faust. University: U of Alabama P, 1978.

Hamlin, Cyrus, ed. *Faust: A Tragedy.* By Johann Wolfgang von Goethe. Trans. Walter Arndt. Norton Critical Edition. New York: Norton, 1976.

Hatfield, Henry. *Aesthetic Paganism in German Literature: From Winckelmann to the Death of Goethe.* Cambridge: Harvard UP, 1964.

————. *Goethe: A Critical Introduction.* New York: New Directions, 1963; Cambridge: Harvard UP, 1964.

Hecht, Wolfgang. Rev. of *Begriffsbestimmung der Klassik und des Klassischen,* by Heinz Otto Burger. *Goethe* 91 (1974): 191–92.

Heffner, R.-M. S., Helmut Rehder, and W. F. Twaddell, eds. *Goethe's* Faust. 2 vols. 1954–55. Madison: U of Wisconsin P, 1975. Rev. ed., 1984.

Heinemann, Karl, ed. *Goethes Werk.* 15 vols. Leipzig: Bibliographisches Inst., n.d. Vol. 5.

Heller, Erich. *The Artist's Journey into the Interior and Other Essays.* 1959. New York: Vintage, 1968.

————. "On Goethe's *Faust.*" Lange 132–44.

Heller, Otto. Faust *and* Faustus: *A Study of Goethe's Relation to Marlowe.* 1931. New York: Cooper, 1972.

Heller, Peter. "Gretchen: Figur, Klischee, Symbol." *Die Frau als Heldin und Autorin.* Ed. Wolfgang Paulsen. Bern: Francke, 1977. 175–89.

Henel, Heinrich. "Goethe und die Naturwissenschaften." *Journal of English and Germanic Philology* 48 (1949): 510–32.

Henning, Hans, ed. Faust-*Bibliographie.* 3 pts. Weimar: Aufbau, 1966–76.

Highet, Gilbert. *The Art of Teaching.* New York: Knopf, 1950.

Hiller, R. I., and John C. Osborne, trans. *The Singular Life Story of Heedless Hopalong.* By H. J. C. von Grimmelshausen. Detroit: Wayne State UP, 1981.

Hofer, P. *Delacroix's* Faust. Cambridge: Harvard UP, 1964.

Hohlfeld, A. R. *Fifty Years with Goethe, 1901–1951.* Madison: U of Wisconsin P, 1953.

Holthusen, Hans Egon. *Kritisches Verstehen: Neue Aufsätze zur Literatur.* München: Piper, 1961.

Honour, Hugh. *Romanticism.* New York: Harper, 1979.

Hoyer, W. *Goethe's Life in Pictures.* Leipzig: VEB, 1963.

Hrotsvit von Gandersheim. *Werke in dt. Übertragung.* Trans. Helene Homeyer. München: Schöningh, 1973.

Hubert, Renée Riese. "Art and Perversity: Barlach's and Dali's Views of *Walpurgisnacht.*" *Journal of European Studies* 13 (1983): 75–95.

Irmscher, Johannes, ed. *Antikerezeption: Deutsche Klassik und socialistische Gegenwart.* Schriften der Winckelmann-Gesellschaft 5. Berlin: Akademie, 1979.

Jaggar, Alison M., and Paula S. Rothenberg. *Feminist Frameworks: Alternative Theoretical Accounts of the Relations between Women and Men.* 2nd ed. New York: McGraw, 1984.

Jamot, P. "Goethe et Delacroix." *Gazette des beaux-arts* 6th ser. 8 (1932): 279–98.

Jantz, Harold. *The Form of* Faust: *The Work of Art and Its Intrinsic Structures.* Baltimore: Johns Hopkins UP, 1978.

———. *Goethe's Faust as a Renaissance Man: Parallels and Prototypes.* Princeton: Princeton UP, 1951; New York: Gordian, 1974.

———. *The Mothers in* Faust: *The Myth of Time and Creativity.* Baltimore: Johns Hopkins UP, 1969.

Jaszi, Andrew Oscar. *Entzweiung und Vereinigung: Goethes Symbol: Weltanschauung.* Heidelberg: Stiehm, 1973.

Jost, Dominik. *Deutsche Klassik—Goethes "Römische Elegien."* 2nd ed. Uni-Taschenbücher 851. Pullach: Dokumentation, 1978.

Kaufmann, Walter, trans. *Goethe's* Faust: *The Original German and a New Translation and Introduction: Part One and Sections from Part Two.* Garden City: Anchor-Doubleday, 1961.

Kehrli, Jakob Otto. *Die Lithographien zu Goethes* Faust *von Eugène Delacroix.* Bern: Lang, 1949.

Keller, Werner, ed. *Aufzätze zu Goethes* Faust. Darmstadt: Wissenschaftliche, 1974.

Kelly, James William. *The Faust Legend in Music.* Diss. Northwestern U, 1960. Detroit: Information Coordinators, 1976.

Kindermann, Heinz. *Das Goethebild des 20. Jahrhunderts.* 2nd ed. Darmstadt: Wissenschaftliche, 1966.

Kippenberg, Anton, Hans Weitz, and Walther Ziesemer, eds. Faust: *Gesamtausgabe.* By Johann Wolfgang von Goethe. Wiesbaden: Insel, 1959.

Kirk, G. S. *Myth: Its Meaning and Functions in Ancient and Other Cultures.* Berkeley: U of California P, 1970.

Kobligk, Helmut. *Johann W. Goethe,* Faust I: *Grundlagen und Gedanken zum Verständnis des Dramas.* Frankfurt: Diesterweg, 1978.

Kolve, V. A. *The Play Called Corpus Christi.* Stanford: Stanford UP, 1966.

Kommerell, Max. *Der Dichter als Führer in der deutschen Klassik.* Berlin: Bondi, 1928.

——. *Geist und Buchstabe der Dichtung: Goethe, Schiller, Kleist, Hölderlin*. 1940. 3rd ed. Frankfurt: Klostermann, 1944.

Kopelew, Lew. "Faust in Russland angeeignet." *Ansichten zu Faust*. Ed. Günther Mahal. Stuttgart: Kohlhammer, 1973. 117–30.

Koskimies, Rafael. *Der nordische Faust: Adam Homo, Peer Gynt, Hans Alienus*. Helsinki: Suomalaisen tiedeakatemian toimituksia, 1965.

Lange, Victor, ed. *Goethe: A Collection of Critical Essays*. Twentieth Century Views. Englewood Cliffs: Prentice, 1968.

Lehmann-Haupt, Christopher. Rev. of *Turing's Man*, by J. David Bolter. *New York Times* 13 Mar. 1984: C16.

Leonard, John. "The Battle of the H-Bomb." Rev. of *Energy and Conflict: The Life and Times of Edward Teller*, by Stanley A. Blumberg and Gwinn Owens. *New York Times* 28 Sept. 1976: L37.

Lessing, Gotthold Ephraim. *Laokoon*. Trans. E. C. Beasley. London: Bell, 1914.

Lewes, George Henry. *The Life and Works of Goethe: With Sketches of His Age and Contemporaries*. 1855. Everyman's Library. London: Dent, 1907.

Liljegren, Sten Bodvar. *The English Sources of Goethe's Gretchen Tragedy: A Study on the Life and Fate of Literary Motives*. Lund: Gleerup, 1937.

Lohmeyer, Dorothea. *Faust und die Welt: Zur Deutung des zweiten Teiles der Dichtung*. 1940. Enl. ed. Potsdam: Athenaion, 1975.

Lüders, Detlev, ed. *Goethe in der Kunst des 20. Jahrhunderts: Weltliteratur und Bilderwelt*. Frankfurt: Freies Deutsches Hochstift/Frankfurter Goethe-Museum, 1982.

Lukács, Georg. *Faust und Faustus: Vom Drama der Menschengattung zur Tragödie der Modernen Kunst*. Reinbek b. Hamburg: Rowohlt, 1967.

——. *Goethe and His Age*. Trans. Robert Anchor. London: Merlin, 1968.

——. *Goethe und seine Zeit*. Bern: Francke, 1947.

Lunatscharski, Anatolii V. *Faust and the City. Three Plays*. Trans. L. A. Magnus and K. Walter. New York: Dutton, 1923.

MacIntyre, C. F., trans. *Faust Part I*. By Johann Wolfgang von Goethe. New York: New Directions, 1949.

MacNeice, Louis, trans. *Goethe's* Faust: Parts I and II. Abr. ver. New York: Oxford UP, 1951.

——. *Goethe's* Faust: Part I. Abr. ver. *The Norton Anthology of World Masterpieces*. 4th ed. 2 vols. New York: Norton, 1979. 2: 353–440.

Madách, Imre. *The Tragedy of Man*. Trans. J. C. W. Horne. Budapest: Corvina, 1963.

Magnus, Rolf. *Goethe as a Scientist*. New York: Schuman, 1949.

Mahal, Günther. *Faust-Museum Knittlingen*. Stuttgart: Daxer, 1980.

——. *Mephistos Metamorphosen: Fausts Partner als Repräsentant literarischer Teufelsgestaltung*. Göppingen: Kümmerle, 1972.

Mann, Klaus. *Mephisto*. Trans. Robin Smith. New York: Penguin, 1983.

Mann, Thomas. *Doctor Faustus: The Life of the German Composer Adrian Lever-kühn, as Told by a Friend*. Trans. H. T. Lowe-Porter. New York: Knopf, 1948.

Marlowe, Christopher. *Doctor Faustus*. Ed. Sylvan Barnet. Signet Classics. New York: NAL, 1969.

Mason, Eudo. *Deutsche und Englische Romantik: Eine Gegenüberstellung*. 2nd ed. Göttingen: Vandenhoeck, 1966.

———. *Goethe's* Faust: *Its Genesis and Purport*. Berkeley: U of California P, 1967.

May, Kurt. Faust II. Teil: *In der Sprachform gedeutet*. Berlin: Junker, 1936.

McDowell, Frederick P. W. "Aestheticism." *Encyclopedia of Poetry and Poetics*. Ed. A. Preminger. Princeton: Princeton UP, 1965.

Mellor, Anne K. *English Romantic Irony*. Cambridge: Harvard UP, 1980.

Meyer, Herman. *Diese sehr ernsten Scherze: Eine Studie zu* Faust II. Heidelberg: Stiehm, 1970.

Middleton, Christopher, ed. *Johann Wolfgang von Goethe. Selected Poems*. Boston: Suhrkamp, 1983.

Mitchell, Breon. *The Complete Illustrations from Delacroix's* Faust *and Manet's "The Raven."* New York: Dover, 1981.

Mommsen, Katharina. *Natur- und Fabelreich in* Faust II. Berlin: Gruyter, 1968.

———, ed. *Who Is Goethe?* Trans. Leslie Willson and Jeanne Willson. Boston: Suhrkamp, 1983.

Mora, Gabriela, and Karen S. Van Hooft, eds. *Theory and Practice of Feminist Literary Criticism*. Ypsilanti: Bilingual, 1982.

Morgan, Bayard Quincy, ed. and trans. *Faust: Part One*. By Johann Wolfgang von Goethe. New York: Liberal Arts, 1954.

Moser, Charles A. *Ivan Turgenev*. New York: Columbia UP, 1972.

Murray, Alexander S. *Manual of Mythology*. New York: Tudor, 1935.

Muschg, Walter. "Die deutsche Klassik, tragisch gesehen." *Abhandlungen der Akademie der Wissenschaften und der Literatur Mainz, Klasse der Literatur, Jahrgang 1952* 4 (1953): 85–101. Rpt. in Burger 157–76.

———. *Tragische Literaturgeschichte*. 3rd ed. Berne: Francke, 1957.

Neubert, Franz. *Vom* Doctor Faustus *zu Goethes* Faust. Leipzig: Weber, 1932.

Nisbet, H. B. *Goethe and the Scientific Tradition*. London: Inst. of Germanic Stud., U of London, 1972.

Orgel, Stephen. *The Illusion of Power: Political Theater in the English Renaissance*. Berkeley: U of California P, 1975.

Orgel, Stephen, and Roy Strong. *Inigo Jones: The Theatre of the Stuart Court*. Berkeley: U of California P, 1973.

Otto, Walter F. *The Homeric Gods*. 1929. Trans. Moses Hadas. 1954. New York: Thames, 1979.

Palmer, Philip Mason, and Robert Pattison More. *The Sources of the Faust Tradition from Simon Magus to Lessing*. 1936. New York: Haskell, 1965.

Pascal, Roy. *The German Sturm und Drang*. Manchester: Manchester UP, 1959.

Passage, Charles, trans. *Faust: Part One and Part Two.* By Johann Wolfgang von Goethe. Library of Liberal Arts. Indianapolis: Bobbs, 1965.

Petriconi, Helmut. *Die verführte Unschuld: Bemerkungen über ein literarisches Thema.* Hamburg: Cram, 1953.

Petsch, Robert, ed. *Das Volksbuch vom Doctor Faust (Nach der ersten Ausgabe, 1587).* 2nd ed. Halle: Niemeyer, 1911.

Prawer, Siegbert Salomon. *Comparative Literary Studies: An Introduction.* London: Duckworth, 1973.

Praz, Mario. *The Romantic Agony.* Rev. ed. New York: Oxford UP, 1960.

Priest, George Madison, trans. *Faust: Parts One and Two.* By Johann Wolfgang von Goethe. New York: Knopf, 1941.

Prodolliet, Ernest. *Faust im Kino.* Freiburg: U Freiburg, 1978.

Pyritz, Hans. "Der Bund zwischen Goethe und Schiller." 1950–51. *Goethe-Studien.* Köln: Böhlau, 1962. 34–51. Rpt. in Burger 306–26.

Pyritz, Hans, et al., eds. *Goethe-Bibliographie.* 2 vols. Heidelberg: Winter, 1965–68.

Reed, T. J. *The Classical Centre: Goethe and Weimar 1775–1832.* New York: Barnes, 1980.

Reinhardt, Kurt F. *Germany: 2000 Years.* Milwaukee: Bruce, 1950.

Requadt, Paul. *Goethes* Faust I: *Leitmotivik und Architektur.* München: Fink, 1972.

Rickert, Heinrich. *Goethes* Faust: *Die dramatische Einheit der Dichtung.* Tübingen: Mohr, 1932.

Robertson, John George. *A History of German Literature.* 3rd ed. Rev. Edna Purdie. Edinburgh: Blackwood, 1959.

———. *The Life and Work of Goethe: 1749–1832.* Rev. of *Goethe.* 1927. London: Routledge; New York: Dutton, 1932.

Rose, Ernst. *A History of German Literature.* New York: New York UP, 1960.

Russell, Douglas A. *Stage Costume Design: Theory, Technique, and Style.* New York: Appleton, 1973.

Safire, William. "The Corporate Faust." *New York Times* 6 Dec. 1981: E23.

Salm, Peter, trans. *Faust, Part I.* By Johann Wolfgang von Goethe. Rev. ed. New York: Bantam, 1985.

Santayana, George. *Three Philosophical Poets: Lucretius, Dante, and Goethe.* 1910. New York: Cooper, 1970.

Schade, R. E. "The *Courasche*-Frontispiece." *Simpliciana* 3 (1981): 73–93.

———. "Junge Soldaten, alte Bettler: Zur Ikonographie des *Springinsfeld*-Titelkupfers." *Der deutsche Schelmenroman im europäischen Kontext.* Ed. G. Hoffmeister. Amsterdam: Rodopi, 1986.

———. "Poet and Artist: Iconography in Grass' *Treffen in Telgte.*" *German Quarterly* 55 (1982): 200–11.

Schapiro, Leonard. *Turgenev: His Life and Times.* New York: Random, 1978.

Schenk, H. G. *The Mind of the European Romantics.* New York: Oxford UP, 1966.

Schlegel, August Wilhelm. "Erste Vorlesung." *Vorlesungen über dramatische Kunst und Literatur.* Vol. 5 of *Kritische Schriften und Briefe.* Ed. Edgar Lohner. Stuttgart: Kohlhammer, 1966. 17–263.

Schlegel, Friedrich. *Literary Notebooks: 1797–1801.* Ed. Hans Eichner. London: Athlone, 1957.

Schmidt, Erich, ed. *Goethes Faust in ursprünglicher Gestalt.* Weimar: Böhlau, 1888.

Schoolfield, G. C., trans. *The German Lyric of the Baroque in English Translation.* Chapel Hill: U of North Carolina P, 1961.

Schuh, Willi. *Goethe-Vertonungen: Ein Verzeichnis.* Zürich: Artemis, 1952.

Schult, Friedrich, ed. *Ernst Barlach: Das graphische Werk.* Hamburg: Hauswedel, 1958.

Schultz, Franz. *Klassik und Romantik der Deutschen.* 1935–40. 2nd ed. 2 vols. Stuttgart: Metzler, 1952.

Schweitzer, Albert. *Goethe: Drei Reden.* München: Biederstein, 1949.

———. *Goethe: Four Studies.* Trans. Charles R. Joy. Boston: Beacon, 1949.

Searle, Humphrey. "Franz Liszt." *The New Grove Dictionary of Music and Musicians.* Ed. Stanley Sadie. London: Macmillan, 1980.

Seuffert, Bernhard, ed. *Goethe: Faust, ein Fragment.* Deutsche Denkmale des 18. Jahrhunderts. Stuttgart: Göschen, 1882.

Shawcross, John, trans. *The First Part of Goethe's Faust.* London: Partridge, 1934.

Smeed, John William. *Faust in Literature.* New York: Oxford UP, 1975.

Spalding, Keith, and Kenneth Brooks. *An Historical Dictionary of German Figurative Usage.* Oxford: Blackwell, 1960–.

Speier, Hans, trans. *Courage, the Adventures.* By H. J. C. von Grimmelshausen. Princeton: Princeton UP, 1964.

Spengler, Oswald. *The Decline of the West.* Trans. Charles Francis Atkinson. New York: Knopf, 1926–28.

Staiger, Emil. *Goethe.* 3 vols. Zürich: Artemis, 1952–59.

Stawell, Florence Melian, and G. Lowes Dickinson. *Goethe and Faust: An Interpretation.* London: Bell, 1928.

Steer, A. G. "Goethe's *Novelle* as a Document of Its Time." *Deutsche Vierteljahrsschrift für Literaturwissenschaft und Geistesgeschichte* 50 (1976): 414–33.

———. *Goethe's Science in the Structure of the* Wanderjahre. Athens: U of Georgia P, 1979.

———. *Goethe's Social Philosophy.* Chapel Hill: U of North Carolina P, 1955.

———. "Sankt-Rochus-Fest zu Bingen." *Jahrbuch des Freien Deutschen Hochstifts.* Tübingen: Niemeyer, 1965. 186–236.

Sternfeld, Fritz. *Goethe and Music.* New York: New York Public Library, 1954.

Stewart, Jean, trans. *Eugène Delacroix: Selected Letters: 1813–1863.* London: Eyre, 1971.

Storz, Gerhard. *Klassik und Romantik: Eine Stilgeschichtliche Darstellung.* Mannheim: Bibliographisches Inst., 1972.

Strich, Fritz. *Deutsche Klassik und Romantik: Oder Vollendung und Unendlichkeit: Ein Vergleich.* 4th ed. Bern: Francke, 1949.

———. *Goethe and World Literature.* Trans. C. A. M. Sym. London: Routledge, 1949.

Taylor, Bayard, trans. *Faust Parts I and II.* By Johann Wolfgang von Goethe. Rev. and ed. Stuart Atkins. New York: Collier, 1963.

Thompson, G. Richard, ed. *Romantic Gothic Tales: 1790–1810.* New York: Harper, 1979.

Trapp, Frank A. *The Attainment of Delacroix.* Baltimore: Johns Hopkins UP, 1970.

Trunz, Erich. "Anmerkungen." *Werke.* By Johann Wolfgang von Goethe. Ed. Trunz. 11th ed. 14 vols. München: Beck, 1981. 3: 497–672.

———, ed. *Faust: Eine Tragödie.* Vol. 3 of *Werke.* By Johann Wolfgang von Goethe. Hamburger Ausgabe. 11th ed. München: Beck, 1981.

Tudor, J. M. "Goethe's Conception of Music as Mediator and 'Element.'" *Studies in Eighteenth-Century Culture* 11 (1982): 321–42.

Turgenev, Ivan. "Faust: A Story in Nine Letters." *The Novels of Ivan Turgenev.* Trans. Constance Garnett. New York: Macmillan; London: Heinemann, 1906. 12: 151–223.

Valéry, Paul. *Mon Faust.* Paris: Gallimard, 1945.

Vaughan, William. *Romantic Art.* New York: Oxford UP, 1978.

Vickery, John B. "Literature and Myth." *Interrelations of Literature.* Ed. Jean-Pierre Barricelli and Joseph Gibaldi. New York: MLA, 1982. 67–89.

Viëtor, Karl. *Geist und Form: Aufsätze zur deutschen Literaturgeschichte.* Bern: Francke, 1952.

———. *Goethe the Poet.* Cambridge: Harvard UP, 1949.

———. *Goethe the Thinker.* Cambridge: Harvard UP, 1950.

Wachsmut, Andreas. "Goethes Naturforschung und Weltanschauung in ihrer Wechselbeziehung." *Jahrbuch der Goethe-Gesellschaft* ns 14–15. Weimar: Böhlau, 1952–53.

Wankmüller, Rike, and Erika Zeise. "Mephisto in Max Beckmanns Illustrationen zu *Faust II.*" *Jahrbuch des Freien Hochstifts.* Tübingen: Niemeyer, 1983. 328–45.

Wayne, Philip, trans. *Faust.* By Johann Wolfgang von Goethe. 2 vols. Harmondsworth: Penguin, 1949.

Weber, Albrecht. *Wege zu Goethes* Faust. Frankfurt: Diesterweg, 1968.

Wegner, Wolfgang. *Die Faustdarstellung vom 16. Jahrhundert bis zur Gegenwart: Eine Enzyklopädie der Faustikonographie und der Faustillustration.* Amsterdam: Erasmus, 1962.

Weinberg, Kurt. *The Figure of Faust in Valéry and Goethe: An Exegesis of* Mon Faust. Princeton: Princeton UP, 1976.

Weinhandl, Ferdinand. *Die Metaphysik Goethes.* 1932. Darmstadt: Wissenschaftliche, 1965.

Wellek, René. *Concepts of Criticism.* New Haven: Yale UP, 1963.

Wendriner, Karl Georg, ed. *Die Faustdichtung vor, neben, und nach Goethe.* Berlin: Morawe, 1913.

Wilkinson, Elizabeth M., and L. A. Willoughby. *Goethe: Dichter und Denker.* Trans. Ingrid Mittenzwei. Frankfurt: Athenäum, 1974.

———. *Goethe: Poet and Thinker.* London: Arnold, 1962.

Willoughby, Leonard Ashley. *The Classical Age of German Literature, 1748–1805.* 1926. London: Oxford UP, 1935.

Winckelmann, Johann Joachim. *Geschichte der Kunst des Altertums.* 1764. Köln: Phaidon, 1972.

Wind, Edgar. *Pagan Mysteries in the Renaissance.* London: Faber, 1958.

Witkowski, Georg, ed. *Goethe:* Faust. 8th ed. 2 vols. Leipzig: Hesse, 1929.

Zimmermann, Rolf Christian. *Das Weltbild des jungen Goethe: Studien zur hermetischen Tradition des deutschen 18. Jahrhunderts.* 2 vols. München: Fink, 1969–79.

Recordings

Adler, Richard, and Jerry Ross. *Damn Yankees.* Book by George Abbott and Douglass Wallop. Orch. Don Walker. With Gwen Verdon. Cond. Hal Hastings. RCA, AYL1–3948(e), 1955.

Berlioz, Hector. *La damnation de Faust.* With Edith Mathis, Stuart Burrows, and Donald McIntyre. Cond. Seiji Ozawa. Tanglewood Festival Chorus and Boston Symphony Orch. Deutsche Grammophon, S 413 197, 1978.

Boito, Arrigo. *Mefistofele.* With Norman Treigle, Placido Domingo, and Montserrat Caballe. Cond. Julius Rudel. Ambrosian Opera Chorus, Chorus of Boys from the Wandsworth School Choir, and London Symphony Orch. Angel, S 3806, 1974.

Busoni, Ferruccio. *Doktor Faust.* With Dietrich Fischer-Dieskau, Karl Christian Kohn, and William Cochran. Cond. Ferdinand Leitner. Bavarian Radio Symphony Orch. and Chorus. Deutsche Grammophon, S 2740 273, 1982.

Goethe, Johann Wolfgang von. *Faust Part One.* Prod. Gustav Gründgens. Deutsche Grammophon, LPMS 43021–43023, 1958.

———. *Faust Part Two.* Prod. Gustav Gründgens. Deutsche Grammophon, LPMS 43040–43042, 1958.

Gounod, Charles. *Faust.* With Victoria de Los Angeles, Nicolai Gedda, and Boris Christoff. Cond. André Cluytens. Orch. and Chorus of the Théâtre National de l'Opéra. Angel, S 3622, 1958. (This production was also recorded and released by Capitol, S 7154, 1959.)

Liszt, Franz. *Eine Faust-Symphonie*. With Lajos Kozma. Cond. Antal Dorati. Concertgebouw Orch. and Chorus. Philips, S 6769 089, 1982.

Moore, Douglas. *The Devil and Daniel Webster*. Book by Stephen Vincent Benét. With Lawrence Winters. Cond. Armando Aliberti. Festival Choir and Orch. Desto, DST-6450, n.d.

Schumann, Robert. *Faust*. With Dietrich Fischer-Dieskau, Elizabeth Harwood, John Shirley-Quirk, Peter Pears, and Jennifer Vyvyan. Cond. Benjamin Britten. English Chamber Orch., Aldeburgh Festival Singers, and the Wandsworth School Choir. London, S OSA 12100, 1974.

Wagner, Richard. *Faust-Ouvertüre*. Cond. Antal Dorati. Concertgebouw Orch. Philips, S 6769 089, 1982.

Films, Filmstrips, Videotapes

Clark, Kenneth. "The Worship of Nature." *Civilization*. Dir. Michael Gill and Peter Montagnon. BBC, 1969. (Script available as ch. 11, "The Worship of Nature," *Civilization: A Personal View*, by Kenneth Clark, New York: Harper, 1969.)

Doctor Faustus. Based on Christopher Marlowe's drama. Dir. Richard Burton and Nevill Coghill. With Richard Burton and Elizabeth Taylor. Columbia Pictures in cooperation with the Oxford Dramatic Society, 1967.

Don Giovanni. Dir. Joseph Losey. Gaumont, 1979. (Information is available from New Yorker Films, 16 W. 61st St., New York, NY 10023.)

Faust. Collaborator, Albert Rapp. Encyclopaedia Britannica Films, 1960. (A filmstrip adaptation of Goethe's *Faust*.)

Faust. Metropolitan Opera Guild, 1966. (A filmstrip showing scenes of the rehearsal and performance of Charles Gounod's opera *Faust* at the Metropolitan Opera.)

Faust: An Adaptation of Goethe's Faust I. By Johann Wolfgang von Goethe. Dir. Peter Groski. Prod. Gustav Gründgens. With Will Quadflieg, Gustav Gründgens, Ella Büchi, and Elizabeth Flickenschildt. Gloria, 1964. Released in the US by Trans-World Films, 1965. 133 min. (color); 111½ min. (black and white). (Information is available from International Film Bureau, 322 S. Michigan Ave., Chicago, IL 60604.)

Faust: Eine deutsche Volkssage. Dir. F. W. Murnau. With Gösta Ekman, Emil Jannings, and Camilla Horn. Ufa, 1926.

Mephisto. Dir. Istvan Szabo. Mafilm-Objectiv Studio, 1981. (Information is available from Almi Libra Cinema 5, 1585 Broadway, New York, NY 10036.)

The Planets. Media Center of the University of Toronto. (Information is available from Media Center, Univ. of Toronto, Toronto, ON M5S 1A6, Canada.)

INDEX